CAT

PRACTICE & REVISION KIT

Level C Paper 5

Managing Finances

This Practice and Revision Kit

BPP is the **official provider** of training materials for the ACCA's CAT qualification. This Practice and Revision Kit forms part of a suite of learning tools, which also includes CD-ROMs for tuition and computer based assessment, and the innovative, internet-based 'virtual campus'.

In this February 2003 edition

- **DO YOU KNOW**? Checklists to test your knowledge and understanding of **Managing Finances** topics

- **QUESTIONS WITH HELP** and questions **HELPING HANDS**

- Feedback on examiner's comments in **WHAT THE EXAMINER SAID** and **EXAMINER'S MARKING SCHEME** at the end of each past examination question

- **TWO MOCK EXAMS -** the June 2002 and December 2002 examinations

FOR JUNE 2003 AND DECEMBER 2003 EXAMS

BPP Professional Education
February 2003

First edition 1998
Sixth edition February 2003

ISBN 0 7517 1083 0 (previous edition 0 7517 5211 8)

British Library Cataloguing-in-Publication Data
A catalogue record for this book
is available from the British Library

Published by

BPP Professional Education
Aldine House, Aldine Place
London W12 8AW

www.bpp.com

Printed in England by W M Print
45-47 Frederick Street
Walsall
West Midlands
WS2 9NE

We are grateful to the Association of Chartered Certified Accountants for permission to reproduce the syllabus, the pilot paper and past examination questions of which the Association holds the copyright. The answers have been prepared by BPP Professional Education.

We are also grateful to the Association of Accounting Technicians for permission to reproduce past examination questions in this Kit. The answers have been prepared by BPP Professional Education.

BPP
PROFESSIONAL EDUCATION

BPP
PROFESSIONAL EDUCATION

HOW TO USE THIS PRACTICE & REVISION KIT

Aim of this Practice & Revision Kit

> To provide the practice to help you succeed in the examination for C5 *Managing Finances*.

To pass the examination you need a thorough understanding in all areas covered by the syllabus and teaching guide.

Recommended approach

- Make sure you are able to answer questions on **everything** specified by the syllabus and teaching guide.

- Learning is an **active** process. Use the **DO YOU KNOW?** Checklists to test your knowledge and understanding of the topics covered in C5 *Managing Finances* by filling in the blank spaces. Then check your answers against the **DID YOU KNOW?** Checklists. Do not attempt any questions if you are unable to fill in any of the blanks - go back to your **BPP Interactive Text** and revise first.

- When you are revising a topic, think about the mistakes that you know that you should avoid by writing down **POSSIBLE PITFALLS** at the end of each **DO YOU KNOW?** Checklist.

- Once you have completed the checklists successfully, you should attempt all of the questions in this Practice & Revision Kit. Each section has one **QUESTION WITH HELP**, and one question without any help or guidance. All of the other questions have **HELPING HANDS** which you should use in order to help you answer the question in the best way.

- Once you have completed all of the questions in the body of this Practice & Revision Kit, you should attempt both of the **MOCK EXAMS** under examination conditions. Check your answers against our answers to find out how well you did.

This approach is only a suggestion. You or your college may well adapt it to suit your needs.

SYLLABUS

MANAGING FINANCES

Aim

To develop knowledge and understanding of the operation of processes and procedure by which organisations plan cash flows, optimise their use of working capital and allocate resources to capital expenditure projects.

Objectives

At the completion of this module candidates should be able to:

- Describe the cash flow cycle
- Describe sources of short, medium and long-term finance
- Prepare cash budgets and cash flow forecasts
- Explain the principles of effective working capital management
- Calculate working capital requirements
- Describe credit management methods and procedures
- Describe cash management methods and procedures
- Evaluate capital expenditure proposals
- Describe processes of internal audit and control

Content

(a)   Cash and the cash flow cycle, cash and accrual accounting, cash in the economy, inflation.

(b)   Cash budgeting; budget profiling, adjustment for timing, preparation of cash flow forecasts, actions to optimise cash flow patterns, financial ratios for financing and liquidity based analysis.

(c)   Working capital management; working capital requirements, cash flow and working capital cycle, optimising - materials, work-in-progress, credit and payments. EOQ, impact of lean manufacturing and just-in-time, creditor control and payment procedures.

(d)   Credit management; sources of information, credit control data, credit policies and implementation, debtors analysis, collection methods, factoring and discounting, insurance.

(e)   Cash management; short-term investing activities, marketable securities (bills of exchange, certificates of deposit, government securities, local authority short-term loans).

(f)   Cash management; short-term financing activities, sources of finance (short, medium and long-term), banking operations; banking system and money markets, impact of monetary policies.

(g)   Capital budgeting; capital investment procedures (authorisation and monitoring), non-DCF methods - accounting rate of return, payback.

(h)   Capital investment appraisal; time preference, discounting, opportunity cost of finance, net present value and internal rate of return, taxation implications, treatment of inflation.

(i)   Internal audit and control processes and procedures.

(j)   Preventing fraud in accounting processes.

THE EXAMINATION PAPER

Format of the paper

Number of marks

Four compulsory questions
(Question 1 40 marks, Questions 2-4 20 marks each)   100

Time allowed: 3 hours.

Prerequisite knowledge

The paper builds on the foundation of accounting knowledge and skills developed in level B papers B1 *Maintaining Financial Records and Accounts* and B2 *Cost Accounting Systems*.

Development of Paper C5

Paper C5 is concerned with the management processes by which the finances of the organisation are planned for, secured, assigned to projects and activities and subsequently optimised and controlled. As such there are clear linkages in the paper with:

C1   Drafting Financial Statements (principally, cash flow statements, elements of financial analysis)

C2   Information for Management (principally, budgetary planning and control, decision making)

C3   Auditing Practice and Procedure (principally, relationship of internal to external audit)

Analysis of past papers

The analysis below shows the topics that have been examined in past exam papers and in the CAT Pilot Paper.

December 2002
1   Ratio analysis; withdrawal; gearing
2   Creditor management
3   ARR and IRR
4   Segregation of duties; fraud detection

The December 2002 exam is Mock Exam 2 in this Kit.

June 2002
1   Net present value; sources of finance
2   Debt factoring; stock and debtor control
3   Economic order quantity; net present value
4   European Union; single currency

The June 2002 exam is Mock Exam 1 in this Kit.

		Question number in this Kit
December 2001		
1	NPV; IRR; abandonment; post-completion audits	40
2	Cash flow forecast; summary profit and loss account	5
3	Working capital finance	21
4	Debt finance	29

> **What the examiner said**
>
> The examiner continued to focus on key syllabus areas. Some question parts were set to reward candidates who had practised old questions or read relevant articles in *Student Accountant*. Performance varied considerably between centres and between questions.

		Question number in this Kit
June 2001		
1	Financial performance; overtrading; cashflow; internal controls	24
2	Projected profit and loss account; ratios; gearing	8
3	Stock control	22
4	Project evaluation and control; post-completion audit	12

> **What the examiner said**
>
> The examiner aims to focus on the key syllabus areas, but also cover the whole syllabus over a number of sittings. Some candidates were disconcerted by the greater percentage of marks available for written answers. However most candidates performed creditably, and should consider taking the main ACCA exams.

December 2000		
1	Net present value; factors in decision-making; control of capital expenditure projects	36
2	Working capital requirements	20
3	Trade credit arrangements; payments to suppliers	23
4	Long-term and short-term financing; fixed interest rates; loan covenants	28

> **What the examiner said**
>
> Performance was disappointing, particularly in questions 2 and 4. Students should prepare by tackling old examination questions and reading relevant articles in *Student Accountant*.

June 2000		
1	Cash flow budgets; cash flow problems, restrictive covenants	2
2	Factoring of debts; trade discounts; payments to suppliers	17
3	IRR and payback	35
4	Financial intermediation; Central Bank; inflation	26

December 1999		
1	Capital investment appraisal	39
2	Monthly cash flow forecast; draft profit and loss account	3
3	Aged debtors' schedules; credit worthiness of new customers; using debtors to raise finance	16
4	Fraud; internal audit and internal control	10

June 1999		
1	Relevant costs; breakeven point; tax and inflation effects	42
2	Factoring; ways of reducing the cash operating cycle	15
3	Financial performance ratios; value for money audit	9
4	Choice between debt and equity finance; stock exchange listing	31

What the examiner said

The overall performance of candidates was very disappointing, with the lowest pass rate since the inception of this paper. Most candidates failed to display a satisfactory understand of even the core topics. On those who failed, a significant number had difficulty with Questions 1 and 2. Question 1 dealt with the core syllabus topic of investment appraisal, and it was disappointing that many candidates failed to cope with the relatively simple data given. Students are advised to focus on core topics of the syllabus and to practice past examination questions to ensure they have an adequate grasp of the topics.

December 1998

		Question number in this Kit
1	Cash operating cycle; effects of change in credit policy; factoring and invoice discounting; assessing creditworthiness; problems in managing debtors	19
2	Forecast P&L account and debtors/trade creditors; actions to improve cash position	6
3	NPV and IRR methods of project appraisal	37
4	Internal control; detection of errors or fraud; internal and external Audit functions	11

What the examiner said

Most candidates demonstrated that they understood and could apply core syllabus topics. As with the previous diet, candidates tended to be stronger on computations but weaker on the written parts of questions. In a small number of cases there was an inability to understand or calculate IRR. Candidates are reminded to study this topic. A significant minority failed to answer all questions in full; the causes might be either poor time management or inadequate preparation. Candidates are advised to practise attempting previous papers and carefully to review their performance before sitting the actual examination. Of those candidates who failed this paper, a significant number had difficulty with Questions 1 and 3. This indicates that insufficient attention is being given to some core syllabus topics.

June 1998

1	Project appraisal: calculations and discussion	38
2	Cash budgeting and cash flow problems	4
3	Overtrading: its consequences, causes and remedies; ratios which indicate overtrading	-
4	Choice of a source of finance. Venture capital and means of realising the venture capitalist's investment	32

What the examiner said

The paper was set to ensure that a focus was maintained on some of the core areas of the syllabus. Most candidates demonstrated a sound grasp of the basics of finance tested in this paper and made credible attempts at all four questions within the designated time. The general level of presentation was good, although there was a tendency for some candidates to confine written answers to a list of points without offering supporting discussion or explanation, especially in Questions 1(b) and 4(a).

BPP)))
PROFESSIONAL EDUCATION

Examiner's approach to the C5 examination

The following extracts are from an article published in the December 1997 issue of the *ACCA Technician Bulletin*.

Approach to the paper

Paper C5 is an optional paper at the final level of the Certified Accounting Technician examinations.

The main objective of this paper is to ensure candidates can demonstrate a clear understanding of:

- The management of working capital (particularly planning and control of cash flows)

- The capital budgeting and investment appraisal process (including an ability to demonstrate both profit based and cash based methods of project evaluation)

- Sources of finance (short/medium/long term) and the treasury functions

Paper C5 will reflect the practical emphasis of the ACCA Technician qualification. Questions set will have a practical emphasis testing skills required of technicians in their work environments. Consequently, clear presentation of workings will be important as will the ability to communicate clearly in written form. Examination questions set will focus on core syllabus areas and will reflect the skill level required of an accounting technician.

This paper will also be designed so that it is a key foundation for those wishing to pursue their studies at a more advanced level through the mainstream ACCA examinations.

Syllabus linkages

C5 will build on knowledge and skills developed in level B, papers B1 and B2. There are also linkages with other level C papers (in particular with C1, C2 and C3). However there will *not* be a presumption of any prior knowledge from any of the other level C papers. This is due to the fact that candidates have considerable flexibility in their approach to level C papers.

Syllabus

The syllabus has six core topics:

1   Working capital management (application of principles and procedures)
2   Cash management (budgeting and control)
3   Sources of finance (short/medium/long-term)
4   Capital investment appraisal (planning, control and application)
5   Analysis of financial positions (including ratio analysis)
6   Internal audit and internal controls [*BPP note:* The topic of fraud is also now in the syllabus.]

MATHEMATICAL TABLES

PRESENT VALUE TABLE

Present value of $1 = (1+r)^{-n}$ where r = discount rate, n = number of periods until payment

This table shows the present value of £1 per annum, receivable or payable at the end of *n* years.

Periods	Discount rates (r)									
(n)	1%	2%	3%	4%	5%	6%	7%	8%	9%	10%
1	0.990	0.980	0.971	0.962	0.952	0.943	0.935	0.926	0.917	0.909
2	0.980	0.961	0.943	0.925	0.907	0.890	0.873	0.857	0.842	0.826
3	0.971	0.942	0.915	0.889	0.864	0.840	0.816	0.794	0.772	0.751
4	0.961	0.924	0.888	0.855	0.823	0.792	0.763	0.735	0.708	0.683
5	0.951	0.906	0.863	0.822	0.784	0.747	0.713	0.681	0.650	0.621
6	0.942	0.888	0.837	0.790	0.746	0.705	0.666	0.630	0.596	0.564
7	0.933	0.871	0.813	0.760	0.711	0.665	0.623	0.583	0.547	0.513
8	0.923	0.853	0.789	0.731	0.677	0.627	0.582	0.540	0.502	0.467
9	0.914	0.837	0.766	0.703	0.645	0.592	0.544	0.500	0.460	0.424
10	0.905	0.820	0.744	0.676	0.614	0.558	0.508	0.463	0.422	0.386
11	0.896	0.804	0.722	0.650	0.585	0.527	0.475	0.429	0.388	0.350
12	0.887	0.788	0.701	0.625	0.557	0.497	0.444	0.397	0.356	0.319
13	0.879	0.773	0.681	0.601	0.530	0.469	0.415	0.368	0.326	0.290
14	0.870	0.758	0.661	0.577	0.505	0.442	0.388	0.340	0.299	0.263
15	0.861	0.743	0.642	0.555	0.481	0.417	0.362	0.315	0.275	0.239

	11%	12%	13%	14%	15%	16%	17%	18%	19%	20%
1	0.901	0.893	0.885	0.877	0.870	0.862	0.855	0.847	0.840	0.833
2	0.812	0.797	0.783	0.769	0.756	0.743	0.731	0.718	0.706	0.694
3	0.731	0.712	0.693	0.675	0.658	0.641	0.624	0.609	0.593	0.579
4	0.659	0.636	0.613	0.592	0.572	0.552	0.534	0.516	0.499	0.482
5	0.593	0.567	0.543	0.519	0.497	0.476	0.456	0.437	0.419	0.402
6	0.535	0.507	0.480	0.456	0.432	0.410	0.390	0.370	0.352	0.335
7	0.482	0.452	0.425	0.400	0.376	0.354	0.333	0.314	0.296	0.279
8	0.434	0.404	0.376	0.351	0.327	0.305	0.285	0.266	0.249	0.233
9	0.391	0.361	0.333	0.308	0.284	0.263	0.243	0.225	0.209	0.194
10	0.352	0.322	0.295	0.270	0.247	0.227	0.208	0.191	0.176	0.162
11	0.317	0.287	0.261	0.237	0.215	0.195	0.178	0.162	0.148	0.135
12	0.286	0.257	0.231	0.208	0.187	0.168	0.152	0.137	0.124	0.112
13	0.258	0.229	0.204	0.182	0.163	0.145	0.130	0.116	0.104	0.093
14	0.232	0.205	0.181	0.160	0.141	0.125	0.111	0.099	0.088	0.078
15	0.209	0.183	0.160	0.140	0.123	0.108	0.095	0.084	0.074	0.065

Mathematical tables

ANNUITY TABLE

Present value of an annuity of 1 ie $\dfrac{1-(1+r)^{-n}}{r}$

where   r = discount rate

n = number of periods

Periods (n)	1%	2%	3%	4%	5%	6%	7%	8%	9%	10%
1	0.990	0.980	0.971	0.962	0.952	0.943	0.935	0.926	0.917	0.909
2	1.970	1.942	1.913	1.886	1.859	1.833	1.808	1.783	1.759	1.736
3	2.941	2.884	2.829	2.775	2.723	2.673	2.624	2.577	2.531	2.487
4	3.902	3.808	3.717	3.630	3.546	3.465	3.387	3.312	3.240	3.170
5	4.853	4.713	4.580	4.452	4.329	4.212	4.100	3.993	3.890	3.791
6	5.795	5.601	5.417	5.242	5.076	4.917	4.767	4.623	4.486	4.355
7	6.728	6.472	6.230	6.002	5.786	5.582	5.389	5.206	5.033	4.868
8	7.652	7.325	7.020	6.733	6.463	6.210	5.971	5.747	5.535	5.335
9	8.566	8.162	7.786	7.435	7.108	6.802	6.515	6.247	5.995	5.759
10	9.471	8.983	8.530	8.111	7.722	7.360	7.024	6.710	6.418	6.145
11	10.37	9.787	9.253	8.760	8.306	7.887	7.499	7.139	6.805	6.495
12	11.26	10.58	9.954	9.385	8.863	8.384	7.943	7.536	7.161	6.814
13	12.13	11.35	10.63	9.986	9.394	8.853	8.358	7.904	7.487	7.103
14	13.00	12.11	11.30	10.56	9.899	9.295	8.745	8.244	7.786	7.367
15	13.87	12.85	11.94	11.12	10.38	9.712	9.108	8.559	8.061	7.606

Periods (n)	11%	12%	13%	14%	15%	16%	17%	18%	19%	20%
1	0.901	0.893	0.885	0.877	0.870	0.862	0.855	0.847	0.840	0.833
2	1.713	1.690	1.668	1.647	1.626	1.605	1.585	1.566	1.547	1.528
3	2.444	2.402	2.361	2.322	2.283	2.246	2.210	2.174	2.140	2.106
4	3.102	3.037	2.974	2.914	2.855	2.798	2.743	2.690	2.639	2.589
5	3.696	3.605	3.517	3.433	3.352	3.274	3.199	3.127	3.058	2.991
6	4.231	4.111	3.998	3.889	3.784	3.685	3.589	3.498	3.410	3.326
7	4.712	4.564	4.423	4.288	4.160	4.039	3.922	3.812	3.706	3.605
8	5.146	4.968	4.799	4.639	4.487	4.344	4.207	4.078	3.954	3.837
9	5.537	5.328	5.132	4.946	4.772	4.607	4.451	4.303	4.163	4.031
10	5.889	5.650	5.426	5.216	5.019	4.833	4.659	4.494	4.339	4.192
11	6.207	5.938	5.687	5.453	5.234	5.029	4.836	4.656	4.486	4.327
12	6.492	6.194	5.918	5.660	5.421	5.197	4.988	4.793	4.611	4.439
13	6.750	6.424	6.122	5.842	5.583	5.342	5.118	4.910	4.715	4.533
14	6.982	6.628	6.302	6.002	5.724	5.468	5.229	5.008	4.802	4.611
15	7.191	6.811	6.462	6.142	5.847	5.575	5.324	5.092	4.876	4.675

Questions and answers

DO YOU KNOW? - CASH FLOWS AND CASH BUDGETING

- *Check that you can fill in the blanks in the statements below before you attempt any questions. If in doubt, you should go back to your BPP Interactive Text and revise first.*

- Working capital is the net difference between a firm's .... and its ....

- The operating cycle measures the period of time between .... and ....

  TRY QUESTION 1

- Cash transactions take different forms. Capital items relate to .... Revenue items relate to ....

- Cash flow can be defined in many ways. Net cash flow is the .... Operational cash flow is the .... Priority cash flows do not relate to trade, but are vital to keep the company afloat. Operational flows can be improved by better management of ...., ... and .... (eg ...., ..., ...).

- Nearly all businesses' accounts are prepared not on a cash basis, but on an .... basis. Under the .... or .... concept, revenue and profits are matched with associated costs and expenses in the same account.

- Cash budgets are prepared on a .... basis.

- A cash budget is a detailed forecast of cash receipts, payments and balances over a planning period. It is formally adopted as part of the .... or .... for the period. It is prepared by taking operational budgets and converting them into forecasts as to when receipts and payments occur. The forecast should indicate the highest and lowest .... in a period as well as the .... at the end of the period.

- A rolling forecast is a forecast that is ....

- There is more than one way of forecasting cash.

  - A forecast can be prepared of cash receipts and payments, and net cash flows (...............based forecasts). These include .... and .... forecasts. They can be used for control reporting.

  - Alternatively, a cash surplus or .... requirement can be prepared by constructing a forecast .... (...............-based forecast). These are used for long-term strategic analysis.

- Cleared funds forecasts are used for short-term planning. They take .... delays into account.

- A forecast might differ from actual cash flows because of .... or ....

  TRY QUESTIONS 2, 3, 4 AND 5

- A business plan sets out how a business intends to achieve its objectives, which might include:

  - ....   o   ....   o   ....   o   ....

- A long-term business plan should show:

  - ....   o   ....   o   ....   o   ....
  - ....

  TRY QUESTION 6

- *Possible pitfalls*

  Write down the mistakes you know you should avoid.

DID YOU KNOW? - CASH FLOWS AND CASH BUDGETING

- *Could you fill in the blanks? The answers are in bold. Use this page for revision purposes as you approach the exam.*

- Working capital is the net difference between a firm's **current assets** and its **current liabilities**.

- The operating cycle measures the period of time between **cash outflows for materials etc** and **cash inflows from sales or debtors**.

  TRY QUESTION 1

- Cash transactions take different forms. Capital items relate to **the long term functioning of the business.** Revenue items relate to **day-to-day operations**.

- Cash flow can be defined in many ways. Net cash flow is the *total* change in a company's cash **balances over a period of time**. Operational cash flow is the **net cash flow arising over a period from trading operations**. Priority cash flows do not relate to trade, but are vital to keep the company afloat. Operational flows can be improved by better management of **stocks, debtors** and **creditors** (eg **fewer stocks, collecting money earlier, paying it later**).

- Nearly all businesses' accounts are prepared not on a cash basis, but on an **accruals** basis. Under the **accruals** or **matching** concept, revenue and profits are matched with associated costs and expenses in the same account.

- Cash budgets are prepared on a **cash** basis.

- A cash budget is a detailed forecast of cash receipts, payments and balances over a planning period. It is formally adopted as part of the **business plan** or **master budget** for the period. It is prepared by taking operational budgets and converting them into forecasts as to when receipts and payments occur. The forecast should indicate the highest and lowest **cash balance** in a period as well as the **cash balance** at the end of the period.

- A rolling forecast is a forecast that is **continually updated**.

- There is more than one way of forecasting cash.

  ° A forecast can be prepared of cash receipts and payments, and net cash flows (**cash flow** based forecasts). These include **cash budgets** and **short-term cleared funds** forecasts. They can be used for control reporting.

  ° Alternatively, a cash surplus or **funding** requirement can be prepared by constructing a forecast **balance sheet** (**balance sheet**-based forecast). These are used for long-term strategic analysis.

- Cleared funds forecasts are used for short-term planning. They take **clearance** delays into account.

- A forecast might differ from actual cash flows because of **poor forecasting techniques** or **unpredicted events**.

  TRY QUESTIONS 2, 3, 4 AND 5

- A business plan sets out how a business intends to achieve its objectives, which might include:

  ° **Maximisation of profits**
  ° **Production of a better quality product**

  ° **Increase in market share**
  ° **Maximisation of shareholder wealth**

- A long-term business plan should show:

  ° **Long-term objectives**
  ° **Projected profits**
  ° **Balance sheet forecasts**

  ° **Projected cash flows**
  ° **Capital expenditure plans**

  TRY QUESTION 6

- *Possible pitfalls*

  ° **Not laying out cash forecasts clearly**
  ° **Not labelling figures clearly**
  ° **Forgetting that depreciation should not be included in a cash budget**
  ° **Calculation errors**

1   QUESTION WITH HELP: MORIBUND

(a)   Explain the term 'operating cycle'.   (6 marks)

(b)   Calculate the operating cycle for Moribund plc for 20X2 on the basis of the following information.

	20X2
	£
Stock:	410,000
Purchases	500,000
Debtors	230,000
Trade creditors	120,000
Sales	900,000
Cost of goods sold	750,000

(8 marks)

(c)   List the steps which might be taken in order to shorten the operating cycle.

(6 marks)

(20 marks)

> *If you are stuck, look at the next page for detailed help as to how you should tackle this question.*

APPROACHING THE ANSWER

(a) *Use this answer plan to construct your answer if you are stuck.*

- Overall definition of the operating cycle

- Explain components of the operating cycle, to do with:

    ° Stockholding
    ° Production time
    ° Credit period
    ° Debt collection period

- Explain effect of changing stock/debtor/creditor turnover periods on the cycle

- Proviso that operating cycle does not indicate *how much* working capital is needed

(b) *Calculate:*

- Average stockholding period (closing stock × 365/cost of goods sold)

    plus

- Debt collection period (closing debtors × 365/sales)

    less

- Length of trade credit taken (closing creditors × 365/purchases)

- The resulting total is the operating cycle, in days

(c) Steps to shorten the operating cycle concern each of its components. The raw materials stockholding period and the finished goods stockholding period can be considered separately.

1   ANSWER TO QUESTION WITH HELP: MORIBUND

(a)   The **operating cycle** of a company is the length of time between the outlay on raw materials, wages and other costs and the inflow of cash arising from the sale of the product. In Moribund plc this can be determined as follows.

Average raw material stockholding period
  plus
Time taken to produce goods
  less
Period of credit taken from suppliers
  plus
Average finished goods stockholding period
  plus
Average debt collection period

Thus as stock and debtor turnover periods improve and the creditor payment period lengthens, the operating cycle shortens and the investment required in working capital falls. The operating cycle therefore represents the relative investment in **working capital**; however it does not by itself indicate the absolute amount of working capital that will be required at different points in the cycle.

(b)   The operating cycle can be found as follows.

Average stockholding period: $\dfrac{\text{Total closing stock} \times 365}{\text{Cost of goods sold}}$

  plus

Debt collection period: $\dfrac{\text{Closing debtors} \times 365}{\text{Sales}}$

  less

Length of **trade credit taken** (creditor days): $\dfrac{\text{Closing creditors} \times 365}{\text{Purchases}}$

	20X2
Total closing stock	£410,000
Cost of goods sold	£750,000
Stockholding period	199.5 days
Closing debtors	£230,000
Sales	£900,000
Debt collection period	93.3 days
Closing creditors	£120,000
Purchases	£500,000
Trade credit period	(87.6 days)
Length of operating cycle (199.5 + 93.3 – 87.6)	205.2 days

(c)   The steps that could be taken to reduce the operating cycle include the following.

(i)   **Reducing the average raw material stockholding period.**

(ii)   **Reducing the time taken to produce goods.** However, the company must ensure that quality is not sacrificed as a result of speeding up the production process.

(iii) **Increasing the period of credit taken from suppliers.** The credit period seems very long - the company is allowed three months credit by its suppliers - and probably could not be increased. If the credit period is extended then the company may lose discounts for prompt payment.

(iv)   **Reducing the average finished goods stockholding period.**

(v)   **Reducing the average debt collection period.** The administrative costs of speeding up debt collection and the effect on sales of reducing the credit period allowed must be evaluated. However, the credit period does seem very long by the standards of most industries. It may be that generous terms have been allowed to secure large contracts and little will be able to be done about this in the short term.

2   COOLSHADES LTD (6/00)

Coolshades Ltd is a prosperous, private company whose five directors each own 20% of the share capital. The company is involved in the distribution of a range of branded sunglasses to various retail outlets. Since its foundation three years ago, the company has grown rapidly. To date, the critical success factors have been the ability to offer a quality product at a competitive price and to guarantee 24 hour delivery to customers.

To date, the company's records have been maintained by a bookkeeper, with the auditors preparing the half-yearly accounts for management review. The bookkeeper has recently retired and you have been recruited as the accounting technician. The role has been expanded to incorporate the preparation of monthly management accounts.

Although Coolshades Ltd is profitable, the company's bank is increasingly concerned about the current liquidity position and the management of working capital. Indications are that the profitability of the company is being significantly eroded, despite the significant growth in sales.

At a recent meeting with the board of directors, you have been given a series of notes in order to prepare a forecast flow for the next six months commencing 1 July 20X1.

Notes

1   Opening debtors are £590,000, of which £307,000 will be paid in July and the remainder in August.

2   Sales for the six months are a total of £1,500,000.

3   10% of sales are for cash, the remainder are on credit. 4% of credit sales end up as bad debts. 50% of debtors pay in the month following sale and the remainder pay in the subsequent month.

4   The gross profit percentage is 30%.

5   Purchases are obtained in the month prior to sale, and the related creditors are paid in the subsequent month (ie July purchases are paid for in August).

6   Opening creditors which will be paid in July are:

Trade creditors	£210,000
Distribution expense creditors	£35,000

7   Distribution expenses for this period will be £33,000 per month, including £7,000 depreciation. Distribution expenses are paid for in the month following the expense.

8   Administration expenses are a total of £120,000, for the half year. This includes a Christmas bonus of £12,000, payable in December. All other expenses accrue evenly over the period.

9   It is proposed that the company purchase new delivery vans from operating cash flows, costing £80,000, and director's cars costing £100,000. Both would be purchased in August and paid for in September.

10   Other payments are as follows:

Corporation tax for year ended 31.12.20X0	£75,000 (due in September)
Dividends for year ended 31.12.20X0	£125,000 (due in August)

11   The bank overdraft limit is capped at £200,000 and the bank has indicated an unwillingness to increase the limit.

12   All earnings are paid out as dividends two months after the year end, of 30 June.

13   Stock levels currently at £825,000 are not expected to change.

14 Loan repayments totalling £25,000 are quarterly in arrears (September and December) and compromise £20,000 principal and £5,000 interest.

Bank overdraft interest of £9,000 is charged at the end of each quarter in arrears.

15 The company intends to undertake a market research project costing £20,000 which is to be paid in October. This project is to investigate the viability of setting up distribution outlets in a neighbouring country.

16 Opening bank balance is £200,000 overdrawn.

Required

(a) (i) Prepare a budgeted cash flow for EACH of the six months to 31 December 20X1, (all figures to the nearest £'000), staring clearly any assumptions you make.

(20 marks)

(ii) Prepare a profit statement for the six month period ending 31 December 20X1 to show profit excluding depreciation.

(5 marks)

(iii) Identify any cash flow problems the company may experience over the coming six months.

(2 marks)

(b) (i) Identify and briefly explain THREE actions which could be considered in an attempt to address any perceived problems in cash flow. Outline potential difficulties with each proposed action.

(9 marks)

(ii) The bank proposes to impose restrictive covenants on the company to force it to reduce its working capital finance requirements. Briefly explain what is meant by a restrictive covenant, giving an example. Identify ONE advantage and ONE disadvantage of restrictive covenants.

(4 marks)

(40 marks)

Helping hand

Period totals will help you answer part (a). In (a)(ii) think carefully about the workings you need.

For (b) think about the effects of control of working capital, also how *current* expenditure can be reduced and whether it is possible to obtain more funds.

---

2   **ANSWER: COOLSHADES LTD**

> **Helping hand**
>
> Although period totals are not strictly necessary in part (a)(i), you should calculate them as a reconciliation check. Calculating the totals will also enable you to answer part (a)(ii) more quickly and accurately.
>
> In part (a)(ii) you should explain your workings clearly, particularly in respect of distribution expenses and tax.
>
> In part (b)(i) and elsewhere in this kit, we provide more examples than you need.
>
> A good approach to (b) is to think about the various elements of the balance sheet and profit and loss account.

(a) (i)   **Budgeted cash flow for the six months to 31 December 20X1**

	Notes	*July* £'000	*Aug* £'000	*Sept* £'000	*Oct* £'000	*Nov* £'000	*Dec* £'000	*Total* £'000
Receipts	1							
Cash sales		25	25	25	25	25	25	150
From opening debtors		307	283					590
Received in month 1			112	112	112	112	112	560
Received in month 2				104	104	104	104	416
Total receipts		332	420	241	241	241	241	1,716
Payments								
Trade creditors	2	210	175	175	175	175	175	1,085
Expense creditors	3	35	26	26	26	26	26	165
Admin expenses	4	18	18	18	18	18	30	120
Bank overdraft interest				9			9	18
Loan interest				5			5	10
Corporation tax				75				75
Dividends			125					125
Loan repayment				20			20	40
Purchase of vans				80				80
Purchase of cars				100				100
Market research					20			20
Total payments		263	344	508	239	219	265	1,838
Net cash flow		69	76	(267)	2	22	(24)	(122)
Opening cash balance		(200)	(131)	(55)	(322)	(320)	(298)	(200)
Closing cash balance		(131)	(55)	(322)	(320)	(298)	(322)	(322)

Notes

1

	£
Six monthly sales	1,500,000
Monthly sales = 1,500,000/6	250,000
Cash sales per month = 250,000 × 10%	25,000
Credit sales per month = 250,000 × 90%	225,000
Paid 1st month = 225,000 × 50%	112,500
Bad debts = 225,000 × 4%	9,000
Paid 2nd month = 225,000 − 112,500 − 9,000	103,500

It is assumed that all bad debts relate to accounts settled after one month.

2   Trade purchases are 70% of sales. Purchases are made in the month prior to sale, and settled in the following month.

Monthly sales are £250,000, and therefore

Monthly purchases = 250,000 × 70% = £175,000

3   Monthly distribution expense creditors = 33,000 – 7,000 = £26,000

These are paid one month in arrears. Depreciation is a non-cash item and is therefore excluded.

4   Monthly admin expenses excluding the Christmas bonus = (120,000 – 12,000) / 6 = £18,000

December expenses = 18,000 + 12,000 = £30,000

It is assumed that expenses are paid in the month in which they are incurred.

(ii)   Budgeted profit statement for the six months to 31 December 20X1

	Note	£'000	£'000
Sales			1,500
Cost of sales			
Opening stock		825	
Purchases	1	1,050	
		1,875	
Less closing stock		825	
			1,050
Gross profit			450
Expenses			
Distribution	2	156	
Administration		120	
Bank & loan interest	3	28	
Bad debts	4	54	
Market research		20	
			378
Profit before depreciation and tax	5		72

Notes

1   Six times £175,000 per month.

2   Six times £26,000 per month, excluding depreciation.

3   Two payments of £9,000, plus two payments of £5,000.

4   Six times £9,000 per month.

5   The tax paid relates to a previous accounting period. No information is given as to the tax liability for the current period, and therefore the profit figure is calculated before tax.

(iii)   The bank overdraft has been capped at £200,000. The forecast suggests that the limit will be **breached** in **September**, and will continue to be breached until the end of December. There is no apparent improving trend in the cash flow, and the problem seems likely to continue into the next year. This issue must be addressed as soon as possible.

(b) (i)   **Defer capital expenditure**

The company is planning to spend £80,000 on new delivery vans, and £100,000 on directors' cars during the period. This is a large amount of capital expenditure to be funded entirely from operating cash flows. It may be possible to **defer** or **stagger** the timing of the **purchases**, and thereby improve the cash flow position. However, the risk is that the vans are necessary for Coolshades to continue to be able to **guarantee twenty-four hour delivery** to customers. If the vans are not purchased, this level of service may be eroded with a consequent impact on competitiveness.

Finance capital expenditure from other sources

Coolshades could alternatively consider financing the assets using **hire purchase or leasing arrangements**, or by taking on **additional medium term debt**. However, if the company is **close** to its **borrowing limits**, it may not be able to arrange further debt finance. If it can obtain debt, the **cost of debt** may be **high** to reflect the additional risk to the lender.

Reduce the level of stocks

Forecasts suggest that stock levels will remain at the current level of £825,000. This is high in relation to the annual sales of £3m, representing a stock turnover period of 100 days (825/3,000 × 365). If the company can **reduce** the **stock level** by reducing the stock levels of slow-moving items, **purchase levels** will **decrease** correspondingly, thereby improving the working capital position and cutting overdraft levels. However this could **jeopardise** the company's ability to provide a guaranteed **24-hour delivery** to its customers, since slower moving items would not be in stock.

Reduce the payout ratio

Currently all earnings are paid out as **dividends.** This means that the company is **not retaining** any **earnings** with which to **finance growth**, or for **investment** in the future **profitability** of the business. In the absence of any new equity, Coolshades should reconsider this policy as soon as possible. The disadvantage of this action would be that it **reduces** the **income** of the **shareholders**. However, since the five shareholders are all directors of the company, it may be easy to obtain their acquiescence.

Review the credit policy

Coolshades currently has bad debts running at 4% of turnover, or £54,000 for the half year. This is a high level both in percentage and absolute terms. The company should look at methods of improving this. Options include a **tighter implementation** of **existing credit policy** – enforcement of credit limits, stopping supplies to customers whose accounts are overdue – and a more rigorous approach to the granting of credit to new customers. This might have the added benefit of **reducing** the **level of debtors** and thereby **improving cash flow.** The potential drawback is that **customers** may be **lost** a result of tighter credit limits and firmer debt collection.

Review operating profitability and expansion plans

Despite the rapid expansion, profitability **appears** to be **falling**. Profit before dividend and tax for the previous year was £200,000 (dividends of £125,000 plus tax of £75,000). The forecast for the next six months is only £72,000, a drop of nearly 30% on the previous year. The company should review the reasons for this, and also **reconsider** the **overseas expansion plans** until the home situation improves. This would have the added benefit of **saving £20,000** in **market research costs.** However, the possible drawback is that the overseas expansion might **compensate** for a **structural downturn** in the home market.

(ii)   Taking out a loan often entails certain obligations for the borrower over and above repaying the loan on demand. These obligations are called **covenants**.

Covenants may be positive, qualitative or restrictive.

A **restrictive covenant** is a promise by a borrower not to do something. Examples include:

(1) The company **pledges not to borrow** more money until the current loan is repaid.

(2) The company **promises not to take over** another company during the period of the loan.

Advantages of restrictive covenants include:

(1) The company may be **forced to solve financial problems** that might otherwise have been put off or ignored.

(2) If the company agrees to covenants, it will find it **easier to obtain** the **finance** it is seeking, since it is effectively giving the lender greater financial security.

Disadvantages of restrictive covenants include:

(1) They **restrict** the management's **freedom of action** in financial matters. This may not be in the best long-term interest of the business.

(2) From the point of view of the lender, **certain covenants** may be **difficult to enforce**. Here for example, the directors may compensate for covenant restrictions on their dividend income by voting themselves more remuneration.

Examiner's marking scheme

			Marks	
(a)	(i)	Determination of correct sales per month	2	
		Cash sales	1	
		Credit sales/bad debts	3	
		Timing of cash flows	2	
		Purchases	1	
		Timing of purchase cash flows	1	
		Distribution expenses net of depreciation	1	
		Administration overheads/Christmas bonus	2	
		Tax/dividends/loan/overdraft interest	3	
		Capital expenditure and market research	2	
		Layout/presentation/assumption	2	
				20
	(ii)	Sales	1	
		Cost of sales (£1.05m)	1	
		Distribution expenses	1	
		Finance expenses	1	
		Layout/workings	1	
				5
	(iii)	Closing balance calculations	1	
		Comment if overdraft > £200,000	1	
				2
(b)	(i)	Each action identified (3 × 1 mark)	3	
		Brief explanation (3 × 1 mark)	3	
		Disadvantages of actions (3 × 1 mark)	3	
				9
	(iii)	Restrictive covenant explained with an example	2	
		Advantages briefly discussed	1	
		Disadvantages briefly discussed	1	
				4
				40

3   BOOKS LTD (12/99)

Books Ltd owns a chain of 10 bookshops selling books and magazines. At the beginning of January 20X1 the company is expected to have an overdraft of £30,000 and the bank has requested that it be eliminated by the end of June 20X1.

As a result of this request, the finance director has asked you, as assistant accountant, to review the financial position to determine if the bank's request can be complied with.

You have been provided with the following information.

	20X0 *Dec* £'000	*20X1* *Jan* £'000	*Feb* £'000	*March* £'000	*April* £'000	*May* £'000	*June* £'000
Sales revenue	200	250	350	250	150	126	100
Purchases	150	200	150	100	76	76	50
Administration expenses	50	60	70	60	50	50	50
Selling expenses	20	26	30	26	20	16	16
Taxation due				30			
Loan repayments (principal & interest)	5	5	5	5	5	5	5
Capital expenditure			10	30	20		

Notes

1   Opening stocks at 1 January 20X1 are estimated at £150,000.

2   Suppliers allow two months credit. Purchases in November were £100,000.

3   The gross profit margin is 50%.

4   50% of sales revenue is for cash. 25% of sales revenue is on credit payable in the month following sale 5% of which is not recovered and is therefore written off as bad debts.

   25% of sales revenue is paid by credit card on which the credit card company charges 2% of credit card sales value. (This is additional to the selling expenses outlined above). The credit card company pays Books Ltd credit card sales revenue net of their 2% charge in the month following the sale.

5   The loan repayments comprise 60% capital repayment and 40% interest.

6   Administration expenses include a monthly depreciation charge of £10,000. This depreciation charge incorporates any depreciation in relation to capital expenditure during the period. All other administration expenses are paid in the month incurred.

7   50% of selling expenses are paid in the month incurred, the remainder being paid in the following month.

Required

(a) (i)   Prepare a monthly cash flow forecast to the nearest £'000 for each of the six months to June 20X1 showing the cash balance at the end of each month.

(12 marks)

   (ii)   Comment briefly on the results obtained.   (3 marks)

(b) Prepare a draft profit and loss account for the 6 months to 30 June 20X1.   (5 marks)

(20 marks)

Helping hand

Try to set out your workings systematically, so that you can obtain the figures for the cash flow forecast and profit and loss account at the same time.

---

3   ANSWER: BOOKS LTD

> **Helping hand**
>
> If you tabulate your workings carefully in the first part of the question, you will find that it is a simple matter to derive the figures required to complete the profit and loss account in part (b). Be careful with your treatment of the bad debts figure and the credit card charges figure in the two schedules. No information is given as to the closing stock level. You must therefore state your assumptions with regard to this item.

(a) (i)   **Books Ltd: Cash flow forecast for the period January to June 20X1**

	Jan £'000	*Feb* £'000	*Mar* £'000	*Apr* £'000	*May* £'000	*Jun* £'000
Income						
From sales	223	297	296	197	136	111
Expenditure						
Operating costs						
Purchases	100	150	200	150	100	76
Administration expenses	50	60	50	40	40	40
Selling expenses	24	29	30	24	19	17
Capital expenditure		10	30	20		
Loan repayments	5	5	5	5	5	5
Taxation			30			
Total expenditure	179	254	345	239	164	138
Excess of income over expenditure	44	43	(49)	(42)	(28)	(27)
Opening cash balance	(30)	14	57	8	(34)	(62)
Closing cash balance	14	57	8	(34)	(62)	(89)

Working

	Dec £'000	*Jan* £'000	*Feb* £'000	*Mar* £'000	*Apr* £'000	*May* £'000	*Jun* £'000	*Jan-Jun* £'000
Receipts from sales								
Sales revenue	200.00	250.00	350.00	250.00	150.00	126.00	100.00	1,226.00
Cash receipts (50%)		125.00	175.00	125.00	75.00	63.00	50.00	
Gross credit receipts (25%)		50.00	62.50	87.50	62.50	37.50	31.50	
Bad debts (5% credit receipts)		(2.50)	(3.13)	(4.38)	(3.13)	(1.88)	(1.58)	(16.60)
Credit cards (gross) (25%)		50.00	62.50	87.50	62.50	37.50	31.50	
Total receipts		222.50	296.87	295.62	196.87	136.12	111.42	
Credit card charge (2%)		1.00	1.25	1.75	1.25	0.75	0.63	6.63
Payments to creditors								
Cost of purchases (100 Nov)	150.00	200.00	150.00	100.00	76.00	76.00	50.00	652.00
Payment		100.00	150.00	200.00	150.00	100.00	76.00	
Administration expenses								
Gross expenses	50.00	60.00	70.00	60.00	50.00	50.00	50.00	
Less depreciation		(10.00)	(10.00)	(10.00)	(10.00)	(10.00)	(10.00)	(60.00)
Net payment		50.00	60.00	50.00	40.00	40.00	40.00	280.00
Selling expenses								
Gross expenses	20.00	26.00	30.00	26.00	20.00	16.00	16.00	134.00
Paid in current month (50%)		13.00	15.00	13.00	10.00	8.00	8.00	
Paid in next month (50%)		10.00	13.00	15.00	13.00	10.00	8.00	
Credit card charge (above)		1.00	1.25	1.75	1.25	0.75	0.63	
Total payment		24.00	29.25	29.75	24.25	18.75	16.63	

It is assumed that stock levels remain constant throughout the period.

(ii)   The figures show that although the **overdraft** will be eliminated by the end of January and Books will continue to be a net depositor until the end of March, the situation deteriorates sharply thereafter. By the end of June the overdraft requirement will have increased to £89,000. This appears to be due mainly to the following factors.

(1) Sales are forecast to fall by more than 50% in the second quarter as compared with the first quarter of the year. This means that even in May and June when there are no unusual items of expenditure, the business will be cash negative.

(2) Funds are required to finance the £60,000 of capital expenditure between February and April. If this expenditure could be deferred, the position at the end of June would be at least no worse than at the start of the year.

It is assumed that the stock levels remain constant throughout the period.

(b) **Books Ltd: Draft profit and loss account for the six months to 30 June 20X1**

	£	£
Sales		1,226,000
Cost of sales (50% sales)		(613,000)
Gross margin		613,000
Overheads		
Selling expenses	(134,000)	
Credit card charges	(6,630)	
Administration expenses	(280,000)	
Depreciation	(60,000)	
		(480,630)
Bad debts		(16,575)
Profit before interest and tax		115,795
Loan interest (40% repayment)		(12,000)
Net profit before tax		103,795

Examiner's marking scheme

				Marks	
(a)	(i)	Cash sales receipts		1	
		Credit sales receipts		2	
		Credit card sales receipts		2	
		Purchase / Admin. expenses		2	
		Selling expenses		2	
		Tax / loan / capital expenditure		1	
		Presentation / layout		2	
					12
	(ii)	Identify deteriorating overdraft	(2 × 1)	1	
		Suggestions to reverse impact		2	
					3
(b)		Sales / cost of sales		1	
		Admin. and selling expenses		1	
		Bad debts		1	
		Credit card fees		1	
		Finance expenses		1	
					5
					20

4   BAT LTD (6/98)

Bat Ltd manufactures and sells a single product for which the following budget details are available:

	£
Selling price per unit	75
Less: Materials 3kg at £10	(30)
Labour 1 hr at £15	(15)
Contribution per unit	30

Notes

1

	Quarter 1 (Jan to Mar)	Quarter 2 (Apr to Jun)	Quarter 3 (Jul to Sep)	Quarter 4 (Oct to Dec)
Budgeted sales units	5,000	2,000	2,500	6,000

2   Opening stocks of finished goods (at the start of quarter one) are 1,000 units. Closing stocks of finished goods at the end of each quarter are budgeted at 10% of sales volume for that quarter.

3   The company operates a Just in Time (JIT) system and consequently the stock of raw materials can be assumed to be always zero.
Raw material purchases are paid for in the quarter of purchase.
Direct labour costs are paid for in the quarter of production.

4   Sales revenue is received as follows: 60% during the quarter of sale, 35% during the following quarter, with the remaining 5% being bad debts.

5   Fixed overheads are £40,000 per quarter. This figure includes depreciation of £10,000. Fixed overheads are paid for in the quarter in which they are incurred.

6   Machinery costing £100,000 is due to be installed in quarter two and paid for in quarter three. A tax liability of £75,000 and a dividend payment of £40,000 are due to be paid in quarter three.

7   Opening debtors balance at the start of quarter one is £60,000 which will be paid during quarter one.

8   The opening bank balance at the start of quarter one is nil.
The company currently has no overdraft facilities.

Required

(a) Prepare a cash budget for each quarter. All relevant calculations must be shown.

(16 marks)

(b) Identify any cash flow problems over the next year and give THREE suggestions as to how the company might deal with this problem. (4 marks)

(20 marks)

Helping hand

Note in (a) that the timing of production and sales may be different. Your answer to (b) should focus on reduction of current costs.

---

4   **ANSWER: BAT LTD**

Helping hand

(a) shows the importance of detailed working for sales and purchases, given the timing difference. Other valid suggestions, focusing on how costs can be reduced to have the desired effect on cash flows, are possible for part (b).

What the examiner said

In part (a), some experienced difficulty in the calculation and use of the quantities produced each quarter. It is important at this level to understand that the timing of production and sales may be different and consequently affect cash flows.

(a) *Bat Ltd: Cash budget*

Quarter	Note	1 £	2 £	3 £	4 £
Cash receipts					
Opening debtors		60,000			
Sales (this Qtr)	1	225,000	90,000	112,500	270,000
Sales (previous Qtr)	1		131,250	52,500	65,625
		285,000	221,250	165,000	335,625
Cash payments					
Materials purchases	2	135,000	51,000	76,500	190,500
Labour	2	67,500	25,500	38,250	95,250
Fixed o/h (excl depn)		30,000	30,000	30,000	30,000
Capital expenditure				100,000	
Taxation				75,000	
Dividends				40,000	
		232,500	106,500	359,750	315,750
Net cash flow		52,500	114,750	(194,750)	19,875
Opening balance		-	52,500	167,250	(27,500)
Closing balance		52,500	167,250	(27,500)	(7,625)

Notes

1   *Sales revenue*

	Q1 £	Q2 £	Q3 £	Q4 £
Sales revenue (Units × £75)	375,000	150,000	187,500	450,000
Received in quarter (60%)	225,000	90,000	112,500	270,000
Received in next quarter (35%)	131,250	52,500	65,625	94,500

2   *Production budget*

	Q1 Units	Q2 Units	Q3 Units	Q4 Units
Sales	5,000	2,000	2,500	6,000
Closing stock (10% of sales)	500	200	250	600
Less: opening stock	(1,000)	(500)	(200)	(250)
Units required	4,500	1,700	2,550	6,350
	£	£	£	£
Materials cost (£30 per unit)	135,000	51,000	76,500	190,500
Labour cost (£15 per unit)	67,500	25,500	38,250	95,250

(b) Bat Ltd faces cash flow problems in quarters 3 and 4, when the cash budget indicates a likely deficit of £27,500 and £7,625 in each quarter respectively. The company has no overdraft facility to cover this deficit.

The company might deal with this problem by the following methods.

(i) **Deferment of capital expenditure.** Perhaps installation of the new machinery can be delayed for two quarters, provided that there are sufficient cash receipts to cover it in later quarters. Alternatively, the financing of the expenditure might be arranged so that it is spread over a longer period, for example, if it can be paid by instalments.

(ii) **Reduction of bad debts.** The total cost of bad debts in the year is ((£375,000 + £150,000 + £187,500 + £450,000) × 5%) = £58,125. Stricter credit terms and improved credit control procedures might result in improved cash flow and enhanced profits.

(iii) **Reduction of costs.** A cost reduction programme aimed at reducing materials and labour costs should also serve to increase profits as well as reduce the deficit.

Examiner's marking scheme		**Marks**	
(a)	Sales revenue/bad debts	2	
	Timing	2	
	Required production	2	
	Material/labour costs	2	
	Cash fixed overheads	2	
	Cash budget layout	2	
	Dealing with opening balances	2	
	Capital expenditure/tax/dividend	2	
			16
(b)	Quarters 3 and 4 overdraft (identified)	1	
	Each valid suggestion	3	
			4
			20

5   AUTOMOTIVE LTD (12/01)

Automotive Ltd imports one type of luxury car (the De-luxe model) from Japan for sale in its domestic market to local motor distributors. The most recent balance sheet of Automotive Ltd as at 30 November 20X1 is as follows.

Automotive Ltd
Balance sheet as at 30 November 20X1

	Cost £'000	Depreciation £'000	Net £'000	£'000
Fixed assets				
Land and buildings	1,000	50	950	
Fixtures and equipment	500	50	450	
	1,500	100		1,400
Current assets				
Stock		1,920		
Trade debtors		3,600		
Cash		80		
			5,600	
Less Creditors:				
(Amounts falling due within one year)				
Trade creditors		960		
Corporation tax		600		
Dividends		440		
			2,000	
				3,600
				5,000
Financed by:				
50p ordinary shares				1,000
Share premium				1,000
Retained earnings				3,000
				5,000

As a result of a slow down in Automotive Ltd's market, the monthly sales of imported luxury Japanese cars have been static for the past year. Deliveries from Japan arrive in one shipment each month. At the beginning of 20X1, Automotive Ltd's sales manager prepared a monthly forecast of the level of De-luxe model car sales. The forecast, upon which orders have been placed with the Japanese supplier, is set out below.

Month	Sales forecast (Number of cars)
December 20X1	40
January 20X2	40
February 20X2	50
March 20X2	70
April 20X2	90
May 20X2	100
June 20X2	100
July 20X2	100

The managing director is not convinced that the above sales forecasts are achievable. She is aware that competitors have been able to import luxury cars from the USA and sell them at a cheaper price than the Japanese imports, mainly due to the weakness in the US dollar and the strength of the Yen over the past year.

The following notes are also relevant.

1   A De-luxe model sells for £30,000 and costs £24,000 to import. Orders from Japan need to be placed six months in advance and are legally binding on Automotive Ltd.

2   Sales to local motor distributors are on two months' credit. Trade debtors (£3,600,000 in the balance sheet as at 30 November 20X1 above) represent the amount outstanding for sales made in October and November 20X1. Sales revenue for October and November were identical amounts.

3   The Japanese supplier allows one month's credit.

4   Stock levels sufficient to meet the following two months' sales are constantly maintained.

5   Automotive Ltd's staff costs are currently £50,000 per month and a bonus of £40,000 is due to be paid during December. Monthly staff costs are due to increase by £10,000 in January 20X2 and remain at this increased level for the foreseeable future.

6   Other costs are £85,000 per month, which include £10,000 depreciation per month for existing assets.

7   The company only moved into its current premises 10 months ago. Redevelopment of an existing warehouse to store cars will be necessary for 20X2. It is estimated that warehouse development will cost £500,000, which will be paid in February.

8   The redeveloped warehouse will be treated as a fixed asset in the accounts. It will be in use from the beginning of February 20X2 and will be depreciated at 6% per annum from the beginning of February. The depreciation charge for this new asset is not included in the £10,000 depreciation charge in note 6 above.

9   The corporation tax and dividends (as shown on the balance sheet as at 30 November 20X1 above) are due for payment in March next. Corporation tax is currently 50%.

10   The company is due to complete a rights issue of 200,000 ordinary shares at £4 each in April 20X2.

Required

(a) Prepare a cash flow forecast for each of the six months for the period ending 31 May 20X2.   (14 marks)

(b) Prepare a summary profit and loss account for the six month period. You may ignore finance costs.   (6 marks)

                                                                                                         (20 marks)

5 **ANSWER: AUTOMOTIVE LTD**

What the examiner said

Most answers to part (a) were very good with candidates scoring high or full marks.

Part (b) was quite well answered, though certain common mistakes did arise, such as including fixed asset expenditure in the profit and loss account and the sequence of deductions being incorrect (especially the taxation charge).

(a) Automotive Ltd: Cash flow forecast for the period ended May 20X2

	December £'000	*January* £'000	*February* £'000	*March* £'000	*April* £'000	*May* £'000
Receipts						
Sales (Working)	1,800	1,800	1,200	1,200	1,500	2,100
Rights issue					800	
Total receipts	1,800	1,800	1,200	1,200	2,300	2,100
Payments						
Supplier (Working)	960	1,200	1,680	2,160	2,400	2,400
Staff costs	90	60	60	60	60	60
Other costs (85–10)	75	75	75	75	75	75
Redevelopment			500			
Tax				600		
Dividends				440		
Total payments	1,125	1,335	2,315	3,335	2,535	2,535
Excess of receipts						
over payments	675	465	(1,115)	(2,135)	(235)	(435)
Opening cash balance	80	755	1,220	105	(2,030)	(2,265)
Closing cash balance	755	1,220	105	(2,030)	(2,265)	(2,700)

Workings

Sales received two months later

Oct £'000	*Nov* £'000	*Dec* £'000	*Jan* £'000	*Feb* £'000	*Mar* £'000	*Apr* £'000	*May* £'000	*Dec-May* £'000
1,800	1,800	1,200	1,200	1,500	2,100	2,700	3,000	11,700

Purchases two months in advance of sales, value 80% of sales

Nov £'000	*Dec* £'000	*Jan* £'000	*Feb* £'000	*Mar* £'000	*Apr* £'000	*May* £'000	*Dec-May* £'000
960	1,200	1,680	2,160	2,400	2,400	2,400	12,240

(b) Automotive Ltd: Summary profit and loss account for period ended 31 May 2002

	£	£
Sales		11,700
Cost of sales		
Opening stock	1,920	
Purchases	12,240	
	14,160	
Less: Closing stock	(4,800)	
		(9,360)
Gross profit		2,340
Expenses		
Staff costs	390	
Other costs	450	
Depreciation (Working)	70	
		(910)
Profit before tax		1,430
Taxation		(715)
Profit after tax		715

Working

Depreciation

	£'000
Existing assets (10×6)	60
Warehouse $(500 \times 6\% \times 4/12)$	10
	70

Examiner's marking scheme

		Marks	
(a)	Opening debtors	2	
	Sales revenue inflows	2	
	Share issue	1	
	Opening creditors	1	
	Payments to creditors	2	
	Staff costs	1	
	Other expenses	1	
	Warehouse development	1	
	Tax/dividend	1	
	Presentation/layout	2	
			14
(b)	Sales revenue	1	
	Cost of sales	1	
	Staff costs/other expenses	1	
	Depreciation	1	
	Taxation	1	
	Presentation	1	
			6
			20

6   TOYZ LTD (12/98)

Toyz Ltd is a medium sized company engaged in the manufacture of a range of educational toys. The business is growing rapidly and the company is experiencing some cash flow difficulties. The company's toys are sold to a number of retail outlets throughout the country. Prior to departing for an extended Christmas holiday, the financial controller had prepared a cash flow forecast for the managing director for the period January to March 20X9.

The managing director has reviewed the cash flow forecast and is concerned with the trend exhibited in the cash position. He has asked you, as assistant accountant, to prepare the profit and loss account for the period January to March 20X9 using the information on which the financial controller had based the cash flow forecast. You have been given the financial controller's working papers which include the following information:

	January 20X9 £	*February 20X9* £	*March 20X9* £	
Inflows				
Receipts from debtors	200,000	125,000	125,000	Note 1
Rental income			40,000	Note 2
Total inflows	200,000	125,000	165,000	
Outflows				
Payments to creditors	(55,000)	(45,000)	(35,000)	Note 3
Wages and salaries	(55,000)	(55,000)	(55,000)	Note 4
Overheads	(30,000)	(30,000)	(30,000)	Note 5
Dividends		(90,000)		Note 6
Production machinery			(50,000)	Note 7
Total outflows	(140,000)	(220,000)	(170,000)	
Net cash flow	60,000	(95,000)	(5,000)	
Opening cash balance	Nil	60,000	(35,000)	
Closing cash balance	60,000	(35,000)	(40,000)	Note 8

Notes

1   Debtors take an average of 3 months to pay. Sales in the period January to March 20X9 are forecast to be £650,000 and no bad debts are expected.

2   Rental income from sub-letting of warehouse space is receivable quarterly in arrears.

3   Toyz Ltd takes an average of 3 months to pay creditors. Raw material purchases in the period January to March 20X9 are budgeted to be £250,000.

4   Wages and salaries are paid in the month incurred.

5   Overheads are paid in the month incurred.

6   The dividends paid in February are the annual dividends for year ended 31 December 20X8.

7   The payment in March relates to the acquisition of a new production machine which will be commissioned (installed) in March. All fixed assets are depreciated at 10% per annum commencing in the month following commissioning. Depreciation on assets held at 1 January is budgeted to be £50,000 for the next year.

8   The company's overdraft limit is £30,000.

9   There is no opening or closing raw material or work-in-progress, but finished goods are expected to be £80,000 higher at the end of March than as at 1 January 20X9.

10   The company's year end is 31 December.

Ignore taxation.

Required

(a) (i) Prepare the forecast profit and loss account for Quarter 1 20X9 to identify the profit after depreciation. (10 marks)

(ii) Calculate the forecast closing debtors and trade creditors figures as at the end of March 20X9. (2 marks)

(b) Briefly outline FOUR possible actions which could be considered by Toyz Ltd, in an attempt to improve the cash position. (8 marks)

(20 marks)

Helping hand

Explain clearly your treatment of wages and salaries and rental income within the profit and loss account, since there is no single correct approach to these items. Remember your answer to earlier questions in part (b).

6 ANSWER: TOYZ LTD

(a) (i) **Toyz Ltd - Forecast profit and loss account for the period January to March 20X9**

	£	Notes
Sales	650,000	1
Direct costs		
Raw materials	(250,000)	2
Wages and salaries	(165,000)	3
	(415,000)	
Stock movement	80,000	4
Gross profit	315,000	
Expenses		
Overheads	(90,000)	
Depreciation	(12,500)	5
	(102,500)	
Rent receivable	40,000	6
Net profit	252,500	

Notes

1 This figure is given.

2 This figure is given.

3 Wages and salaries amount to £55,000 × 3. It is assumed that these costs are effectively direct costs of production.

4 The increase in the stock level during the period must be credited to the profit and loss account.

5 Depreciation is calculated as 25% of the annual charge of £50,000. No depreciation will be chargeable on the new production machine until the second quarter.

6 It is assumed that there is no change in the level of rent receivable from the previous quarter. This item has been included with overheads since it is not a trading revenue.

7 Dividends have been excluded since these are payable out of the net profit figure.

(ii) Closing debtors will be the same as the turnover figure for the quarter since the payment period is three months. The closing debtors will therefore be £650,000.

Similarly, the closing creditors figure will be £250,000, since the December creditors will have been paid in March, and there will be three months' purchases outstanding.

(b) The cash forecast indicates that Toyz Ltd will **breach** its **overdraft limit** before the end of February, and therefore the company must at the very least seek to take measures to bring its borrowings into line with this limit. Possible courses of action include the following.

    (i) **Deferring** the **acquisition** of the **new production machinery** until the cash position is better.

    (ii) **Financing** the **acquisition** of the **new production machinery** using some form of operating or finance lease to spread the cost of the payment over a longer period.

    (iii) **Negotiating with the bank** either to **raise the overdraft limit** for a temporary period to ease the cash position following payment of the dividend, or to take on some form of **fixed term loan**. Alternatively, additional equity could be sought.

    (iv) **Taking action** to shorten the **debtors' collection period**. This may be difficult to achieve in the short time available since it could involve the renegotiation of credit terms.

    (v) Using **debt factoring** or **invoice discounting** to free funds locked up in debtors.

    (vi) **Cutting back the level of production** so that there is a smaller increase in the level of finished goods stock. However, this could impact upon the operating position for the next quarter.

    (vii) Undertake a **cost reduction programme**. Although this will help both the cash flow and profits, it may not show results quickly enough to solve the immediate liquidity problems.

Examiner's marking scheme

			Marks	
(a)	(i)	Presentation	1	
		Identification of sales figure	2	
		Identification of purchases figure	2	
		Wages calculated	1	
		Overheads calculated	1	
		Stock increase adjustment	2	
		Depreciation	1	
				10
	(ii)	Calculation of debtors	1	
		Calculation of creditors	1	
				2
(b)		Each valid suggestion briefly discussed (4 × 2 marks each)		8
				20

DO YOU KNOW? - FINANCIAL ANALYSIS AND CONTROL

- *Check that you can fill in the blanks in the statements below before you attempt any questions. If in doubt, you should go back to your BPP Interactive Text and revise first.*

- Profit margin = ... ÷ ....

- Contribution = ... less ....

- ROCE (...............) = ... ÷ ...., as a percentage.

- Asset turnover = ... ÷ ....

- Profit margin × Asset turnover = ...

- Current ratio = ... ÷ ....

- Quick ratio (or .... ratio) = ... ÷ ....

- Debtors days = ... × ....

- Stock turnover period = ... × ....

- Creditor days = ... × ....

- Debt ratio = ... ÷ ....

- Capital gearing ratio = ... ÷ ....

- Interest cover = ... ÷ ....

  TRY QUESTIONS 7 AND 8

- An independent internal audit function can be of great benefit to the efficiency of the organisation.

- .... audits are concerned with all areas of an operation's activities.

- Instead of auditing around the computer, auditors now generally audit ....

- VFM audits involve testing the ...., ... and .... of an organisation.

- In controls over cash handling, ... of duties is particularly important.

  TRY QUESTIONS 9, 10, 11 AND 12

- *Possible pitfalls*

  Write down the mistakes you know you should avoid.

DID YOU KNOW? - FINANCIAL ANALYSIS AND CONTROL

- *Could you fill in the blanks? The answers are in bold. Use this page for revision purposes as you approach the exam.*

- Profit margin = **Net profit** ÷ **Sales**

- Contribution = **Sales** less **Variable costs**

- ROCE (**Return on capital employed**) = **Profit before interest and tax** ÷ **Capital employed**, as a percentage.

- Asset turnover = **Sales** ÷ **Capital employed**

- Profit margin × Asset turnover = **ROCE**

- Current ratio = **Current assets** ÷ **Current liabilities**

- Quick ratio (or **acid test** ratio) = **Current assets less stocks** ÷ **Current liabilities**

- Debtors days = **Trade debtors** × **365/Sales**

- Stock turnover period = **Stock** × **365/Cost of sales**

- Creditor days = **Trade creditors** × **365/Purchases**

- Debt ratio = **Total liabilities** ÷ **total assets**

- Capital gearing ratio = **Prior charge capital (long-term borrowings)** ÷ **Total capital**

- Interest cover = **Profit before interest and tax** ÷ **Net interest payable**

TRY QUESTIONS 7 AND 8

- An independent internal audit function can be of great benefit to the efficiency of the organisation.

- **Operational** audits are concerned with all areas of an operation's activities.

- Instead of auditing around the computer, auditors now generally audit **through the computer**.

- VFM audits involve testing the **economy**, **efficiency** and **effectiveness** of an organisation.

- In controls over cash handling, **segregation** of duties is particularly important.

TRY QUESTIONS 9, 10, 11 AND 12

- *Possible pitfalls*
  - **Getting ratio analysis / formulae wrong**
  - **Miscalculating ratios**
  - **Remember: ratios are for comparison**

7   **QUESTION WITH HELP: TRADE ASSOCIATION**

WH Limited is a member of a trade association which operates an inter-company comparison scheme. The scheme is designed to help its member companies to monitor their own performance against that of other companies in the same industry.

At the end of each year, the member companies submit detailed annual accounts to the scheme organisers. The results are processed and a number of accounting ratios are published and circulated to members. The ratios indicate the average results for all member companies.

Your manager has given you the following extract, which shows the average profitability and asset turnover ratios for the latest year. For comparison purposes, WH Limited's accounts analyst has added the ratios for your company.

	Results for year 4	
	Trade association	
	average	*WH Limited*
Return on capital employed	20.5%	18.4%
Net (operating) profit margin	5.4%	6.8%
Asset turnover	3.8 times	2.7 times
Gross margin	14.2%	12.9%

Required

As assistant accountant for WH Limited, your manager has asked you to prepare a report for the Senior Management Committee. The report should cover the following points.

(a)   An explanation of what each ratio is designed to show   (7 marks)

(b)   An interpretation of WH Limited's profitability and asset turnover compared with the trade association average   (8 marks)

(c)   Comments on any limitations of these ratios and of comparisons made on this basis   (5 marks)
                    (20 marks)

> *If you are stuck, look at the next page for detailed help as to how you should tackle this question.*

APPROACHING THE ANSWER

Use this answer plan to construct your answer if you are stuck.

(a) (i)   ROCE   -   how calculated
                          -   what it measures and responsibility for it

   (ii) Net operating -   how calculated
       profit margin -   what it measures and responsibility for it

   (iii) Asset turnover -   how calculated
                          -   what it measures

   (iv) Gross margin   -   how calculated
                          -   what it highlights

(b) (i)   ROCE   -   reasons for difference

   (ii) Operating profit margin -   reasons for difference

   (iii) Asset turnover   -   reasons for difference

   (iv) Gross profit margin   -   reasons for difference (costs and sales)

(c) • Averages
   • Movements around year-end
   • Different accounting policies
   • Different methods of calculation
   • Impact of diversification

7   **ANSWER: TRADE ASSOCIATION**

WH LIMITED

REPORT

To: Senior Management Committee
From: Assistant accountant
Date: 12 December 20X4
Subject: Profitability and asset turnover ratios

We have received the trade association results for year 4 and this report looks in detail at the profitability and asset turnover ratios.

(a) **What each ratio is designed to show**

(i)   **Return on capital employed (ROCE)/Return on investment (ROI)**

This ratio shows the percentage rate of profit which has been earned on the capital invested in the business, that is the return on the resources controlled by management. The expected return varies depending on the type of business and it is usually calculated as follows.

$$\text{Return on capital employed} = \frac{\text{Profit before interest and tax}}{\text{Capital employed}} \times 100\%$$

Other profit figures can be used, as well as various definitions of capital employed.

(ii) **Net operating profit margin**

This ratio shows the operating profit as a percentage of sales. The operating profit is calculated before interest and tax and it is the profit over which operational mangers can exercise day to day control. It is the amount left after all direct costs and overheads have been deducted from sales revenue.

$$\text{Net operating profit margin} = \frac{\text{Operating profit}}{\text{Sales revenue}} \times 100\%$$

(iii) **Asset turnover**

This ratio shows how effectively the assets of a business are being used to generate sales.

$$\text{Asset turnover} = \frac{\text{Gross profit}}{\text{Sales revenue}}$$

If the same figure for capital employed is used as in ROCE, than ratios (i) to (iii) can be related together as follows.

(i) ROCE = (ii) net operating profit margin × (iii) asset turnover

(iv) **Gross margin**

This ratio measures the profitability of sales.

$$\text{Gross margin} = \frac{\text{Gross profit}}{\text{Sales revenue}} \times 100\%$$

The gross profit is calculated as sales revenue less the cost of goods sold, and this ratio therefore focuses on the company's manufacturing and trading activities.

(b)   **WH Limited's profitability and asset turnover**

    (i)   WH Limited's ROCE is lower than the trade association average, possibly indicating that the company's assets are not being used as profitably as in the industry as a whole.

    (ii)   WH Limited's **operating profit margin** is **higher** than the **trade association average,** despite a lower than average gross profit margin. This suggests that non-production costs are lower in relation to sales value in WH Limited than in the industry as a whole.

    (iii)   WH Limited's **asset turnover ratio** is **lower** than the **trade association average.** This may mean that assets are not being used as effectively in our company as in the industry as a whole, which could be the cause of the lower than average ROCE.

    (iv)   WH Limited's **gross profit margin** is **lower** than the **trade association average.** This suggests either that WH Limited's production costs are higher than average, or that selling prices are lower than average.

(c)   **Limitations of the ratios and inter-company comparisons**

There are a number of limitations of which management should be aware before drawing any firm conclusions from a comparison of these ratios.

    (i)   The **ratios are merely averages,** based on year-end balance sheet data, which may not be representative.

    (ii)   These ratios could be **affected** by any **new investment** towards the end of the financial year. Such investment would increase the value of the assets or capital employed, but the profits from the investment would not yet have accumulated in the profit and loss account. Generally, newer assets tend to depress the asset turnover and hence the ROCE in the short term. It is possible that this is the cause of our company's lower asset turnover and ROCE.

    (iii)   Although the trade association probably makes some attempt to standardise the data, different member companies may be using **different accounting policies,** for example in calculating depreciation and valuing stock.

    (iv)   Our company's analyst may have used a **different formula** for calculating one or more of the ratios. For example, as noted above, there are a variety of ways of calculating capital employed. It is likely, however, that the trade association would provide information on the basis of calculation of the ratios.

    (v)   The member companies will have some **activities in common,** hence their membership of the trade association. Some may, however, have a **diversified range of activities,** which will distort the ratios and make direct comparison difficult.

If you would like any further information please do not hesitate to contact me.

8   CATERER LTD (6/01)

Caterer Ltd produces a standard meal for consumption by airline passengers, which it sells to various airlines throughout Europe. Each meal is sold to the airlines for £2.00.

At present, the company's plant is operating at full capacity and it is not possible to increase sales above the current level, unless further investment is made in premises and equipment.

The most recent set of company accounts reveals the following.

Profit and loss account for year ending 31 May 20X1

	£m
Sales (2m meals)	4.0
Less variable costs	(2.0)
	2.0
Less fixed costs	(1.0)
Profit before interest and taxation	1.0
Less interest payable	(0.2)
Profit before tax	0.8
Less taxation (25%)	(0.2)
Profit after tax	0.6
Ordinary dividends	(0.3)
Retained earnings	0.3

Balance sheet extracts as at 31 May 20X1

	£m	£m
Share capital		
5m ordinary shares (par value 50p)	2.5	
Share premium	2.0	
Retained earnings	0.5	
		5.0
Medium term finance		
10% debentures 20Y0		2.0
		7.0

Notes

1   The production manager has indicated that the building of an extension and the installation of a new packaging process at a cost of £2m will increase output by 20%. It is expected that this additional capacity will be fully utilised.

2   The financial controller has indicated that this expansion would be financed by £2m 10% debentures, issued at par.

3   The new proposed investment will reduce variable costs of all meals by 20p per meal, but will increase fixed costs by £200,000 per annum.

4   Installation of the new facilities could be put in place immediately.

5   There is no change expected in the tax rate.

6   The company intends to increase the dividend per share by 10%.

Required

(a)   Assuming the company decides to install the new facilities immediately, prepare a projected profit and loss account for the year ended 31 May 20X2.   (8 marks)

(b)   (i)   Calculate and briefly comment on the following ratios as at 31 May 20X1 and those projected as at 31 May 20X2:

   Gearing ratio (Total debt/total equity)
   Interest cover (Times interest earned)   (4 marks)

(ii)   Briefly state two items of additional information you would require before deciding whether or not to invest in the new facilitates.   (2 marks)

(c)   Identify and discuss four practical factors that are likely to have an influence on the level of gearing which can be achieved. (Where possible, relate your answer to a company such as Caterer Ltd.)   (6 marks)

(20 marks)

Helping hand

In (a) be careful about the change in variable costs; remember also you are presenting a profit and loss account that includes financing costs.

In (b) think about the levels, the changes and what would be regarded as an acceptable level.

Your answer to (c) should address variability, security and formal restrictions on Caterer's borrowing.

---

8   **ANSWER: CATERER LTD**

Helping hand

Your answer to (a) should not just have considered operating profits. Extra funding does mean extra interest and dividends.

In (b) you need more specific information about the present value of the project, but also need to consider the wider issues of variability of returns and non-financial factors.

Your answer to (c) should have identified that much depends on the attitudes of borrowers and lenders. Do the directors want to bear a heavy interest burden, and risk the consequences of not being able to pay what they owe. What can the company offer to lenders (security)? What is the attitude of lenders to the possibility of default?

What the examiner said

Generally this question was answered well by most candidates. The most significant weakness was an inability to calculate the gearing ratios in (b)(i).

(a)   Projected profit and loss account for the year ended 31 May 20X2

	Note	£m
Sales (2.4m meals at £2)		4.80
Less: variable costs	1	(1.92)
		2.88
Less: fixed costs	2	(1.20)
Profit before interest and tax		1.68
Less: interest payable	3	(0.40)
Profit before tax		1.28
Less: taxation at 25%		(0.32)
Profit after tax		0.96
Ordinary dividends	4	(0.33)
Retained earnings		0.63

Notes

1   Variable costs are currently 50% sales = £1 per meal. This will be reduced by 20% to £0.80 per meal. Total cost will therefore be 2.4m × £0.80 = £1.92m.

2   Fixed costs will increase by £200,000 to £1.2m.

3   Interest on existing debenture = £2m × 10% = £0.2m
Interest on new expenditure = £2m × 10% = £0.2m

4   Dividends will be increased by 10% = £0.3m × 1.1 = £0.33m

(b)   (i)   **Gearing ratio**

	20X1		*20X2*
Total debt	£2m	£2m + £2m =	£4m
Total equity	£5m	£5m + £0.63m =	£5.63m
Gearing	40%		71%

The gearing ratio has risen sharply over the year, based on book values. This will **restrict** the company's **ability** to **borrow further** in the future and may impact on the attractiveness of the shares. However, the calculations have been based on book values. Although we do not know the current share price, it is probable that the effect will be less marked if market values are used.

Interest cover

	20X1	*20X2*
Profit before interest and tax	£1.0m	£1.68m
Interest payable	£0.2m	£0.40
Interest cover	5 times	4.2 times

Although there has been a reduction in the level of interest cover, it has not fallen to what would normally be regarded as a **critical level**. An interest cover in excess of three times is generally regarded as acceptable.

(ii) Additional items of information that would be required include:

- A **financial appraisal** of the **proposed investment**, ideally using present value techniques

- An **appraisal** of the **non-financial factors** such as the effect on the competitive position

- An **assessment** of the **risk** of the proposals

(c) Practical factors that influence the level of gearing that can be achieved include:

(i) **Stability of earnings**. If earnings are stable and consistent the company will be able to sustain a higher level of gearing since there will be less risk of its being able to service the debt.

(ii) **Security**. Companies with a good quality asset base will be able to raise more finance and sustain a higher level of gearing than will those with poorer quality fixed assets.

(iii) **The nature of the industry**. The range of acceptable gearing tends to vary from industry to industry. Similarly, this will be affected by the growth prospects for the industry, companies in sectors with better prospects being able to achieve higher gearing in anticipation of future earnings growth.

(iv) **Attitude to risk**. The attitude of the directors and shareholders to risk will be significant in determining what is an acceptable level of gearing for the company to achieve.

(v) **Reputation of the company**. The trading history and reputation of the company will influence the ease with which it will be able to gain credit, and therefore the level of gearing that it will be able to achieve.

(vi) **Memorandum and articles of association**. These may restrict the amount that the company is permitted to borrow, and therefore its maximum gearing level.

(vii) **Existing loan covenants**. There may be covenants on existing loans that restrict the company's ability to borrow further.

			Marks	
Examiner's marking scheme				
(a)	Sales volume/revenue		2	
	Variable costs/fixed costs		2	
	Interest payable/taxation		2	
	Dividends		1	
	Presentation		1	
				8
(b)	(i) Gearing ratios		2	
	Interest cover		2	
				4
	(ii) NPV analysis		1	
	Non-financial factor evaluation		1	2
(c)	Each factor identified and briefly explained	(4 × 1½ marks)		6
				20

9   MEASURES PLC (6/99)

Measures plc, a quoted company, manufactures electronic weighing scales. The accounting statements for the most recent year are summarised below. Fixed assets are shown at historical cost, net of depreciation.

Balance sheet as at 31 December 20X0

	£m	£m
Fixed assets		
Land and premises	12	
Equipment	28	
		40
Current assets		
Stocks	14	
Debtors	15	
Cash	1	
	30	
Less liabilities due within 1 year		
Trade creditors	20	
Bank overdraft	5	
	(25)	
Net current assets		5
Total assets less current liabilities		45
Less creditors due after 1 year		
10% debenture 20X7		(30)
Net assets		15

Financed by	£m
Issued share capital (10m par value £0.50)	5
Share premium	2
Retained earnings	8
Shareholder's funds	15

Profit and loss account for the year ending 31 December 20X0

	£m
Sales	110.0
Cost of sales	(97.0)
Operating profit	13.0
Interest charges	(4.0)
Profit before tax	9.0
Corporation tax 40%	(3.6)
Profits after tax	5.4
Dividends	(0.4)
Retained earnings	5.0

BPP PROFESSIONAL EDUCATION

Note 1. The following information is available for the industry in which Measures plc operates.

Financial Statistics - Industry Averages

Return on capital employed	24%
Return on shareholders' capital	15%
Operating profit margin	10%
Current ratio	2:1
Acid test	1:1
Debtors days	30 days
Gearing (total debt: total equity)	80% by book value
Times interest earned (interest cover)	5 times
Price earnings (P/E) ratio	14 times

Note 2. Measures plc shares are currently trading at £5.40 each.

Note 3. When calculating gearing, use the book value of total debt (including bank overdraft) as a percentage of the book value of equity.

Required

(a) Discuss the financial performance of Measures plc compared to the industry as a whole, supporting your answer with key ratios.

(Approximately 8 marks are available for calculation and 8 marks for relevant discussion.) (16 marks)

(b) In an effort to improve profitability, the board of directors is considering a value-for-money audit throughout the company, commencing with the purchasing department.

Briefly explain what is meant by a value for money (VFM) audit. (4 marks)

(20 marks)

Helping hand

In (a) the best way to organise your answer is to group the answers under four main headings.

* Profitability and return
* Liquidity
* Debt and gearing
* Shareholder investment ratios

In (b) you should focus on the three key elements of VFM.

---

9   ANSWER: MEASURES PLC

(a)   Ratios can be grouped into four main categories.

	Measures plc	*Industry*

Profitability and return

1   **Return on capital employed**

$$\frac{\text{Profit before interest and tax}}{\text{Capital employed}} = 13/45$$

	Measures plc	*Industry*
	29%	24%

2   **Operating profit margin**

$$\frac{\text{Profit before interest and tax}}{\text{Sales}} = 13/110$$

	Measures plc	*Industry*
	12%	10%

Measures plc is much more profitable than the industry as a whole, both in terms of return on sales and return on capital employed.

Liquidity: control of cash and other working capital items

3   **Current ratio**

Current assets current liabilities 30:25

	Measures plc	*Industry*
	1.2:1	2:1

4   **Acid test**

Current assets excluding stock current liabilities

	Measures plc	*Industry*
	0.64:1	1:1

5   **Debtors days**

$$\frac{\text{Average debtors}}{\text{Sales}} \times 365$$

Liquidity is **very poor** compared with the rest of the industry. In particular, the **current** and **quick ratios appear dangerously low** for a manufacturing company, and Measures could face liquidity problems. **Control of working capital** is **poor** compared with the rest of the industry, with the collection period for debtors well above the industry average. Improved control of working capital would help to ease the liquidity problems and improve the current and quick ratios.

Debt and gearing

6   **Gearing (book values)**

$$\frac{\text{Total debt (incl overdraft)}}{\text{Total equity}} = (30 + 5)/15$$

	Measures plc	*Industry*
	233%	80%

7   **Interest cover (times interest earned)**

$$\frac{\text{Profit before interest and tax}}{\text{Interest}} = 13/4$$

                                                             3.25 times   5 times

Gearing is much **higher than the industry average**, with debt being the major source of finance. As would be expected, the interest cover is lower than the industry average, although at 3.25 times there would not appear to be a high risk of default.

Shareholder investment ratios

8   **Return on shareholders' capital**

$$\frac{\text{Profit available for dividend}}{\text{Shareholders' funds}} = 5.4/15$$

                                                             36%   15%

9   **Price earnings (P/E) ratio**

$$\frac{\text{Market price of a share}}{\text{Earnings per share}} = 5.40/0.54$$

                                                             10 times   14 times

Earnings per share = profit after tax (£5.4m) ÷ Number of shares in issue (10m)

Return on capital is well **above the industry average**, but the **P/E ratio is lower**. Presumably this is because investors recognise the high gearing and the liquidity problems, and therefore perceive this company to be a riskier investment than others in the industry. This perception is reflected in the share price, and therefore in the P/E ratio.

(b) A **value for money (VFM) audit** is an evaluation of the performance of a particular function of the business, such as credit control. The aim is to assess performance in terms of the following.

    (i)   **Economy.** The department should be meeting its given performance targets with the minimum use of resources, without compromising quality. For example, in the credit control function this might involve regularly assessing the market to ensure that the credit rating agency used is competitive with other agencies.

    (ii)   **Efficiency.** The department should be maximising its output per unit of resource input. In credit control this could mean increasing the number of invoicing queries resolved each day.

    (iii)   **Effectiveness.** This means achieving the targets set for the department. For example, in credit control this might be reducing the level of bad debts as a percentage of sales by 0.5%.

Examiner's marking scheme		**Marks**
(a) Calculation of each ratio to compare with the industry sector average (8 × 1 mark)	8	
Relevant comment on each ratio (8 × 1 mark)	8	
		16
(b) VFM briefly explained	1	
Economy/efficiency/effectiveness (3 × 1 mark)	3	
		4
		20

10   TOM, DICK AND HARRY (12/99)

Ten years ago, three business acquaintances, Tom, Dick and Harry, jointly formed an ice-cream manufacturing and distribution company TDH Ltd. Since its inception it has been very successful and has grown to become one of the country's major ice-cream companies, with six manufacturing outlets and over ten retail units in various shopping centres. Its turnover is now approaching £10 million per annum. Tom recently attended a business conference entitled 'Fraud and its prevention'. The conference has made him concerned about the risk of fraud in TDH Ltd, as there is no internal audit function and neither himself, Dick nor Harry has an expertise in accounting or auditing. As a result, he has proposed that a review of internal control procedures to be undertaken and that consideration be given to the establishment of an internal audit function.

Required

(a)   Identify and briefly describe FOUR different types of fraud which may occur within a business such as TDH Ltd.   (8 marks)

(b)   (i)   Briefly explain TWO ways in which an internal audit function could help prevent or detect fraud.   (2 marks)

      (ii)   Briefly explain FOUR features of an internal control system, which could help prevent or detect fraud.   (6 marks)

      (iii) Briefly outline TWO ways in which the personnel department could help prevent or reduce fraud.   (4 marks)

(20 marks)

10   **ANSWER: TOM, DICK AND HARRY**

(a)   **Types of fraud which may occur within a business such as TDH Ltd**

    (i)   Fraud in connection with **cash handling in retail outlets**. Staff may take money for ice creams and put it in their own pockets rather than in the till. This is especially possible with this type of product which is scooped by hand from a large tub. It is harder where all products sold are individually recorded within a stock control and invoicing system.

    (ii)   Fraud in connection with **cash handling in manufacturing units**. This can arise when false petty cash vouchers are raised, and cash paid against them.

    (iii)   **Payroll fraud**. This can occur in various ways, for example by recording higher levels of hours than were actually worked, or by setting up payroll records for non-existent employees.

    (iv)   Fraud connected with the **creditors' ledger**. For example accounts can be set up for imaginary suppliers, and then invoices raised and paid on these accounts.

(b)   (i)   An internal audit function can help prevent or detect fraud as follows.

        (1)   It can carry out **independent special investigations** into situations where fraud is suspected.

        (2)   The presence of the function and the knowledge that procedures will be regularly monitored may **deter the perpetrators** of fraud from acting illegally.

    (ii)   **Features of an internal control system that could help prevent or detect fraud**

        (1)   **Segregation of duties.** An important means of control is to separate the duties of various individuals so that no one person is in a position to record and process a complete transaction. There should be a division of responsibilities for:

- **Authorising** or initiating the transaction
- The physical **custody** and control of assets involved
- **Recording** the transaction

        (2)   **Physical controls.** These relate to the custody of assets and aim at restricting access to assets such as stock and cash to specified authorised personnel. Such controls are particularly important in the case of valuable, portable or attractive assets.

        (3)   **Supervision controls.** Responsible officials should supervise on a day-to-day basis the carrying out and recording of transactions.

        (4)   **Authorisation and approval controls.** All transactions should require approval or authorisation by a responsible official whose duties and authorisation limits are clearly defined.

    (iii)   Ways in which the personnel department could help prevent or reduce fraud include the following

        (1)   Establishing **clear lines of responsibility** within the organisation, and making it easy for staff who suspect fraudulent practice to report their suspicions in a 'safe' manner.

        (2)   Exercising controls over the **selection and training** of staff so that the abilities of members of staff match up to their responsibilities.

Examiner's marking scheme

				Marks
(a)	(i)	Identification	(4 × 1)	4
		Description	(4 × 1)	4
				8
(b)	(i)	Each method identified and discussed	(2 × 1)	2
	(ii)	Each feature identified	(4 × ½)	2
		and discussed	(4 × 1)	4
				6
	(iii)	Each suggestion identified	(2 × 1)	2
		and briefly discussed	(2 × 1)	2
				4
				20

11   SPARX LTD (12/98)

Sparx Ltd is a rapidly expanding chain of retail outlets specialising in electrical goods. The board of directors has recently decided to implement improvements in internal controls and to investigate the possibility of creating an internal audit function.

Required

(a) (i)   Briefly describe the concept of internal control.   (2 marks)

    (ii)   Identify and briefly describe FOUR fundamental requirements in the design of internal controls which may help Sparx Ltd to prevent or detect errors or fraud.
                                                                                              (8 marks)

(b) (i)   Briefly outline THREE advantages to Sparx Ltd of having an internal audit function.   (6 marks)

    (ii)   Briefly outline TWO main difference between the internal and external audit functions.   (4 marks)

                                                                                      (20 marks)

Helping hand

In (a) (ii) think about management's role and also recording.

In your answer to part (b)(i) you may find it helpful to consider the specific issues that will be facing Sparx because of the nature of its business activity. In (b) (ii) think about who appoints auditors and what auditors are trying to do.

---

11   ANSWER: SPARX LTD

> **Helping hand**
>
> Additional points have been included in the suggested solution to parts (a)(ii), (b)(i) and (b)(ii). Recording and commitment by management are key components of internal control. In (b) (i) the geographical spread of the business has to be addressed. In (b) (ii) main differences are summarised under three headings.
>
> **What the examiner said**
>
> A question on internal and external audit seemed to come as a surprise to some candidates. This is an important section of the syllabus. Some candidates produced very good answers while others did not attempt the question at all, even though all questions on the paper were compulsory.

(a)   (i)   An **internal control** is any action taken by management to enhance the likelihood that established objectives and goals will be achieved. Management plans, organises and directs the performance of sufficient actions to provide reasonable assurance that objectives and goals will be achieved. Thus, control is the result of proper planning, organising and directing by management.

   (ii)   Key fundamental requirements in the design of internal controls to help Sparx Ltd in the prevention and detection of **fraud** include the following.

      (1)   **Responsibilities** should be **delegated** so as to ensure that there is a **segregation** of key roles to avoid fraudulent activity. For example, the same person as the one who banks the receipts should not carry out the bank reconciliation.

      (2)   All **financial transactions** should require **appropriate authorisation**. For example, local managers might have to receive head office authorisation for capital purchases in excess of a given size.

      (3)   Managers must be committed to the **control function**, taking care to **review accounts and reports** thoroughly, and to follow up recommendations made by the internal audit team.

      (4)   There should be an acceptance and an expectation throughout the organisation that their work will be subject to **periodic checks**. This will reduce the temptation to commit fraud or simply to be satisfied with poor quality work.

      (5)   There should be **clear lines of responsibility and accountability**.

      (6)   There should be a comprehensive **audit trail** of the movement of the physical assets of the company.

(b)   (i)   (1)   The very presence of an **internal audit function** may act as a deterrent to restrict people from the temptation to defraud or simply to carry out tasks to a poor standard. The function thereby safeguards resources and encourages excellence in the quality of work carried out.

      (2)   Sparx is expanding fast through a large number of geographical locations. The presence of an internal audit function can help to ensure that **consistent approaches and standards** are used throughout the organisation, and in particular, that **accounting and internal control systems** are **appropriate**.

      (3)   The role of internal audit goes beyond that of **external audit**, and the department can ensure that there is **compliance throughout the**

organisation with laws, regulations and other external requirements that affect the business.

(4) The presence of an internal audit function can **reduce** the **costs of the external audit**. If the internal audit team is operating efficiently, the external auditors will be able to rely on their work, particularly in the area of systems audit, thus reducing the scale of the annual audit.

(ii) The main differences between internal and external audit are as follows.

(1) **Appointment.** External auditors are appointed by the company or its shareholders and must be independent of the company, whereas internal auditors are employees of the organisation.

(2) **Responsibility.** External auditors are responsible to the owners (shareholders, the public or Parliament), whereas internal auditors are responsible to senior management.

(3) **Objectives.** The objectives for external auditors are defined by statute, whereas those for internal auditors are set by management. Thus management decides what parts of the organisation or what systems they are to look at, and what type of audit should be carried out.

		Examiner's marking scheme		**Marks**
(a)	(i)	Identification of management responsibility		1
		Systems, procedures, policies to ensure orderly and efficient conduct of business		1
	(ii)	Each concept identified and briefly explained	(4 × 2 marks)	8
				10
(b)	(i)	Each advantage briefly explained	(3 × 2 marks)	6
	(ii)	Each difference identified and briefly explained	(2 × 2 marks)	4
				10
				20

12   SOKE PLC (6/01)

Soke plc, an international soft drinks company, has recently acquired Fizz Ltd, which produces high quality soft drinks for its local domestic market. Following the acquisition, the internal audit department of Soke plc examined the capital investment appraisal procedures in Fizz Ltd.

The report summary was critical of processes in use and concluded that:

1   There is no apparent structure or formalised process for evaluation of capital investment projects.
2   Post completion controls do not exist in any meaningful way.

Required

(a)   As the financial assistant, prepare a draft report to the finance director, identifying and briefly explaining the major stages in evaluating and controlling expenditure projects.

(8 marks)

(b)   (i)   Identify and briefly explain two advantages of a post completion audit. (4 marks)

(ii)   Prepare a proposed procedure for a post completion audit, identifying key features which need to be incorporated into such a procedure.   (8 marks)

(20 marks)

Helping hand

(a) requires a knowledge of the procedures of project management. Try planning the question by drawing a flow diagram, and think about what each stage is designed to achieve.

In (b) (i) think about the timescales. Your answer to (b) (ii) should cover the attributes staff should possess, the key concerns of the audit, and what should be communicated about the work done.

---

12   ANSWER: SOKE PLC

Helping hand

In (a) your answer needs to bring out the phased nature – initial general investigation and then a more detailed overview. The other key aspect is control – authorisation, monitoring and the post-completion audit.

In (b) (i) ideally the results should influence projects currently in progress as well as projects that will be started in the future. The suggested solution to (b) (i) contains more points than are required by the question. Other sensible suggestions would be equally valid.

For (b) (ii) the audit team have to be competent and independent (as all auditors should be!), and need to focus on the variations. Constructive relationships with staff being audited are important, and this should feed through to recommendations and feedback given by the audit team.

(a)   To: Finance Director
      From: Financial Assistant
      Date: 16 October 20X2
      Subject: Evaluating and controlling expenditure projects

The main stages involved in evaluating and controlling capital expenditure projects are as follows:

1   **Initial investigation**

    We need to consider whether the project is **technically and commercially feasible,** what are the **main risks** and whether it fits with the company's **long-term strategic objectives.**

2   **Detailed evaluation**

    Once the feasibility of the project has been established, a **detailed investigation** will examine expected cash flow arising from the project, using DCF and other appropriate techniques.

    The effects of risk should be analysed using **sensitivity analysis.**

    Sources of finance should be considered. If there are insufficient funds to undertake all the proposed projects, they should be ranked in order of priority.

3   **Authorisation**

    For capital projects that are significant relative to the size of the company, **authorisation rules** should require that the decision to go ahead be made by **senior management** or the board of directors. Those making the decision must be satisfied that an appropriately detailed evaluation has been carried out, that the proposal meets the necessary criteria to contribute to profitability, and that it is consistent with the overall strategy of the enterprise.

4   **Implementation**

    Once the decision has been made that the project will be undertaken, **responsibility** for the project should be **assigned** to a project manager or other responsible person. The **required resources** will need to be made available to this manager, who should be given specific targets to achieve.

5   **Project monitoring**

    After the start of the project, **progress** should be **monitored** and senior management should be informed regularly on the development of the project.

6   **Post-completion audit**

At the end of the project, a **post-completion audit** should be undertaken in order to learn from the experience in the planning of future projects.

Signed: Financial Assistant

(b) (i)   Benefits of a post-completion audit include the following.

(1) **Better future investment decisions.** The audit can identify where mistakes have been made, so that similar mistakes can be avoided in the future. It might also identify areas of success that could be replicated in future projects.

(2) **Better current investment decisions.** Awareness that an audit will be carried out at a later date may encourage managers involved to be more realistic and not unduly optimistic in their judgements.

(3) **Contribution to performance evaluation.** A project audit can provide feedback to senior management which is of use in the process of management control and performance assessment.

(ii)   The procedures to be adopted will depend on the type of project being considered. However, key features to be addressed include the following:

(1) Staff involved in the audit should be **independent** from those involved in carrying out the project.

(2) They should also have the technical and market **competence** to carry out the review.

(3) The original **objectives** of the project should be identified, and performance should be evaluated against these objectives.

(4) **Financial performance** should be compared with the original plan, and **material deviations** should be **investigated**. If financial performance is well below that anticipated, then the option of abandoning the project should be evaluated.

(5) **Communication** with those directly involved in the project is important throughout the process. If the audit team is seen as the 'hit squad' there will be little incentive to learn from the process. Audit should not be about apportioning blame.

(6) **Significant variations** from the forecast costs and revenues should be investigated to improve the way in which risk is handled in project evaluation.

(7) The audit team should make specific **recommendations** at the end of the audit that will **improve** the **cost effectiveness** of future project management. Benefits of the process should exceed its costs.

(8) There should be **feedback** of the outcomes to all the relevant personnel to ensure that the maximum is learned from the exercise and that project management is improved as a result.

Examiner's marking scheme				**Marks**
(a)	Each stage identified and briefly described		(4 × 2 marks)	8
(b)	(i)	Each advantage identified and discussed	(2 × 2 marks)	4
	(ii)	Each guideline identified		8
				20

DO YOU KNOW? - WORKING CAPITAL MANAGEMENT

- *Check that you know the following basic points before you attempt any questions. If in doubt, you should go back to your BPP Interactive Text and revise first.*

- A situation of excessive working capital is referred to as ....

- A situation where a business tries to do too much with too little long-term capital is called ....

- The functions of a treasurer include ...., ..., ..., and ....

  TRY QUESTION 13

- When a company has debtors, it is effectively lending money interest-free. Debtors can therefore be a major cost. Strict control must be maintained to ensure that credit limits are not exceeded and that debtors pay by the due date.

  ° Discounts may be allowed for prompt payment. .... must be compared with ....

  ° If credit terms are relaxed to increase sales, ... must be compared with ....

- Creditors should be paid just early enough so as to ....

- Credit control deals with a firm's management of its working capital. .... credit is offered to business customers. .... credit is offered to household customers.

- A firm must consider suitable payment terms. .... can be offered, if cost-effective and if they improve liquidity.

- Credit risk is the possibility that .... High risk customers can be profitable, but need to be managed carefully.

- Data about potential debtors can be obtained from a number of sources.

  ° .... owe a duty of care to their customers and to the enquirer: their assessments of a debtor's credit statement are likely to be precisely worded.

  ° .... references are useful, but should not be used uncritically.

  ° .... agencies supply legal and business information and give suggested ratings.

- .... analyses can be prepared by customer or in any useful aggregation. Aggregated information may highlight disputed items or overdues as a percentage of debtors.

- Factoring can be *with* or *without* .... Where the factor is exposed to the risk of bad debts the fees are likely to be higher.

- Credit insurance can be obtained against .... However, the insurers will rarely insure the entire debt portfolio.

- Some customers are reluctant to pay. A staged process of reminders and demands, culminating in ...., is necessary.

  TRY QUESTIONS 14, 15, 16, 17, 18 AND 19

- Management of trade creditors involves seeking ...., ..., and ....

- Methods of paying creditors include ...., ..., ..., ..., ..., and ....

- The optimal quantity of order to minimise stock costs is called the ....

- JIT stands for .... procurement and involves obtaining goods from suppliers at the latest possible time, thus avoiding the need to carry materials or components stocks.

  TRY QUESTIONS 20, 21, 22, 23 AND 24

- *Possible pitfalls*

  Write down the mistakes you know you should avoid.

DID YOU KNOW? - WORKING CAPITAL MANAGEMENT

- *Could you fill in the blanks? The answers are in bold. Use this page for revision purposes as you approach the exam.*

- A situation of excessive working capital is referred to as **over-capitalisation**.

- A situation where a business tries to do too much with too little long-term capital is called **overtrading**.

- The functions of a treasurer include **advising on capital structure, managing cash flows to minimise associated costs, maintaining good banking relationships** and **managing foreign currency transactions to avoid risk.**

  TRY QUESTION 13

- When a company has debtors, it is effectively lending money interest-free. Debtors can therefore be a major cost. Strict control must be maintained to ensure that credit limits are not exceeded and that debtors pay by the due date.
  - ° Discounts may be allowed for prompt payment. **The interest saving from obtaining prompt payment** must be compared with **the cost of the discount**.
  - ° If credit terms are relaxed to increase sales, **the benefit from increased sales** must be compared with **the interest cost and any increased bad debt cost**.

- Creditors should be paid just early enough so as to **avoid costly penalties or to secure worthwhile discounts**.

- Credit control deals with a firm's management of its working capital. **Trade** credit is offered to business customers. **Consumer** credit is offered to household customers.

- A firm must consider suitable payment terms. **Settlement discounts** can be offered, if cost-effective and if they improve liquidity.

- Credit risk is the possibility that **a debt will go bad**. High risk customers can be profitable, but need to be managed carefully.

- Data about potential debtors can be obtained from a number of sources.
  - ° **Banks** owe a duty of care to their customers and to the enquirer: their assessments of a debtor's credit statement are likely to be precisely worded.
  - ° **Trade** references are useful, but should not be used uncritically.
  - ° **Credit reference** agencies supply a variety of legal and business information, and give suggested ratings.

- **Debtor ageing** analyses can be prepared by customer or in any useful aggregation. Aggregated information may highlight disputed items or overdues as a percentage of debtors.

- Factoring can be *with* or *without* **recourse**. Where the factor is exposed to the risk of bad debts the fees are likely to be higher.

- Credit insurance can be obtained against **bad debts**. However, the insurers will rarely insure the entire debt portfolio.

- Some customers are reluctant to pay. A staged process of reminders and demands, culminating in **debt collection or legal action**, is necessary.

  TRY QUESTIONS 14, 15, 16, 17, 18 AND 19

- Management of trade creditors involves seeking **satisfactory credit from suppliers, extended credit during cash shortages,** and **good relations with key suppliers.**

- Methods of paying creditors include **cheque, BACS, banker's draft, standing order, direct debit**, and **mail transfer**.

- The optimal quantity of order to minimise stock costs is called the **economic order quantity**.

- JIT stands for **Just-In-Time** procurement and involves obtaining goods from suppliers at the latest possible time, thus avoiding the need to carry materials or components stocks.

  TRY QUESTIONS 20, 21, 22, 23 AND 24

- *Possible pitfalls*
  - ° **Not looking at working capital as a whole: controlling working capital means controlling costs.**
  - ° **Not calculating costs and benefits of new policies carefully, from the point of view of the business.**

13   QUESTION WITH HELP: P&Q

(a)   What are the three main issues underlying the management of cash and the control of credit? Would you say that one of them was always more important than the others?

(5 marks)

(b)   P & Q plc is a UK-based manufacturing company having subsidiary companies in the USA and various European countries and also a number of overseas agencies.

The company has been growing rapidly and the finance director has recently put in hand a major reorganisation of the finance department, including the setting up of a separate treasury function.

Required

Draft a report from the finance director to the board describing the proposed responsibilities of the treasury function.

(7 marks)

(c)   Explain why the reported profit figure for a period does not normally represent the amount of cash generated in that period.

(3 marks)

(15 marks)

If you are stuck, look at the next page for detailed help as to how you should tackle this question.

APPROACHING THE ANSWER

Use this answer plan to construct your answer if you are stuck.

(a)   Three issues:

- Profitability
- Liquidity
- Security

(b)   • Use report format

- Responsibilities

  ° Funding management
  ° Liquidity management
  ° Investment management
  ° Currency management

(c)   Why profit does not equal cash flow:

- The matching concept: costs and revenues are not equivalent to payments and receipts
- Items in profit statement which are not a cash flow (give an example)
- Items in cash flow but not in profit statement (give an example)

13   ANSWER TO QUESTION WITH HELP: P&Q

(a)   The three issues underlying the management of cash and the control of credit are as follows.

   (i)   **Profitability** relates to maintaining a surplus of income over expenditure, for example obtaining the best return on an investment. However, some cash management activities incur costs (eg interest payments, discount allowed) which are incurred as expenses necessary in the course of business: a discount may be offered to secure a sale, for example. These costs should be minimised.

   (ii)   **Liquidity** refers to a business's ability to pay its debts as they fall due. A firm must have access to cash in order to pay its creditors. A failure of liquidity can lead to insolvency, in which case the firm will go out of business.

   (iii) **Security** involves minimising the risk that, for example, a debt will not be collected, cash will be stolen, or that an 'investment' will turn out to be worthless.

All are equally important, but in different ways and over different timescales. As the recent example of Barings shows, unacceptable risk (a safety issue) can lead to insolvency. However, insolvency may only be a short term problem. In the long term a failure to be profitable can lead to collapse.

(b)   REPORT

   To: The Board of Directors
   From: B Brown, Finance Director
   Date: 20 May 20X9
   Subject: Proposed responsibilities of the treasury function

Following the decision at the group board meeting of 15 May 20X9, I present this report on the responsibilities of a specialist treasury function.

Proposed responsibilities of the treasury function

A treasury function's responsibilities can be usefully divided into four areas.

   (i)   **Funding management:** advising the finance director and the board on appropriate sources for the group's capital. The treasurer will advise on the cost of different types of capital, anticipate future changes, and identify where such funds can be obtained, in the light of the overall strategy for the group's capital structure.

   (ii) **Liquidity management:** co-ordinating the group's cashflows to ensure that:

      (1) Transaction costs are minimised
      (2) Short-term cash deficits and surpluses amongst group companies are set off
      (3) Banking relationships are properly managed

   (iii) **Investment management:** ensuring that surplus short-term funds awaiting investment in the group's businesses are obtaining the best possible yield, subject to the group's risk strategy.

      Where surplus funds are held on a longer term basis, the treasury department will also co-ordinate investment to yield maximum return, consistent with realising the investments for planned group expenditure.

   (iv) **Currency management:** co-ordination of group policy as regards foreign currency transactions.

(c)   The principal reasons why profit will not equal cash flow are as follows.

(i)   The '**matching concept**' means that costs and revenues do not equal payments and receipts. Revenue is recognised in the profit statement when goods are sold, and any revenue not received is recorded as a debtor. Similarly, costs are incurred when a resource is acquired or subsequently used, not when it happens to be paid for.

(ii)   Some items appearing in the profit statement do not affect cash flow. For example, **depreciation** is a 'non-cash' deduction in arriving at profit.

(iii)   Similarly, items may affect cash flow but not profit. **Capital expenditure** decisions (apart from depreciation) and stock level adjustments are examples.

14   CREDIT CONTROL DEPARTMENT

(a)   Briefly describe the role of the credit control department.   (8 marks)

(b)   A company is proposing to increase the credit period it gives to customers from one calendar month to one and a half calendar months in order to raise turnover from the present annual figure of £24 million representing 4m units per annum. The price of the product is £6 and it costs £5.40 to make. The increase in the credit period is likely to generate an extra 150,000 unit sales. Is this enough to justify the extra costs given that the company's required rate of return is 20%? Assume no changes to stock levels, as the company is increasing its operating efficiency. Assume that existing debtors will take advantage of the new terms.   (6 marks)

(c)   Specify the factors a company should take into account when considering offering cash discounts to credit customers.   (6 marks)

(20 marks)

14   ANSWER: CREDIT CONTROL DEPARTMENT

(a)   The **role of the credit control department** can include the following.

(i)   In some cases, maintaining the sales ledger (an up-to-date sales ledger is essential for adequate credit control)

(ii)   Dealing with customer queries, in some cases

(iii)   Reporting to sales staff about new enquiries

(iv)   Giving references about customers to third parties (eg credit reference agencies)

(v)   In addition to checking out customers' creditworthiness, advising on payment terms

(vi)   Setting credit limits

(vii) Visiting clients

(viii) Monitoring customer payments

In fact, the credit control function's jobs occupy a number of stages of the order cycle (from customer order to invoice despatch) and the collection cycle (from invoice despatch to the receipt of cash).

The role of the credit control department in the order and collection cycles are as follows.

(i)   **Establish credit status** for new customers or customers who request a credit extension.

(ii)   **Check credit limit.** If the order is fairly routine, and there is no problem with credit status, then credit control staff examine their records or at least the sales ledger records to see if the new order will cause the customer to exceed the credit limit.

(iii)   Issuing the delivery note, invoicing etc is not the job of the credit control department, but the credit control department will need to have **access to information**, such as invoice details, to do its job. Indeed the credit control department might well help in the design of the invoice, to ensure issues relating to payment are given their due prominence.

(iv)   The credit control department takes over the **collection cycle**, although the final payment is ultimately received by the accounts department. This includes:

(1) Issuing statements
(2) Sending demands
(3) Employing debt collectors
(4) Initiating legal action

(b)   The existing value of debtors is:

$$\frac{£24m}{12\ months} = £2m$$

If sales increased by 150,000 units, the value of debtors would be:

$$1^{1}/_{2} \times \frac{£24m + (150,000 \times £6)}{12\ months} = £3,112,500.$$

The debtors have to be financed somehow, and the additional £1,112,500 will cost £1,112,500 × 20% = £222,500 in financing costs.

The profit on the extra sales is: 150,000 units × (£6 – £5.40) = £90,000

The new credit policy is not worthwhile, mainly because existing customers would also take advantage of it.

(c) Factors that need to be taken into account when considering whether to offer **cash discounts** are detailed below. The general effects will be to shorten the collection period and to alter the level of demand.

(i) **Current trade practice.** If it is common practice within the industry to offer cash discounts, then it may be difficult to avoid doing so.

(ii) **Cost of capital.** The financial effect on speed of payment of offering cash discounts should be evaluated against the cost of capital to the company.

(iii) **Effect on liquidity.** If cash resources are scarce, the firm may not be able to offer discounts.

(iv) **Cost and ease of administration.** Such a scheme could potentially either increase costs or reduce them due to more prompt payment by customers. The effect of this must be evaluated.

(v) **Impact on sales.** The effect on encouraging customers to buy must be considered. This will depend on the elasticity of demand for the product and on the competitive structure of the industry.

15 TAC LTD (6/99)

TAC Ltd manufactures and distributes a range of cosmetic products to a wide variety of small retailers. The business has recently been expanding rapidly and the company is beginning to experience cash flow difficulties. The bank manager has expressed her concern regarding the company's continued high overdraft level and, as a result, the managing director has decided that action must be taken immediately to improve the cash flow position.

Credit sales for year ending 31 December 20X8 were £1,650,000 and average debtors during 20X8 amounted to £490,000.

The managing director initially wishes to review the working capital (cash operating) cycle of the business, with a view to identifying areas for corrective action. Following this initial review, he needs to have a proposal evaluated from a factoring institution, Finance plc.

The details of the factoring proposal are as follows.

(i)   Finance plc is prepared to provide factoring facilities to TAC Ltd and advance 80% of the value of sales advances. If the factoring proposal is accepted, TAC Ltd would be required to take advantage of the 80% advance.

(ii) Finance plc will charge 1% turnover for the factoring service and an interest rate of 15% per annum on advances.

(iii) TAC Ltd estimates factoring will save sales administration costs of £25,000 per annum.

(iv) Sales are expected to remain at 20X8 levels for the foreseeable future (all sales are on credit). As a result of the stricter credit control procedures adopted by the factoring company, average debtors days are expected to fall to 90 days.

Current overdraft rates are 13%.

Ignore taxation and inflation.

Required

(a)   Calculate whether it is financially beneficial for TAC Ltd to factor its debtors. (Note: a net present value analysis is not required.)   (14 marks)

(b)   Identify and briefly discuss, SIX specific other actions that could be taken by TAC Ltd in the management of its debtors and its stocks to reduce the cash operating cycle.

(6 marks)

(20 marks)

Helping hand

In (a) you need to start off by calculating the current cost of financing debtors, the relevant rate of interest being the overdraft rate.

Then calculate the various costs of the factoring arrangement, and consider the effect of any savings.

In (b) for debtors, consider how time could be saved, and whether changing the profile of customers would help.

For stocks the best approach is to consider each of the three components of stock.

15   ANSWER: TAC LTD

> **Helping hand**
>
> Don't forget the sales administration savings in (a). In part (b), note the question is only concerned with the management of stocks and debtors. It is therefore a waste of time to talk about the management of creditors in the cash operating cycle. The answer is a combination of immediate steps (prompt banking) and longer-term steps (changing customer base, introducing TQM).
>
> **What the examiner said**
>
> This question dealt with factoring of debtors in the management of working capital. Part (a) required a financial analysis to determine if it was financially viable for the company to factor its debtors.
>
> Many candidates provided good answers to part (b), although some wrote about actions to manage creditors and cash rather than debtors and stocks. This highlights the tendency for some candidates not to read the requirements carefully enough.

(a)   The first step is to calculate the current cost to TAC of financing its debtors at 13% pa: £490,000 × 13% = £63,700 per year

If the factoring proposal is accepted, the costs will become:

(i)   *Cost of financing debtors*

		£	£
Average debtors would become £1,650,000 × 90/365		406,849	
20% of this balance would be financed by TAC		81,370	
The cost of finance at 13% would be			10,578

(ii)   *Cost of taking the 80% advance on the value of the sales*

	£	£
Average level of advance = 80% average debtors	325,479	
Cost of advance at 15%		48,822

(iii)   *Sales administration cost charged by factor*

	£
1% of annual turnover (£1,650,000 × 1%)	16,500

(iv)   *Saving in sales administration costs at TAC*

	£
As per question	(25,000)
Net annual cost of factoring	50,900

The factoring proposal would save £12,800 per year, and therefore on financial grounds it should be accepted.

(b)   Other actions that could be taken by TAC in the management of stocks and debtors to reduce its cash operating cycle include the following.

Debtors

(i)   Ensure that the **sales invoicing system** is efficient and that invoices and credit notes are issued promptly.

(ii)   Ensure that all **receipts** are **banked promptly** so as to minimise the float time.

(iii)   Encourage customers to use **electronic settlement** methods such as BACS to reduce the time and cost of clearance.

(iv)   TAC could consider **selling to wholesalers** rather than direct to small retailers in order to reduce the costs of sales administration.

(v)   It may be possible to realise cash from the sales ledger by **invoice discounting**.

Raw material stocks

(i)   Review the way in which **stock is ordered** to ensure that the costs of purchasing are minimised through use of the economic order quantity.

(ii)   Consider moving to **Just In Time (JIT)** systems.

(iii)   Review the **range of raw materials** used to try and reduce the number of different components held in stock.

Work in progress

(i)   Review the **factory layout** to ensure that there is an efficient flow of work through the factory and to eliminate potential bottlenecks.

(ii)   Introduce a **Total Quality Management (TQM)** programme to reduce the level of scrap and waste.

(iii)   **Speed up production** through the use of automation where appropriate.

(iv)   It may be possible to **contract out** some of the production processes.

Finished goods stocks

(i)   Where possible TAC should try to **manufacture** to order to minimise this area of stock.

(ii)   It should constantly **review obsolete and slow-moving stocks,** and scrap or rework these where possible to reduce the overall level of stocks being held.

Examiner's marking scheme

		Marks	
(a)	Existing finance costs	2	
	Revised debtors	2	
	Finance plc finance cost	3	
	Own finance cost	3	
	Finance plc factor charge	1	
	Administration savings	1	
	Conclusion/recommendation	2	
			14
(b)	Identification and brief explanation of each of six actions (6 × 1 mark)		6
			20

16   EXPANDER LTD (12/99)

Expander Ltd has recently decided to set up a new factory so it can enter as both a manufacturer and wholesaler into the rapidly expanding mobile telephone market.

Expander Ltd will manufacture a single type of mobile telephone and sell it to a variety of retail outlets. The retail outlets have been categorised into three distinct groupings.

1   Mobile telephone shops

2   Chain stores specialising in a variety of telecommunications equipment

3   Internet service providers who include mobile telephones which can be linked to the internet as part of their product range

The new telephone will be launched on 1 January 20X0. Forecast sales data for the first year are as follows.

Customer type	Sales price £	January 20X0 sales Units	Monthly compound growth %	Credit period allowed Months
Mobile phone shops	50	2,000	5	1
Specialist chain stores	40	5,000	5	3
Internet service providers	30	5,000	10	3

All sales to retail outlets are on credit and are invoiced at month end, except for 10% of mobile telephone shop sales, which will be for cash.

The company is currently experiencing liquidity difficulties due to the rate of expansion being undertaken. The recently appointed financial controller is concerned about the financial implications of launching the new product, particularly in light of the fact that at present there is no credit control function in the company. This is a new market sector for the company and there will be a need to assess the creditworthiness of new customers.

Required

(a) (i)   Prepare three aged debtors schedules, one for each of the first three months of 20X0. These schedules should show the amount outstanding for each customer type, and the business as a whole appropriately aged.   (12 marks)

    (ii)   Briefly comment on the results obtained.   (2 marks)

(b) Identify and briefly discuss FOUR factors which need to be considered when assessing the credit-worthiness of new customers.   (4 marks)

(c) Briefly explain ONE method by which Expander Ltd could raise finance, using its trade debtors.   (2 marks)

(20 marks)

Helping hand

In (a) detailed workings will help you, with sales and outstanding balances from each type of customer shown separately.

Your discussion in (a) should focus on the specific issues facing this company.

In (b) think about the different sources of information on creditworthiness.

In (c) think about who could 'take over' debtors.

---

16 ANSWER: EXPANDER LTD

Helping hand

Construction of the aged debtors schedules is easier if in your workings you tabulate the monthly sales and date of receipt for each of the customer types. When commenting on the figures in (a) you should take into account the situation of the company as described, and think in practical terms of the risks that it faces.

In (b) remember the distinction between internal sources (generated by the company) and external sources (maintained by somebody else). Both types of source can provide useful information.

(a) (i) **Expander Ltd: Aged debtors forecast as at 31 January 20X0**

Customer type	2 mths (Nov) £	1 mth (Dec) £	Current (Jan) £	Total £
Mobile phone shops			90,000	90,000
Specialist chain stores			200,000	200,000
Internet service providers			150,000	150,000
Total outstanding	0	0	440,000	440,000

Expander Ltd: Aged debtors forecast as at 29 February 20X0

Customer type	2 mths (Dec) £	1 mth (Jan) £	Current (Feb) £	Total £
Mobile phone shops			94,500	94,500
Specialist chain stores		200,000	210,000	410,000
Internet service providers		150,000	165,000	315,000
Total outstanding	0	350,000	469,500	819,500

Expander Ltd: Aged debtors forecast as at 31 March 20X0

Customer type	2 mths (Jan) £	1 mth (Feb) £	Current (Mar) £	Total £
Mobile phone shops			99,225	99,225
Specialist chain stores	200,000	210,000	220,500	630,500
Internet service providers	150,000	165,000	181,500	496,500
Total outstanding	350,000	375,000	501,225	1,226,225

Workings

	£ per unit	Units sold Jan	Growth rate %	Sales Jan £	Feb £	Mar £
Mobile phone shops	50	2,000	5	100,000	105,000	110,250
Cash sales				10,000	10,500	11,025
Credit sales				90,000	94,500	99,225
Month received				Feb	Mar	Apr
Outstanding at month end				90,000	94,500	99,225
Specialist chain stores	40	5,000	5	200,000	210,000	220,500
Month received				Apr	May	Jun
Outstanding at month end				200,000	410,000	630,500
Internet service providers	30	5,000	10	150,000	165,000	181,500
Month received				Apr	May	Jun
Outstanding at month end				150,000	315,000	496,500

(ii) The figures show that by the end of March the debtors will total in excess of £1.25m. Only £216,025 will have been collected from customers by this time, although the income stream should begin to build up from April onwards as debts from specialist chain stores and internet service providers become due.

Expander Ltd will be in a risky position since it will have a **high level of debt**, all from **new customers** with whom it has no trading history, and there are currently no systems in place to assess the creditworthiness of new customers. The company therefore faces the twin risks of late payment and default, and it is recommended that effective credit control and debt collection procedures are introduced as soon as possible.

(b) **Factors to be considered when assessing creditworthiness of new customers**

(i) New customer should give **two good references**, including one from a bank, before being granted credit.

(ii) Credit ratings can be checked using a **credit rating agency**.

(iii) For large value customers, **a file** should be maintained of any available **financial information** about the customer, and its contents regularly reviewed.

(iv) The company could send a member of staff to **visit** the customer's premises, to get a first hand impression of the company and its prospects. This is particularly important in the case of prospective major customers.

(c) Expander Ltd could consider **factoring** its debtors. The main aspects of factoring are:

(i) **Administration** of the client's invoicing, sales accounting and debt collection function

(ii) **Credit protection** for the client's debts, whereby the factor takes over the risk of loss from bad debts and so 'insures' the client against such losses

(iii) **Making payments** to the client **in advance** of collecting the debts. This is sometimes referred to as **factor finance** because the factor is providing cash to the client against outstanding debts

---

Helping hand

An alternative would be to discuss **invoice discounting**. This is the purchase by the discounter of selected invoices, at a discount. Administration of the debtors ledger remains with the company, and the arrangement is purely for the advance of cash. It is usually arranged to provide temporary 'one-off' finance rather than a regular source of short-term finance.

Examiner's marking scheme

				Marks
(a)	(i)	January credit sales	(3 × 1)	3
		February credit sales	(3 × 1)	3
		March credit sales	(3 × 1)	3
		Layout for each aged schedule	(3 × 1)	3
				12
	(ii)	Relevant comments	(2 × 1)	2
(b)		Each factor discussed	(4 × 1)	4
(c)		Identification of method		1
		Brief explanation		1
				2
				20

17   PAINTER LTD (6/00)

Painter Ltd produces a range of paint for distribution to hardware stores and paint shops. Annual credit sales are £3m. Recently, the company has experienced credit control problems. Customers are taking an average of 60 days to pay, even though the agreed credit period is for payment within 30 days. Currently 2% of sales are written off as bad debts.

The company has recently approached a factoring organisation, which is prepared to advance 80% of sales. Due to the efficiency of the factor, the average credit period is expected to be reduced to 45 days. The factor will change 10% per annum on any advances.

The factoring organisation will also undertake sales administration for a fee of 3% of sales. This will result in a permanent reduction of one staff member, currently engaged in credit control, who is paid £15,000 per annum. The factoring arrangement will also free up 25% of the financial controller's time for work on other tasks. The financial controller will continue to be paid £40,000 per annum whether or not the factoring arrangement proceeds. As a result of using the factoring organisation, bad debts are expected to fall to 1% of sales, which are to be borne by the factoring organisation. Sales are expected to remain at the current levels.

Painter Ltd is also considering a change in policy with regard to payments to suppliers. Credit purchases are currently £1m per annum. At present, suppliers offer 2½% discount for a payment within 10 days. Painter Ltd has thus far not taken advantage of the discount, and pays suppliers in 60 days, even though payment is required 45 days from the date of invoice. The company is now considering availing itself of the discount, paying on day 10. Painter Ltd currently finances working capital using a bank overdraft which has an interest of 12%.

Required

(a) Evaluate if it is financially viable for Painter Ltd to factor its trade debts, assuming that it will take advantage of 80% advances.   (10 marks)

(b) (i) Determine if it is financially viable for the company to take advantage of the trade discounts.   (6 marks)

   (ii) Identify and briefly discuss TWO additional factors which would be considered in order to determine whether the change in policy towards paying suppliers is made.   (4 marks)

(20 marks)

Helping hand

The key to both parts (a) and (b) is determining what information is relevant and what data would not be included. In (b) (ii) think how the company could benefit from improving its credit rating.

---

17   ANSWER: PAINTER LTD

(a)   **Annual cost of the existing credit policy**

	£
Cost of financing existing debtors	
£3m × (60/365) × 12%	59,178
Cost of bad debts written off	
£3m × 2%	60,000
	119,178

Cost of the proposed system

	£
Cost of financing remaining debtors	
£3m × 20% × (45/365) × 12%	8,877
Factor's finance charge	
£3m × 80% × (45/365)× 10%	29,589
Factor's administration fee	
£3m × 3%	90,000
	128,466
Less staff savings	15,000
	113,466

Conclusion

Painter Ltd should factor its trade debts, since this should result in cost savings of £5,712 per annum (£119,178 − £113,466).

(b)   (i)   The cost to Painter Ltd of not taking the discount can be estimated using the formula:

$$\frac{d}{100 - d} \times 365/t$$

where   d = size of discount (%)

t = reduction in the payment period in days which would be necessary to obtain the early payment discount

In this case:

$$\text{Cost of not taking the discount} = \frac{2.5}{100 - 2.5} \times 365/50 = 18.7\% \text{ per annum}$$

Painter should thus take advantage of the discount unless it is able to invest the funds in an alternative manner that would yield a return in excess of 18.7%.

(ii)   Creditor payment policy does not only depend on the financial aspects of the transactions. Other factors to be considered include:

(1)   Painter should aim to **keep** the **goodwill** of its **suppliers**. Painter currently exceeds its credit terms on a regular basis. If it were to improve its speed of payment this would improve its relationship with the suppliers, and this might be reflected in the **level of service** that it receives.

(2)   Since Painter consistently exceeds its terms, it may risk having its **credit restricted** by some suppliers, or of being **charged interest** on amounts overdue. Changing the payment policy would reduce these risks.

(3)   Significant amounts of **administration time** may be taken up with dealing with suppliers who are chasing for payment. This time would be saved if payments were made more promptly.

(4)   Consistent late payment to all suppliers is likely to result in a **poor credit rating**. This will affect Painter's ability to get credit from new suppliers in the future.

(5)   Although reducing the payment period and taking the discount is financially beneficial, Painter must be able to **source** the additional **working capital** that such a change in policy will demand; in particular reducing the payment policy might **strain** the **company's overdraft limit**.

			Marks	
	Examiner's marking scheme			
(a)	Cost of financing existing debtors		2	
	Existing bad debts		1	
	Factor's fee		1	
	Factor's finance charge on advances		2	
	Overdraft costs		2	
	Staff savings		1	
	Conclusion		1	
				10
(b)	(i)	Discount available	1	
		Amount due net of discount	1	
		Formula and correct application	2	
		Annualised	1	
		Conclusion	1	
				6
	(ii)	Factor identified and briefly discussed (2 × 2 marks)		4
				20

18   BUILDING SUPPLIES (Pilot Paper)

You have recently taken over the position of credit manager in a building supplies company. The company sells building materials on credit to building contractors. Yours is a new position established on the advice of the company's auditors to deal with poor credit controls and a high incidence of bad debts. The auditors have suggested that an early priority should be the development of a credit control manual which covers policy and procedures in respect of:

(a)   New customer credit acceptance
(b)   Setting credit levels
(c)   Setting credit terms
(d)   Ensuring prompt payment

Required

Write an introductory note, suitable for inclusion in the proposed credit control manual, for each of the four credit control procedures listed above.   **(20 marks)**

18   ANSWER: BUILDING SUPPLIES

The introductory notes below cover aspects of the company's procedures for granting credit and collecting debts. In the building supplies industry, we are exposed to **credit risk** for a number of reasons, as follows.

(a) We deal with a **large number of customers**, many of which are small in turnover terms.

(b) Many of our customers suffer from **cash flow problems** from time to time.

(c) There are **high levels of business failure** in our industry.

The **credit control manual** of which these notes form a part is designed to give guidance in the light of these general circumstances.

New customer credit acceptance

In this section, we detail the checks which are carried out when a trader applies to us to become a credit customer. This set of checks, which aims to assess the trading record of the business, its capacity to pay its debts and any special risk factors, is designed to **balance the risk of debts turning out** to be **bad** with the **commercial objective of maximising turnover**. In some cases, acceptance may be granted for a 'probationary' period and reviewed at the end of that specified period. New customers, or customers on which information is limited or is adverse, may be restricted to cash sales, or to sales on **pro forma paid invoices** only.

Setting credit levels

A **credit limit** is set for each prospective credit customer at the stage when they are accepted. This limit, which must be **authorised** as appropriate and will be reviewed regularly, is set with reference to **information** obtained about the customer together with the past trading record as a cash customer, if any. Procedures exist, as set out below, to ensure that sales which breach customers' credit limits are not made.

Setting credit terms

All credit control staff need to be fully familiar with our **standard terms and conditions** of sale, which are set out below and are also shown on the reverse side of invoice forms. Note that these cover various matters including retention of title, our reservation of a right to charge interest on overdue payments and the option to offset debts against any reciprocal trading account we may hold with the customer. Note that **specific credit terms** for particular customers must be in **writing and must be authorised** by the Credit Manager.

Ensuring prompt payment

Prompt payment is a key objective of all credit controllers. If **payment is late**, there is a **loss in interest**, or an **increase in overdraft interest**, for us, and a **risk of cash flow problems** in our business. We are not in the business of providing interest-free loans for our customers! There is also the risk that slow payers will turn into non-payers, and therefore into a greater loss to our business. Here, we outline the steps which can be taken to ensure prompt payment, ranging from the use of initial reminder letters and telephone calls, through personal visits to customers and the eventual sanction of resorting to legal action, by which stage the Credit Manager will be involved. The steps must be followed consistently for all accounts.

BPP
PROFESSIONAL EDUCATION

19   FRAMES LTD (12/98)

Frames Ltd is a small wholesaler of building materials. The company sells on credit to a wide variety of building contractors.

You have recently been appointed to the newly created position of credit manager to implement credit control procedures in order to avoid potential bad debts.

Extracts from the company's most recent accounts are as follows.

Balance sheet as at 30 June 20X8

	£'000	£'000	£'000
Fixed assets			
Land and buildings at cost		600	
Less accumulated depreciation		200	
			400
Fixtures and fittings at cost		200	
Less accumulated depreciation		75	
			125
			525
Current assets			
Stocks		400	
Trade debtors		400	
Bank		2	
		802	
Creditors: (Amounts falling due in less than 1 year)			
Trade creditors	346		
Taxation	30		
		376	
			426
			951
Creditors: (Amounts falling due after 1 year)			
Term loan (10%)			300
			651
Capital and reserves			
Called up share capital (50p par value)			100
Share premium			200
Revenue reserves (retained profit)			351
			651

Profit and loss account for the year ended 30 June 20X8

	£'000	£'000
Sales		2,000
Less Cost of sales		
Opening stock	400	
Purchases	1,400	
	1,800	
Less Closing stock	400	
		1,400
Gross profit		600
Administration expenses	200	
Selling expenses	270	
Finance expenses	30	
		500
Pre-tax profit		100
Taxation 30%		30
Profit after taxation		70

Notes

1   All sales and purchases are on credit.

2   The managing director is considering increasing the credit period given to customers by 15 days. It is anticipated that:

     (a)   This will increase annual sales by 20%.

     (b)   To cope with the increase in sales, stocks will be increased by 10% effective immediately, and are forecast to remain constant at this increased level.

     (c)   Gross profit margin on the additional sales will be the same as at present (ie 30%).

     (d)   Credit period received from suppliers will remain unchanged.

     (e)   Administration and selling expenses are not expected to change.

3   To finance any extra working capital requirement the company intends to increase its term loan effectively immediately. Interest on this term loan is currently 10% per annum. (Any increase in the term loan will result in an increase in the finance expenses in the profit and loss account.)

Required

(a)   (i)   Explain the term net working capital (cash operating) cycle.   (2 marks)

     (ii)   Calculate the existing cash operating cycle to the nearest day. (Use 30 June 20X8 year end figures.)   (6 marks)

     (iii)   If the proposed credit policy change is implemented, calculate the increase or decrease in each of the following:

         -    Cash operating cycle to the nearest day
         -    Net investment in stock, debtors and creditors to the nearest £'000
         -    Net profit after tax to the nearest £'000

     (Use 30 June 20X9 year end figures.)   (14 marks)

(b)   It has been suggested that Frames Ltd considers factoring and/or invoice discounting to finance the expansion of the business. You are required to explain THREE ways in which factoring differs from invoice discounting.   (6 marks)

(c)   (i)   Identify and briefly discuss FOUR factors which need to be taken into account when assessing the creditworthiness of new customers.   (8 marks)

     (ii)   Briefly outline FOUR reasons why small companies like Frames Ltd may find the management of debtors a particular problem.   (4 marks)

                                                               (40 marks)

Helping hand

When calculating the operating cycle in (a) you will need to make an assumption about the time taken to produce the goods. This should be stated clearly in your answer.

Remember to focus on the differences in (b). (c) (i) is about the information available. Think in (c) (ii) about the priorities of small companies.

---

19   ANSWER: FRAMES LTD

> **Helping hand**
>
> In part (a)(iii) you are required to calculate the **increase or decrease** in the various figures – not just the revised figures themselves.
>
> Differences in (b) relate to administration, insurance and who has responsibility for the debtors.
>
> In (c) (i) there are a number of sources of external information, but the most convincing guide is how the customer pays the company itself. A payment patterns take time to emerge, the credit limit should initially be set low. In (c) (ii) small companies cannot afford to staff a full-time credit control department.
>
> **What the examiner said**
>
> Parts (b) and (c) were generally well answered, but there were some very poor answers to part (a).

(a)   (i)   The **working capital cycle** may be expressed as the average number of days between the outlay on raw materials, wages and other expenses and the inflow of cash from the sale of the company's product. In a manufacturing business, the length of the working capital cycle equals:

The average time that raw materials remain in stock
Less the credit period taken from suppliers
Plus the time taken to produce the goods
Plus the time taken by customers to pay for the goods

(ii)   The various elements of the existing cycle based on the balance sheet figures as at 30 June 20X8 can be calculated as follows.

Raw material stock period

It is assumed that all the stocks are raw materials. Since there has been no change in the level of stock during the year, the purchases figure equates to the raw material usage figure.

Purchases for the year	£1,400,000	
Usage per day (£1.4m ÷ 365)	£3,835.62	a
Closing stock value	£400,000	b
Stock-holding period (to nearest day)	104 days	b ÷ a

Credit period taken from suppliers

It is assumed that the figure for trade creditors relates exclusively to the purchases figure.

Purchases for the year	£1,400,000	
Purchases per day (£1.4m ÷ 365)	£3,835.62	a
Closing trade creditors	£346,000	b
Credit period taken (to nearest day)	90 days	b ÷ a

Credit period allowed to debtors

Sales for the year	£2,000,000	
Sales per day (£2m ÷ 365)	£5,479.45	a
Closing trade debtors	£400,000	b
Credit period allowed (to nearest day)	73 days	b ÷ a

It is assumed that the time taken to produce the goods is **negligible**.

The cash operating cycle is therefore:

Raw material stock period	104 days
Less the credit period taken from suppliers	(90 days)
Plus the credit period allowed to debtors	73 days
Cash operating cycle	**87 days**

(iii)   The elements of the operating cycle will change as follows:

Raw materials stock period

Purchases will increase by 20% in line with the increase in sales so as to maintain a gross margin of 30%.

Purchases for the year (£1.4m × 1.2)	£1,680,000	
Usage per day (£1.68m ÷ 365)	£4,602.74	a
Closing stock value (£0.4m × 1.1)	£440,000	b
Stock-holding period (to nearest day)	96 days	b ÷ a

The credit period taken from suppliers will be unchanged at 90 days, while the credit period allowed to debtors will increase by 15 days to 88 days. The operating cycle will therefore become:

Raw material stock period	96 days
Less the credit period taken from suppliers	(90 days)
Plus the credit period allowed to debtors	88 days
Cash operating capital cycle	**94 days**

The cash operating cycle will therefore **increase by 7 days** from 87 days to 94 days.

Net investment in stock

This will **increase by £40,000** from £400,000 to £440,000 as calculated above.

Net investment in debtors

This can be calculated as follows:

Sales for the year (£2m × 1.2)	£2,400,000	
Average daily sales (£2.4m ÷ 365)	£6,575.34	A
Credit period allowed to debtors	88 days	B
Average level of debtors	£578,630	a × b

The net investment in debtors will therefore **increase by £178,630** from £400,000 to £578,630.

Net investment in creditors

It is assumed that the increase in the stock level will occur immediately and that the long-term level of creditors will be unaffected by this.

Purchases for the year (above)	£1,680,000	
Average daily purchases (above)	£4,602.74	A
Credit period taken (above)	90 days	B
Average level of creditors	£414,247	a × b

The level of creditors will therefore **increase by £68,247** from £346,000 to £414,247.

Note. Provided that your assumptions are clearly stated, it would be equally correct to include the additional investment in stock in the purchases figure, giving a revised creditors figure as follows.

	£'000	
Purchases for the year	£1,720,000	
Average daily purchases	£4,712.33	A
Credit period taken (above)	90 days	B
Average level of creditors	£424,110	a × b

Frames Ltd - redrafted profit and loss account

	£'000	£'000	Note
Sales (£2m × 1.2)		2,400	
Less cost of sales:			
Opening stock	400		1
Purchases	1,720		2
	2,120		
Less closing stock	440		2
		1,680	
Gross profit		720	
Administration expenses	200		
Selling expenses	270		
Finance expenses	45		3
		515	
Pre-tax profit		205	
Taxation 30%		62	
Profit after taxation		143	

This is an increase in the annual profit after tax of £73,000.

Notes

1   The opening stock is taken to be unchanged from the closing stock from the previous period.

2   The closing stock is increased by 10% to £440,000. The purchases must also be increased by a similar amount in addition to the 20% increase so as to maintain the gross margin at 30%.

3   The additional investment in working capital is as follows:

	£'000
Stock	40
Debtors	179
Creditors	(68)
Total	151

This increase must be financed by an increase in the term loan at a cost of 10%. The finance expenses will therefore increase by £15,000 to £45,000 per year.

(b) **Factoring** is an arrangement to have debts collected by a factor company, which advances a proportion of the money it is due to collect. **Invoice discounting** is similar in that it involves the purchase of trade debts at a discount, thereby speeding up the liberation of cash from the debtors. The principal differences between the two services are:

(i)   The invoice discounter does not take over the **administration of the debtors ledger** as the factor does.

(ii)   The factor can provide **credit protection** for the clients' debts, whereby the risk of loss from bad debts is transferred to the factor, effectively 'insuring' the client against such losses. This is known as **non-recourse** factoring.

(iii)   The factor may make **payments to the client in advance** of collecting the debts, otherwise known as **factor finance**. **Invoice discounting** is different in this respect since it involves the outright purchase of given invoices, at a discount. The level of risk to the discounter is higher since he will still rely on the client to collect the debt.

(c) (i) (1) The prospective customer's track record in payment of suppliers and their financial security should be checked. The customer should supply two good **references**, including one from a bank, before being granted credit.

(2) **Credit rating** checks can be made using agencies such as Dun and Bradstreet.

(3) The initial **credit limit** should be set at a low level and only increased gradually as the payment record warrants it.

(4) If the customer is likely to do a large volume of business with the company, then a member of staff could be sent to **visit** in order to gain a first hand impression of the company and its prospects.

(5) **Press reports** should be studied in order to gain information about the current position of the company.

(6) The historical situation disclosed in documents such as the **annual accounts** is also relevant.

(7) If the company is not a UK company, advice can be sought from the **DTI** and the **ECGD** (Export Credit Guarantee Department).

(ii) (1) A small company will **not be able** to **employ a full-time specialist** person to deal with credit control and debt collection. This makes it harder to ensure high quality management of debtors, and there may be a lack of proper procedures in place.

(2) There is only likely to be **one person** whose main task it is to deal with **debtor management**. At times of holiday or sickness this work must be covered by other people who are less skilled in this area and who do not have a lot of time available to ensure that everything is done correctly and on time.

(3) Small companies may be **exploited by larger companies** who keep them waiting for payment because the unequal trading relationship is exploited – the large company's business is usually much more important to the small company than the small company's business is to the large company.

(4) Small companies are often run by **entrepreneurs** who are more **concerned to get sales** and satisfy customers than with the day to day administration of the business. This may mean that bad credit control decisions are made in the interests of winning orders.

Examiner's marking scheme

				Marks	
(a)	(i)	Explanation		2	
	(ii)	Use of formulae	(3 × 1 mark)	3	
		Each calculation	(3 × 1 mark)	3	
	(iii)	Revised cycle	(3 × 1 mark)	3	
		Comment on increase/decrease		1	
		Revised stocks, debtors and creditors	(3 × 1 mark)	3	
		Comment on increase/decrease		1	
		Change in net profit	(3 × 1 mark)	3	
		Comment on increase/decrease		1	
		Presentation/explanation		2	
					22
(b)		Each difference identified and explained	(3 × 2 marks)		6
(c)	(i)	Each factor identified	(4 × 1 mark)	4	
		Brief explanation	(4 × 1 mark)	4	
	(ii)	Each reason briefly explained	(4 × 1 mark)	4	
					12
					40

BPP
PROFESSIONAL EDUCATION

20   AB LTD (12/00)

AB Ltd manufactures and sells two types of project. Brief details are as follows.

	Product A	Product B
Projected annual sales volume	100,000	400,000
Selling price per unit	£10	£20
Costs as a % of sales		
Raw material	25%	40%
Direct labour	25%	20%
Overheads	25%	20%
Working capital statistics		
Average debtors collection period	4 weeks	6 weeks
Average raw material stock holding period	4 weeks	4 weeks
Average work-in-progress holding period (see notes 1 and 2)	2 weeks	4 weeks
Average finished goods stock holding period	3 weeks	3 weeks
Average raw material supplier credit received	6 weeks	5 weeks
Average period of credit on overhead expenses	4 weeks	4 weeks
Average period of credit on direct labour	1 week	1 week

Notes

1   All raw materials are input at the start of the production process.

2   Work-in-progress is valued at the entire raw material content and 50% of labour and overhead.

3   During the year, production volume is expected to equal sales volume, which is anticipated to be spread evenly over the year.

Required

(a)   Calculate the estimated average working capital finance required to the nearest £'000.

(16 marks)

(b)   Identify and briefly explain TWO significant weaknesses in the calculations completed in part (a).

(Note: Assume a 52 week year)   (4 marks)

(20 marks)

Helping hand

In (a) WIP and finished goods will require detailed calculation. In (b) think about the assumptions, the basis of calculation and what is included and not included.

---

20   ANSWER: AB LTD

Helping hand

The calculations in (a) have been set out more fully than is strictly necessary, in order to make the workings clear for WIP and finished goods stocks. (b) is quite a common type of question. For this sort of calculation you will always need to make simplifying assumptions. In addition lack of detailed information may mean that certain items that should be excluded are included because you cannot separate them out, and certain items which should be included are excluded because you are not given details about them. Note the examiner's comment that this is a key topic area; a very similar question was set in December 2001, only two sittings after this one was set.

What the examiner said

Some candidates failed to answer this question at all. Calculation of working capital requirements is however a core syllabus topic.

(a)   The annual costs and revenues for Product A will be as follows.

Expected annual sales volume (units)		100,000
Selling price per unit		£10

		£'000
Sales		1,000
Direct materials	25% × £1,000	250
Direct labour	25% × £1,000	250
Overheads	25% × £1,000	250
Total cost		750

The average value of current assets will be as follows.

Raw materials	4/52 × 250		19
Work in progress			
Materials (100% complete)	2/52 × 250	10	
Labour (50% complete)	2/52 × 50% × 250	5	
Overheads (50% complete)	2/52 × 50% × 250	5	
			20
Finished goods			
Materials (100% complete)	3/52 × 250	14	
Labour (100% complete)	3/52 × 250	14	
Overheads (100% complete)	3/52 × 250	14	
			42
Debtors	4/52 × 1,000		77
Total current assets			158

Current liabilities			
Raw materials	6/52 × 250	(29)	
Labour	1/52 × 250	(5)	
Overheads	4/52 × 250	(19)	
			(53)
Total working capital requirement			105

The annual costs and revenues for Product B will be as follows.

Expected annual sales volume (units)		400,000
Selling price per unit		£20
		£'000
Sales		8,000
Direct materials	40% × £8,000	3,200
Overheads	20% × £8,000	1,600
Total cost	20% × £8,000	1,600
		6,400

The average value of current assets will be as follows.

Raw materials	4/52 × 3,200		246
Work in progress			
Materials (100% complete)	4/52 × 3,200	246	
Labour (50% complete)	4/52 × 50% × 1,600	62	
Overheads (50% complete)	4/52 × 50% × 1,600	62	
			370
Finished goods			
Materials (100% complete)	3/52 × 3,200	185	
Labour (100% complete)	3/52 × 1,600	92	
Overheads (100% complete)	3/52 × 1,600	92	
			369
Debtors	6/52 × 8,000		923
Total current assets			1,908
Raw materials	5/52 × 3,200	(308)	
Labour	1/52 × 1,600	(31)	
Overheads	4/52 × 1,600	(123)	
			(462)
Total working capital requirement			1,446

The total working capital requirement is therefore £105,000 + £1,446,000 = 1,551,000

(b) **Weaknesses in the calculations**

(i) **Production** and **sales** are **assumed** to **occur evenly** throughout the year. In reality, there will be peaks and troughs in activity, and this means that at times more working capital will be required than is suggested by the calculations.

(ii) It is assumed that the workers are paid a **regular amount** each week. In reality, a weekly paid workforce are likely to receive holiday pay in advance of their holiday being taken, particularly if holiday money is accrued. This will cause peaks and troughs in the level of working capital, which will be exacerbated if the whole factory shuts down at specific holiday times.

(iii) All the statistics given are **averages**. It may be that certain customers are granted different terms than others, and this means that if the balance of trade between customers changes, the actual period of credit granted will at times differ significantly from the average.

(iv) The overheads may include **non-cash overheads** which are not relevant to working capital.

(v) The calculations **ignore other influences** on the level of working capital, such as the need to pay tax or dividends.

Examiner's marking scheme

			Marks
(a)	Debtors		2
	Raw material stocks		2
	WIP stocks		2
	Finished goods stocks		2
	Trade creditors		2
	Overhead creditors		2
	Payroll creditors		2
	Totals and conclusion		2
			16
(b)	Weakness identified	(2 × 2 marks)	
	And briefly discussed/explained		4
			20

BPP PROFESSIONAL EDUCATION

21   SEATS LTD (12/01)

Seats Ltd manufactures and sells two types of chair, the Comfyseat and the Bigseat. The Comfyseat uses less expensive materials, but has a lower profit margin than the Bigseat.

	Comfyseat	Bigseat
Projected annual sales volume	25,000	25,000
Selling price per unit	£100	£245
Contribution as a % mark up on variable costs	25%	40%
Variable cost elements breakdown in %		
Raw material	40%	50%
Direct labour	30%	25%
Variable overheads	30%	25%
	100%	100%
Working capital statistics		
Average debtors collection period	6 weeks	8 weeks
Average raw material stock holding period	4 weeks	6 weeks
Average work-in-progress holding period (See notes 1 & 2)	4 weeks	4 weeks
Average finished goods stock holding period	3 weeks	3 weeks
Average raw material supplier credit received	5 weeks	5 weeks
Average period of credit on overhead expenses	6 weeks	3 weeks
Average period of credit on direct labour	1 week	1 week

Notes:

1   All raw materials are input at the start of the production process.

2   Work-in-progress is valued at the entire raw material content and 40% of the labour and variable overhead elements.

3   During the year, production volume is expected to equal sales volume, which is anticipated to be spread evenly over the year.

Required

(a)   Calculate the estimated average working capital finance required to the nearest £'000, assuming a 52 week year.   (16 marks)

(b)   Identify and briefly explain TWO significant weaknesses in the calculations completed in part (a).

(4 marks)

(20 marks)

Helping hand

Have another look at question 20.

---

21   ANSWER: SEATS LTD

(a)   The annual costs and revenues for Comfyseat will be as follows.

Expected annual sales volume (units)	25,000
Selling price per unit	£100

	£'000
Sales	2,500
Materials (40% × 100/125 × 2,500)	800
Labour (30% × 100/125 × 2,500)	600
Overheads (30% × 100/125 × 2,500	600
Total cost	2,000

The average value of current assets will be as follows.

		£'000	£'000
Raw materials	4/52 × 800		62
Work in progress			
Materials (100% complete)	4/52 × 800	62	
Labour (40% complete)	40% × 4/52 × 600	18	
Overheads (40% complete)	40% × 4/52 × 600	18	
			98
Finished goods			
Materials (100% complete)	3/52 × 800	46	
Labour (100% complete)	3/52 × 600	35	
Overheads (100% complete)	3/52 × 600	35	
			116
Debtors	6/52 × 2,500		288
Total current assets			564
Current liabilities			
Materials	5/52 × 800	(77)	
Labour	1/52 × 600	(12)	
Overheads	6/52 × 600	(69)	
			(158)
Total working capital requirement			406

The annual costs and revenues for Bigseat will be as follows.

Expected annual sales volume (units)	25,000
Selling price per unit	£245

		£'000
Sales		6,125
Materials	50% × 100/140 × 6,125	2,188
Labour	25% × 100/140 × 6,125	1,094
Overheads	25% × 100/140 × 6,125	1,094
Total cost		4,376

The average value of current assets will be as follows.

		£'000	£'000
Raw materials	6/52 × 2,188		252
Work in progress			
Materials (100% complete)	4/52 × 2,188	168	
Labour (40% complete)	40% × 4/52 × 1,094	34	
Overheads (40% complete)	40% × 4/52 × 1,094	34	
Finished goods			236
Materials (100% complete)	3/52 × 2,188	126	
Labour (100% complete)	3/52 × 1,094	63	
Overheads (100% complete)	3/52 × 1,094	63	
			252
Debtors	8/52 × 6,125		942
Total current assets			1,682
Materials	5/52 × 2,188	(210)	
Labour	1/52 × 1,094	(21)	
Overheads	3/52 × 1,094	(63)	
			(294)
Total working capital requirement			1,388

The total working capital requirement is therefore £406,000 + 1,388,000 = £1,794,000

(b) Weaknesses in the calculations include the following:

(i) **Production** and **sales** are **assumed** to **occur evenly** throughout the year. In reality, there will be seasonal peaks and troughs, and this means that at times more working capital will be required than is suggested by the calculations.

(ii) It is assumed that the workers are paid a **regular amount** each week. In reality, a weekly paid workforce are likely to receive holiday pay in advance of their holiday being taken, particularly if holiday money is accrued. This will cause peaks and troughs in the level of working capital, which will be exacerbated if the whole factory shuts down at specific holiday times.

(iii) All the statistics given are **averages**. It may be that certain customers are granted different terms than others, and this means that if the balance of trade between customers changes, the actual period of credit granted will at times differ significantly from the average.

(iv) The overheads may include **non-cash overheads** which are not relevant to working capital.

(v) The calculations **ignore other influences** on the level of working capital, such as the need to pay tax or dividends.

Examiner's marking scheme			Marks
(a)	Debtors		2
	Raw material stocks		2
	WIP stocks		2
	Finished goods stocks		2
	Trade creditors		2
	Overhead creditors		2
	Payroll creditors		2
	Totals and conclusion		2
			16
(b)	Weakness identified and briefly discussed/explained	(2 × 2 marks)	4
			20

22   VICTORY LTD (6/01)

Victory Ltd is a retailer, specialising in vitamin supplements and health foods claimed to enhance performance. One of the products purchased by Victory Ltd for resale is a performance enhancing vitamin drink called 'Buzz'.

Victory Ltd sells a fixed quantity of 200 bottles of Buzz per week. The estimated storage costs for a bottle of Buzz are £2.00 per annum per bottle.

Delivery from Victory Ltd's existing supplier takes two weeks and the purchase price per bottle delivered is £20. The current supplier charges a fixed £75 order processing charge for each order, regardless of the order size.

Victory Ltd has recently been approached by another supplier of Buzz with the following offer:

1   The cost to Victory Ltd per bottle will be £19 each.

2   There will be a fixed order processing charge of £250 regardless of order size.

3   Delivery time will be one week.

4   Victory Ltd estimates that due to packaging differences, the storage cost per bottle will be £1.80 per annum per bottle.

Note

The economic order quantity Q, which will minimise costs, is:

$$Q = \sqrt{\frac{2CoD}{Ch}}$$

Where Co = The cost of making one order
       D   = Annual demand
       Ch = The holding cost per unit per annum

Required

(a) Assuming Victory Ltd continues to purchase from the existing supplier, calculate:

   (i)   Economic order quantity
   (ii)   Reorder level
   (iii) Total cost of stocking Buzz for one year to the nearest £   (6 marks)

(b) (i)   Calculate the economic order quantity if Victory Ltd changes to the new supplier and determine if it would be financially viable to change to this new supplier.   (4 marks)

     (ii)   Discuss two limitations of the above calculations and briefly describe three other non-financial factors to be taken into account before a final decision is made.

(5 marks)

(c) Explain what is meant by a Just-in-Time (JIT) system and briefly describe four of its main features.   (5 marks)

(20 marks)

Helping hand

(a) (i) just involves plugging the figures into the formula. The key elements in (a) (ii) are how long orders will take to be delivered, and how much will be demanded during that time. In (a)(iii) you are being asked for the total costs.

For (b) (i) consider what elements of cost will differ if the supplier is changed. Think for (b) (ii) about the assumptions, and also the factors that financial calculations do not take into account.

In (c) think what is necessary for a just-in-time system to be implemented, and think also beyond stock delivery to the rest of the production process.

22   **ANSWER: VICTORY LTD**

> **Helping hand**
>
> You should be given the stock control formula. Always note how long it will take to deliver orders as this is an important detail, even though it isn't brought into the economic order quantity calculation.
>
> In (a) (iii) and (b) (i) you need to bring purchasing costs in as they will be affected by the discount.
>
> For questions like (b) (ii) focus on what might differ in the real world from what is assumed to happen for the purposes of the calculation, and think about non-financial factors.
>
> Remember for questions such as (c) that just-in-time is a philosophy that impacts upon the whole production process, not just delivery of stock. That said, relationships with suppliers are critical and do need to be stressed.
>
> **What the examiner said**
>
> Answers to this question were very disappointing. Most candidates could not use the EOQ formula, and calculate reorder levels and total cost. Candidates in future exams should make sure that they revise these topic areas.

(a)   (i)   Using the economic order quantity (EOQ) model:

$$Q = \sqrt{\frac{2C_oD}{C_h}}$$

where: C_o = cost of making one order   = £75
         D = annual demand   = $200 \times 52 = 10,400$
         C_h = holding cost per unit per annum   = £2

$Q = \sqrt{(2 \times £75 \times 10,400)/£2}$

$Q = \sqrt{780,000}$

$Q = 883.2$ units

The economic order quantity is therefore 883 units (to the nearest unit).

(ii) Demand is fixed at 200 bottles per week, and delivery from the supplier takes two weeks. Victory must therefore reorder when stocks fall to 400 units (2 weeks demand).

(iii) The total cost of stocking Buzz for one year will be:

		£
Purchase cost		
10,400 units £20 each		208,000
Ordering cost		
Annual demand (units)	10,400	
Order size (units)	883	
Number of orders per year	11.78	
Cost of placing one order	£75	
Annual ordering cost		883
Holding cost		
Average stock (883/2)	441.5	
Holding cost per unit pa	£2	
Annual holding cost		883
Total annual cost		209,766

(b) (i) The factors for the new supplier are as follows:

C_o = £250

D = 10,400

C_h = £1.80

Q = $\sqrt{(2 \times £250 \times 10,400)/£1.80}$

= 1,699.7

The economic order quantity is therefore 1,700 units (to the nearest unit).

To determine whether it is financially viable to change supplier we must calculate the total annual cost of ordering from this supplier and to compare this with the existing annual cost.

		£
Purchase cost		
10,400 units £19 each		197,600
Ordering cost		
Annual demand (units)	10,400	
Order size (units)	1,700	
Number of orders per year	6.12	
Cost of placing one order	£250	
Annual ordering cost		1,530
Holding cost		
Average stock (1,700/2)	850	
Holding cost per unit pa	£1.80	
Annual holding cost		1,530
Total annual cost		200,660

This is £9,106 less than the existing annual purchasing cost, and therefore it would be financially beneficial to switch suppliers.

(ii) Limitations of the calculations include the following:

(1) **Demand is assumed to be the same** throughout the year. In practice, there are likely to be variations.

(2) **It is assumed that the lead-time is constant** and that the **suppliers** are both **completely dependable.**

(3) **It is assumed that purchase costs are constant.** In practice it is necessary to allow for the effects of differing discount and credit policies.

Non-financial factors to be considered include:

(1) **Quality** must be consistent and reliable from both suppliers.

(2) **Packaging differences** must be acceptable, and the product from both suppliers must be equally attractive to consumers.

(3) **Flexibility.** Both suppliers must be able to respond quickly and efficiently to variations in the level of demand.

(4) **Environmental effects.** Victory must ensure that the suppliers' production facilities meet any agreed environmental standards that the company requires.

(c) **Just-in-time (JIT) manufacturing** involves obtaining goods from suppliers at the **latest possible time** (ie when they are needed on the production line), thereby **avoiding the need to carry** any materials or components stock. Reduced stock levels mean that a **lower level of investment in working capital** will be required. In certain environments where the cost of a stock-out is high, JIT is inappropriate, eg in a hospital, the cost of a stock-out for certain items could be fatal.

The main features of a JIT system include the following:

(i)   **Deliveries** will be **small and frequent**, rather than in bulk. **Production runs** will also be shorter.

(ii)   **Supplier relationships** must **be close**, since high demands will be placed on suppliers to deliver on time and with 100% quality.

(iii) **Unit purchasing prices** may need to be **higher** than in a conventional system to compensate suppliers for their need to hold higher stocks and to meet more rigorous quality and delivery requirements. However, savings in production costs and reductions in working capital should offset these costs.

(iv)   **Improved labour productivity** should result from a smoother flow of materials through the process.

(v)   **Production process improvements** may be required for a JIT system to function to full effectiveness. In particular set-up time for machinery may have to be reduced, workforce teams reorganised, and movement of materials within the production process minimised.

			Marks	
Examiner's marking scheme				
(a)	(i) EOQ formula and solution		2	
	(ii) Reorder level		1	
	(iii) Cost of holding, ordering and purchasing		3	
				6
(b)	(i) EOQ		1	
	Cost of holding, ordering and purchasing		2	
	Recommendation		1	
				4
	(ii) Limitations	(2 × 1 mark)	2	
	Non-financial factors	(3 × 1 mark)	3	
				5
(c)	JIT explanation		1	
	Each feature identified and briefly discussed	(4 × 1 mark)	4	
				5
				20

23   ONTIME PLC (12/00)

Ontime plc, a manufacturer of sundials has four main suppliers. The company's finance director has asked you as his assistant to prepare an analysis of the cost of using trade credit as a source of finance. Your initial analysis has identified that each supplier offers different terms of trade. Specific details are as follows:

Supplier No. 1   Charges 1½% of the invoice value per monthly period from the date on which payment is due. This charge is only made if the payment is one month or more past the due date.

Supplier No. 2   Charges a fixed penalty of 2½% of the invoice for late payment. This penalty is charged even if the payment is only one day late.

Supplier No. 3   Offers a 2½% discount if payment is received within one month of the invoice date. Payment after one month is net invoice value.

Supplier No. 4   Charges 12% per annum simple interest on the invoice value if payment is made after the due date.

Notes

1   Total purchases from all suppliers are £10m.

2   40% of purchases are made from supplier No. 1 with the remainder being equally split between suppliers 2, 3 and 4.

3   All four suppliers have a due date for payment one month from the invoice date.

4   Ontime plc takes three months to pay each of the four suppliers.

5   Ontime plc's cost of funds is normally 10%.

Required

(a)   Calculate the NET annual cost of delaying payment beyond the agreed time, as is currently being practised by Ontime plc, to each of the four suppliers. Identify which, if any, of the trade credit arrangements is financially beneficial to Ontime plc.

(11 marks)

(b)   Identify and briefly discuss THREE advantages and THREE disadvantages to Ontime plc of using the delaying of payments to suppliers as a source of finance.   (9 marks)

(20 marks)

Helping hand

In (a) you can either base your calculations on monthly rates of interest or use effective annual rates of interest.

In (b) think about the financial advantages and the actions suppliers might take.

---

23   ANSWER: ONTIME PLC

> **Helping hand**
>
> In (a) the calculations have been built up from monthly invoicing amounts to aid clarity. However, it would be equally acceptable to calculate effective annual rates of interest, and to compare these with the cost of other funds. If this approach is used, you will need to be careful when calculating the total net annual cost of delaying payment.
>
> In (b) although costs of borrowing may be reduced, the effects of suppliers setting tougher limits may be significant.
>
> **What the examiner said**
>
> This question was reasonably well-answered. Answers to (a) were generally adequate, although few were completely correct. Discussions in (b) were generally good.

(a)   **Supplier 1**

		£
Annual purchases	£10m × 40%	4,000,000
Monthly purchases	£4,000,000/12	333,333

Each month there will be two invoices that are overdue, and on which interest will be charged.

		£
Monthly interest charge	£333,333 × 1.5% × 2	10,000
Annual interest charge	£10,000 × 12	120,000

Ontime plc currently has 3 × £333,333 outstanding at any one time. If it were to pay the supplier according to terms, this would fall to 1 × £333,333. It would therefore have to borrow 2 × £333,333 to replace the lost finance. The cost of this would be £666,667 × 10% per year = £66,667.

If the supplier was paid according to terms, Ontime plc would therefore save £120,000 – £66,667 = £53,333 per year.

Supplier 2

		£
Annual purchases	£10m × 20%	2,000,000
Monthly purchases	£2,000,000/12	166,667

Each month there would be a single penalty of 2.5% of the invoice value as the next invoice became overdue.

		£
Monthly interest charge	£166,667 × 2.5%	4,166.67
Annual interest charge	£4,166.67 × 12	50,000

Ontime plc currently has 3 × £166,667 outstanding at any one time. If it were to pay the supplier according to terms, this would fall to 1 × £166,667. It would therefore have to borrow 2 × £166,667 to replace the lost finance. The cost of this would be £333,333 × 10% per year = £33,333.

If the supplier was paid according to terms, Ontime plc would therefore save £50,000 – £33,333 = £16,667 per year.

Supplier 3

		£
Annual purchases	£10m × 20%	2,000,000
Monthly purchases	£2,000,000/12	166,667

Each month, Ontime forgoes a settlement discount of 2.5% × £166,667 = £4,166.67 by paying late. This amounts to £50,000 per year.

Ontime plc currently has 3 × £166,667 outstanding at any one time. If it were to pay the supplier according to terms, this would fall to 1 × £166,667. It would therefore have to borrow 2 × £166,667 to replace the lost finance. The cost of this would be £333,333 × 10% per year = £33,333.

If the supplier was paid according to terms, and the discount was taken Ontime plc would therefore save £50,000 – £33,333 = £16,667 per year.

Supplier 4

		£
Annual purchases	£10m × 20%	2,000,000
Monthly purchases	£2,000,000/12	166,667

Each month, Ontime has two invoices that are overdue ie £166,667 × 2 = £333,333. The supplier will charge 12% per annum on overdue balances. The annual cost of this is therefore £333,333 × 12% = £40,000.

Ontime plc currently has 3 × £166,667 outstanding at any one time. If it were to pay the supplier according to terms, this would fall to 1 × £166,667. It would therefore have to borrow 2 × £166,667 to replace the lost finance. The cost of this would be £333,333 × 10% per year = £33,333.

If the supplier was paid according to terms, Ontime plc would therefore save £40,000 – £33,333 = £6,667 per year.

The net annual cost to Ontime plc of delaying payment is therefore:

	£
Supplier 1	53,333
Supplier 2	16,667
Supplier 3	16,667
Supplier 4	6,667
Total net annual cost	93,334

Ontime plc would be better off with all the suppliers by paying according to terms and taking discounts where available. The discount terms offered by Supplier 3 are beneficial to Ontime, but the credit charges levied by the other suppliers are not.

(b) **Advantages of delaying payments to suppliers as a source of finance include the following.**

(i) Delaying payments is a **cheap source of finance**, provided that suppliers do not charge interest on overdue payments.

(ii) There are no **application formalities** nor **arrangement fees** for creditor finance as there are for bank loans.

(iii) The company **does not have to provide security** for the finance.

(iv) The **level of working capital** is **reduced**.

Disadvantages of delaying payments to suppliers include the following.

(i) The company may **lose the goodwill** of **suppliers**. This means that the supplier may be less willing to help when materials are needed urgently.

(ii) The company will **lose any** available cash **discounts** for the early payment of debts.

(iii) A **poor payment record** will result in a **lower credit rating**. This means that the company may find it harder to obtain credit from other suppliers in the future.

(iv) The company may find that the **total amount of credit** that it is able to obtain from the supplier is **limited** if it consistently fails to pay to terms.

Examiner's marking scheme

			Marks	
(a)	Purchases per supplier		1	
	Additional finance charges each of 4 suppliers	(4 × 1 mark)	4	
	Savings in finance costs each of 4 suppliers	(4 × 1 mark)	4	
	Conclusion and presentation		2	
				11
(b)	Each advantage identified and briefly explained	(3 × 1½ marks)	4½	
	Each disadvantage identified and briefly explained	(3 × 1½ marks)	4½	
				9
				20

24   VDO PLC (6/01)

VDO plc manufactures and sells DVD playing devices for use with conventional video recorders, avoiding the need for customers to replace their existing video player in order to move to DVD technology. In recent years, the business has been growing rapidly as the availability of films on DVD has increased.

In the last year, the company has encountered cash flow difficulties and the board of directors has become increasingly concerned about this development. Extracts from VDO plc's financial statements are as follows.

	Balance sheet as at 31 May 20X1			Balance sheet as at 31 May 20X0		
	£'000	£'000	£'000	£'000	£'000	£'000
Fixed assets			550			450
Current assets						
Stocks	250			100		
Debtors	250			120		
Cash	nil			80		
		500			300	
Current liabilities						
Trade creditors	200			150		
		(200)			(150)	
Net current assets			300			150
			850			600
Medium term liabilities						
Bank term loan			(200)			nil
			650			600
Financed by						
Issued share capital (10p shares)			50			50
Retained earnings			600			550
Shareholders funds			650			600

	Profit & loss account y/e 31 May 20X1	Profit & loss account y/e 31 May 20X0
	£'000	£'000
Sales revenue	4,000	2,000
Profit before interest and tax	120	120
Interest	(20)	nil
Profit before tax	100	120
Taxation 20%	(20)	(24)
Profit after tax	80	96
Dividends	(30)	(36)
Retained earnings	50	60

Other information

		20X1	20X0
1	Industry average statistics		
	Debtor days	35 days	33 days
	Current ratio	2:1	2:1
	Total debt: total equity (Book value)	20%	20%
	P/E ratio	20 times	18 times
	ROCE	20%	18%
2	Average market value of VDO plc's shares	240p	346p

Required

(a) Assess the financial performance of VDO plc in comparison to the industry average. (6 marks are available for calculations and 6 marks are available for relevant comments.)   (12 marks)

(b) Explain what is meant by overtrading and briefly explain three causes of overtrading.
                                                                                   (6 marks)

(c) Identify and briefly discuss four possible reasons, other than overtrading, for a manufacturing company such as VDO plc to experience cash shortages, despite the considerable growth in sales.   (6 marks)

(d) Suggest and briefly explain four ways by which VDO plc could resolve its current cash flow difficulties, identifying a disadvantage associated with each suggestion.   (8 marks)

(e) Overtrading is one set of circumstances that would give rise to internal controls being compromised. Identify and briefly describe four types of fraud which may occur when internal controls are compromised.   (8 marks)

                                                                              (40 marks)

Helping hand

In (a) there are six marks available for calculations, so you have to use the information you are given to come up with a further calculation and comment. Think in (b) about activity levels, finance and control of the business. Your answer to (c) does not need to be confined to VDO. Your answer to (d) should link into the problems identified in (b).

---

24   ANSWER: VDO PLC

Helping hand

In (a) there are only five pieces of information given for industry comparison. Since six marks are available for calculations and comments, you can therefore infer that a further calculation is required beyond those suggested by the comparative figures. The suggested solution includes two that you could choose – the quick ratio and the EPS – however, others could also be used.

In (b) overtrading is most commonly caused by a mismatch between increasing activity levels and limited finance. Only three causes of overtrading are required. Sensible alternative suggestions to those included in the suggested solution would be equally valid.

In (c) the question asks for reasons for a manufacturing company such as VDO to experience cash shortages in spite of sales growth. It is not asking specifically for reasons for VDO's problems, although these may be relevant to parts of your answer.

In (d) the suggestions need to address the mismatch between activity and finance. Five reasons have been given in the suggested solution. However, you are only required to provide four in your answer. Sensible alternative suggestions would be equally valid.

What the examiner said

In (a) some candidates found the ratio calculations to be too difficult. (b) and (c) were generally answered satisfactorily; however many candidates failed to discuss disadvantages in (d). (e) was well answered, indicating that many candidates had read the articles in *Students' Newsletter.*

(a) (All figures £000)

Profitability

This is measured by the **return on capital employed** (ROCE).

$$ROCE = \frac{\text{Profit on ordinary activities before interest and tax (PBIT)}}{\text{Capital employed}}$$

For VDO plc:

	20X1	20X0
PBIT	120	120
Capital employed	850	600
ROCE	14.1%	20%
Industry averages	20%	18%

While VDO's profitability compared favourably with industry averages in 20X0, it has fallen back in 20X1, while average profitability for the industry has increased. Capital employed has risen, reflecting a significant **investment** in both **fixed and current assets**. Although this investment has generated a doubling in the level of sales, this has been at the expense of profit margins, actual profits being unchanged at £120,000. This should be a major concern for the shareholders. The company needs to address its **sales and pricing policies,** and also its **product cost base,** as a matter of urgency.

Liquidity

This is measured by (i) The **current ratio** (current assets: current liabilities) and (ii) The **quick ratio** (current assets excluding stock: current liabilities).

	20X1	20X0
Current assets	500	300
Stock	250	100
Current assets excl stock	250	200
Current liabilities	200	150
Quick ratio	1.25:1	1.33:1
Current ratio	2.5:1	2:1
Industry current ratio	2:1	2:1

At 31 May 20X0, the current ratio was in line with the industry average. By 31 May 20X1, it had risen above the industry average, while at the same time the quick ratio had decreased. This suggests that VDO may be holding an **excessive amount of stock**. The deterioration in the quick ratio suggests a **reduction** in the **liquidity** of the company.

Working capital ratios

The only working capital ratio that can be compared with the industry averages is the **debtor days**. This measures the average length of time taken by customers to pay their bills. It is calculated as:

$$\frac{\text{Trade debtors}}{\text{Sales}} \times 365$$

	20X1	20X0
Trade debtors	250	120
Sales	4,000	2,000
Debtor days	23 days	22 days
Industry average	35 days	33 days

Debtor days compare very favourably with the industry average, which suggests that VDO has tight control over its debtors. However, it must consider whether it is damaging its competitive position by imposing **tighter restrictions** on its debtors than does the rest of the industry.

Gearing ratio

This is measured by the debt : equity %.

	20X1	20X0
Long term liabilities	200	0
Shareholders' funds	650	600
Debt:Equity %	30.8%	0%
Industry average	20%	20%

The gearing ratio has risen from zero to a level significantly above the industry average. This indicates that the **financial risk** faced by the shareholders has **increased**.

Stock market ratios

These include (i) **Earnings per share (EPS)** and (ii) **Price/earnings (P/E) ratio**. The P/E ratio is calculated as the market price of the share divided by the earnings per share. EPS is calculated as earnings available for dividend divided by the number of shares in issue.

	20X1	20X0
Number of shares	500	500
Earnings	80	96
EPS	16 pence	19.2 pence
Market price	240p	346p
P/E ratio	15 times	18 times
Industry average	20 times	18 times

Both the earnings per share and the share price have fallen significantly over the past year. The proportionately greater drop in the share price (a fall of 30%) has resulted in a drop in the P/E ratio. This ratio was previously in line with the industry average, indicating that at that time the market believed VDO's growth prospects to be in line with the rest of the industry. However, the position has now changed, and the market perception is that VDO's **earnings prospects** are **significantly below** those for the rest of the industry. These facts taken together should give the shareholders real cause for concern about their investment in the company.

(b) **Overtrading** describes the situation that arises when a business tries to do too much too quickly with too little long-term capital. It is trying to support too large a volume of trade with the capital resources at its disposal. A business that is overtrading may generate a profit, but it can easily run into **liquidity problems**. These may be manifested in **breaches** of **the overdraft limits** or in **late payment** of **creditors and interest**. A further consequence is that the business may have problems in **meeting its production and sales schedules** due to shortages of stocks.

Causes of overtrading include the following.

(i) A business may seek to **increase its turnover too quickly** without an **adequate capital base**. In this situation, the ambition of the managers and/or the inability of the company to raise sufficient additional finance cause overtrading.

(ii) When a business repays a loan, it often replaces the old loan with a new one. However a business might repay a loan without replacing it, with the consequence that it has **less long-term capital** to finance its current level of operations.

(iii) A business might be profitable, but in a period of inflation, its retained profits might be insufficient to pay for the **replacement of fixed assets and stocks**, the cost of which have risen due to inflation. The business would become increasingly dependent on credit, and find itself unable to support its current volume of trading with a capital base that has fallen in real terms.

(iv) If management have **inadequate information available**, or **exercise poor supervision**, different elements of working capital may be far from their ideal levels (for example poor control over debtor payments leading to excessive debtors and a shortage of cash.)

(c) Possible reasons for cash shortages include the following:

(i) **Lower profit margins** may cause a **fall** in the **level of cash** available in the business. In the case of VDO sales have doubled, but profits have remained unchanged. This could be due to pressure on prices, increases in direct costs, or to increased overheads. The amount of cash generated from operations is therefore unchanged, but the amount of cash required by the increases in working capital needed to generate the additional sales has increased significantly. This is reflected in the conversion of the £80,000 cash resources into a £200,000 term loan – a depletion of the cash level by £280,000.

(ii) Businesses with **long working capital cycles** will need large amounts of cash to finance high levels of stock and debtors.

(iii) **Seasonal businesses** may have cash flow difficulties at certain times of the year when cash inflows are low but outflows are high, often because the company is producing at a high level ready for the **next period** of **high sales**. An example of this would be a company manufacturing fireworks; pressure on cash would be worst during the summer when fireworks are being produced ready for the increase in demand during the autumn.

(iv) **One-off large items of expenditure** such as the purchase of a freehold property may stretch the cash resources of a company for a long time to come.

(v) **Increased competition** may force a business to reduce prices just to retain its existing volume of sales. This will reduce profit margins and therefore the amount of cash generated by the business will fall.

(vi) **Inflation** means that a company may need **increasing amounts** of cash to **replace used up** and worn out assets. Thus a business that is profitable in historic cost terms may still not be making sufficient money to sustain itself in the long term.

(d) VDO could take the following steps to resolve its cash difficulties.

(i) **Rationalisation of its product/market areas**. VDO should analyse its profitability by product and market areas to identify which areas of its business are making the greatest profits, and which areas are generating little contribution. It could then withdraw from the unprofitable areas and concentrate effort on the more profitable parts of the business. The drawback to this is that there may be long-term strategic reasons for supplying the less profitable parts of the market, and withdrawal may reduce the company's ability to compete in the more profitable areas.

(ii) **Cost reduction programme**. The company should analyse its cost base to determine if reductions are possible, for example in the sourcing of cheaper raw materials, the reduction of overtime or overheads. Possible drawbacks include a reduction in the quality of the products, which may be unacceptable to customers, and resistance on the part of staff.

(iii) **Reduction in the level of working capital**. While the figures suggest that the company has tight control of debtors, the level of stock has increased by two and a half times compared with an increase in sales of two times. This suggests that there is scope to reduce the level of stocks, perhaps by concentrating on the **levels of obsolete and slow moving stock**. The drawback is that unless this is done carefully there could be a negative impact on the level of customer service.

(iv) **Refinancing fixed assets**. If the company has a marketable property, it may be able to raise cash by arranging a **sale and leaseback agreement**. The drawbacks to this are that it would then be vulnerable to future rent rises, and that it would have reduced its ability to offer security for future borrowings.

(v) **Raise additional external finance**. VDO could seek to raise additional equity in the form of a rights issue, or debt in the form of a **term loan or debenture**. However, it will be difficult to persuade shareholders to make a further investment given the recent performance of the share price, and raising new equity is a lengthy and expensive process. The company has already taken on a new loan in the last twelve months, and it may find it difficult to raise further debt given its recent financial performance.

(e) Types of fraud that may arise when internal controls are compromised include the following.

(i) **Ghost employees** are imaginary employees for whom the wages department prepare wage payments, which are then distributed amongst the fraudsters. This type of fraud arises when there is extensive reliance on casual workers for whom there is minimal record keeping.

(ii) **Inflated overtime claims** can be made when there is pressure on production with insufficient time for managers to check timesheets.

(iii) **Miscasting the payroll** allows an inflated amount to be approved for the week's payroll, with the fraudster collecting the additional amount. This type of fraud is hard to trace when employees are paid in cash.

(iv) **Collusion with external parties** can involve suppliers or customers and their staff. Possible frauds are overcharging on purchase invoices, undercharging on sales invoices or the sale of confidential information to a competitor.

Helping hand

Only four suggestions are required. Other valid examples include:

- Teeming and lading
- Altering cheques and inflating expenses
- Stealing assets such as DVDs
- Issuing false credit notes
- Failing to record all sales

Examiner's marking scheme

			Marks
(a)	Comparison with each industry ratio and calculation of EPS/Acid test	(6 × 1 mark)	6
	Interpretation/comment on each ratio	(6 × 1 mark)	6
			12
(b)	Overtrading explained		3
	Each cause identified (max 4)	(3 × 1 mark)	3
			6
(c)	Each reason identified and briefly explained	(3 × 2 marks)	6
(d)	Each action identified and briefly described	(4 × 2 marks)	8
(e)	Each weakness identified and briefly explained	(4 × 2 marks)	8
			40

DO YOU KNOW? - FINANCIAL MARKETS AND THE ECONOMY

- *Check that your knowledge covers the following basic points before you attempt any questions. If in doubt, you should go back to your BPP Interactive Text and revise first.*

- .... exist to smooth the flow of funds from surplus sectors of the economy to deficit sectors. They may be either banks or non-banks.

- .... banks are banks that operate the payments mechanism and are usually called commercial banks or clearing banks. .... banks deal mostly with wholesale business in the secondary money markets, not in the High Street.

- The role of the .... bank is particularly important for the government's monetary policy. The main instrument of monetary policy is the use of .... to influence the demand for bank loans and other forms of credit, and also to influence exchange rates.

- Other functions of central banks include:
  - ....
  - ....
  - ....
  - ....
  - ....

- The 'wholesale' markets through which financial institutions borrow and lend are called the ....

- Financial instruments traded on these markets include:
  - ....
  - ....
  - ....
  - ....
  - ....

- The government's management of the economy is directed towards certain objectives such as .... and ....

- The UK government prefers to regulate the money supply indirectly, through ...., rather than quantitative or qualitative controls on amounts that can be lent.

- The desire to hold money, rather than other forms of wealth, is termed '............... preference'.

- Nominal and real rates of interest, and the rate of inflation, are linked by the following approximate formula.

  .... – .... = ...

- If interest rates in Country A rise while those in Country B remain unchanged, other things being equal the exchange rate for Country A currency relative to Country B currency will ....

- The term structure of interest rates reflects the fact that different financial instruments have different ....

  TRY QUESTIONS 25 AND 26

- *Possible pitfalls*

  Write down the mistakes you know you should avoid.

DID YOU KNOW? - FINANCIAL MARKETS AND THE ECONOMY

- *Could you fill in the blanks? The answers are in bold. Use this page for revision purposes as you approach the exam.*

- **Financial intermediaries** exist to smooth the flow of funds from surplus sectors of the economy to deficit sectors. They may be either banks or other institutions.

- **Primary** banks are banks that operate the payments mechanism and are usually called commercial banks or clearing banks. **Secondary** banks deal mostly with wholesale business in the secondary money markets, not in the High Street.

- The role of the **central** bank is particularly important for the government's monetary policy. The main instrument of monetary policy is the use of **interest rates** to influence the demand for bank loans and other forms of credit, and also to influence exchange rates.

- Other functions of central banks include:
  - **Acting as banker to government**
  - **Acting as banker to commercial banks**
  - **Issuing bank notes**
  - **Supervising banks**
  - **Acting as lender of last resort**

- The 'wholesale' markets through which financial institutions borrow and lend are called the **money markets**.

- Financial instruments traded on these markets include:
  - **Treasury bills**
  - **Local authority bonds**
  - **Certificates of Deposit**
  - **Commercial paper**
  - **Eurocurrency deposits**

- The government's management of the economy is directed towards certain objectives such as **price stability** and **economic growth**.

- The UK government prefers to regulate the money supply indirectly, through **interest rates**, rather than quantitative or qualitative controls on amounts that can be lent.

- The desire to hold money, rather than other forms of wealth, is termed '**liquidity** preference'.

- Nominal and real rates of interest, and the rate of inflation, are linked by the following approximate formula.

  Nominal interest rate – Real interest rate = Inflation rate

- If interest rates in Country A rise while those in Country B remain unchanged, other things being equal the exchange rate for Country A currency relative to Country B currency will **rise**.

- The term structure of interest rates reflects the fact that different financial instruments have different **periods to maturity**.

  TRY QUESTIONS 25 AND 26

- *Possible pitfalls*
  - **Confusing terminology**. (Note, for example, that eurocurrency has nothing to do with the 'euro', the European single currency.)
  - **Not keeping your knowledge of the financial markets and the economy up to date.**

25   QUESTION WITH HELP: MONEY SUPPLY

(a)   What is meant by the term 'the money supply'? What is its significance to a business?

(7 marks)

(b)   Briefly explain the principal functions of a central bank.   (7 marks)

(c)   Why might a commercial bank operate with various different rates of interest?

(6 marks)

(20 marks)

If you are stuck, look at the next page for detailed help as to how you should tackle this question.

APPROACHING THE ANSWER

Use this answer plan to construct your answer if you are stuck.

(a) Define the money supply.

Outline the concepts of narrow and broad money, illustrating by reference to M0 and M4 or equivalent.

Outline the role of the commercial banks in the creation of money.

Demonstrate how monetary policy, particularly interest rate policy affects business.

(b) Answer the question with reference to a particular central bank, for example, that of your country. Factors to consider include:

- Relationship with government and government policy

- Role in relation to the rest of the banking system

- Role in relation to foreign exchange and currency issues

(c) Factors influencing interest rates:

- Risk
- Duration
- Size
- Margin
- Overseas

25 ANSWER TO QUESTION WITH HELP: MONEY SUPPLY

(a) The **money supply** in an economy is the total stock of money in that economy.

There are different ways of defining the total stock of money in an economy. **Money** may be defined 'narrowly', meaning that financial assets have to be very liquid to be counted in the definition. M0 is the most commonly used measure of **narrow money** in the UK, consisting of **notes and coin in circulation** with the public plus banks' till money and banks' operational balances with the Bank of England.

Broad money definitions of the money supply embrace forms of money held for **transaction purposes** and also money held as a form of **saving**. Such definitions provide an indicator of the private sector's holdings of relatively liquid assets, ie those which can be converted with relative ease and without capital loss into spending on goods and services. M4 is a measure of broad money which counts private sector deposits in banks and building societies as money in addition to notes and coin in circulation with the public.

The **commercial banks** are **agents** in the **creation of money** because money is created through the expansion of bank deposits. As a result, measures to limit or to reduce the growth of the money supply need to take account of the importance of the liquidity of the banks, which provides the means by which money is created.

In recent years, the UK government has rejected reliance upon most methods of seeking to control the supply of money and has instead sought to influence its demand through the policy instrument of the interest rate. Since 1997, **interest rate decisions** have been made by the Bank of England, in line with the government's inflation target.

Rises in interest rates will **reduce** the **profitability** of **new investment** by firms. Investment demand may also be inhibited by any measures which make it more difficult for firms to borrow from the commercial banks. Reduced demand for investment, together with reduced consumer demand, will have a deflationary effect on the economy overall.

In summary, business could find themselves squeezed by falling demand on one hand and rising costs on the other, leading to the possibility of a rising level of business failures.

(b) The fact that all developed countries have a **central bank** indicates the existence of a general consensus that central banks perform indispensable functions. In the UK the central bank is the **Bank of England** and although it has certain special functions, its major activities are the same as any other central bank.

    (i) One of the functions of the Bank is that it acts as **banker to the government.** This embraces various activities including the handling of receipts, such as tax revenues, paid to the government and releasing funds to meet the spending commitments of the different government departments.

    (ii) Another major function of the Bank is to **implement the government's monetary policy:** by manipulating or influencing the liquidity position of the banks and hence their ability to make loans, and (since 1997) by setting short-term interest rates at a level designed to meet the government's inflation target.

    (iii) The Bank functions as the **lender of last resort** to the banking system by making loans to the banking system when it is short of liquidity.

    (iv) The Bank of England is also **banker to the monetary system**. All banks and licensed deposit takers are required to hold operational deposits at the Bank and these are effectively used as current accounts.

(v)   In England and Wales, the Bank is the sole **note-issuing authority**.

(vi)   The Bank has responsibility for **converting foreign exchange** receipts are converted into sterling and vice versa.

(c) A **commercial bank** operates with a widely varying pattern of **interest rates** for the following reasons.

(i)   Banks will lend money at a lower rate of interest to lower **risk** customers. This is apparent in short-term lending, where very low interest rates are charged on lending in the interbank market to leading banks, whereas higher interest rates are charged on similar short-term lending to even large and well-established companies. Higher interest rates will also be charged on personal loans to customers in a higher risk category.

(ii)   Interest rates vary with the **duration of a loan or deposit**. Saving schemes requiring some notice of withdrawal will attract a higher yield than an ordinary deposit account. With an ordinary current account, where customers can withdraw funds on demand, no interest at all is paid.

(iii)   Banks' interest rates vary with the **size of loans and deposits**. Generally, a lower interest rate will be charged for larger 'wholesale' loans and a higher interest rate offered for larger 'wholesale' deposits.

(iv)   The need to make a **profit** on re-lending is clearly evident in the banks' rate of interest. For example, retail loans to customers will be at an interest rate higher than the bank's base rate, whereas low or nil interest is paid on current accounts, and the rate paid on deposit accounts is less than the bank's base rate.

(v)   A substantial proportion of a bank's business is conducted in **foreign currencies**. The interest rate in which a bank deals, in the eurocurrency markets, will vary according to the currency, and the general level of interest rates in that country.

26 FINANCIAL INTERMEDIARIES (6/00)

In order to facilitate the efficient operation of financial markets, the Central Bank (in the case of the UK, the Bank of England), and the major financial intermediaries have important roles to play.

Required

(a) (i) Briefly explain what is meant by financial intermediation, giving specific examples of types of organisations that take on this role. (4 marks)

(ii) Identify and briefly describe FOUR roles of financial intermediaries which help improve market efficiency. (8 marks)

(b) (i) Explain FOUR main roles of a central bank (in the case of the UK, the Bank of England). (4 marks)

(ii) One of the roles of a central bank is to provide advice to the government on strategies to control inflation. Briefly outline FOUR possible consequences of inflation on organisations engaged in business. (4 marks)

(20 marks)

26   ANSWER: FINANCIAL INTERMEDIARIES

(a) (i)   Financial intermediation is the process by which **providers** and **users** of finance are brought together. The organisations that promote this process are known as financial intermediaries.

Examples of financial intermediaries include:

(1) Clearing banks
(2) Building societies
(3) Merchant banks
(4) Finance houses
(5) Insurance companies
(6) Pension funds
(7) Unit trust companies
(8) Investment trust companies
(9) Venture capital houses
(10) Bank of England

(ii) The roles played by financial intermediaries in the efficient operation of the markets include:

(1) They **link lenders** of money with potential **borrowers**. Their activity in this process means that trading of securities is made easier, and hence the **marketability** of securities is **enhanced**.

(2) The intermediary is able to '**package**' the **amounts** lent by savers into the amounts that borrowers require. For example, large numbers of small building society deposits are packaged together to provide mortgages of the size needed by borrowers.

(3) **Risk** to the individual lender is **reduced** by the **pooling** of the risks of lending money to borrowers among the various lenders who deposit money with the intermediary. Similarly, risk is reduced by unit and investment trust companies that carry a much larger portfolio of securities than the individual investor could manage.

(4) Intermediaries such as unit and investment trusts **reduce** the **level of transaction costs** to the individual investor, who does not have to make a large number of small transactions in order to achieve diversification.

(5) The intermediaries **facilitate 'maturity transformation'**. By this process borrowers are able to borrow over longer periods than would be realistic for an individual lender to provide. An example of this is the provision of mortgages described in (2) above.

(6) The intermediaries **provide information and advice** to investors and thereby improve the efficiency of the markets by improving the flow of information.

(b) (i)   The main roles of a central bank such as the Bank of England are as follows:

(1) It is responsible for the **control and issue of currency** notes and coins.

(2) It acts as **banker to government and the other banks** in the financial system. It provides the mechanism for the transfer of funds between the banks, and between the government and the banks. It is also the **lender of last resort** in the banking system.

(3)   The Bank **manages the National Debt** by issuing government securities, trading in government securities, and administering the repayment of government debt.

(4)   It **manages the Exchange Equalisation Account**. This is the means by which the government can intervene in the currency markets to stabilise the exchange rate of sterling against other currencies.

(5)   It is influential in a number of areas of **monetary policy,** in particular now being responsible for **setting interest rates** as appropriate to meet the government's inflation targets. It will also advise government on areas such as the money supply and exchange rate policy.

(ii)   Some of the consequences of inflation are as follows:

(1)   The **costs** of materials, labour and energy will **rise.** If the market is competitive, it may not be possible to pass these increases on to the customer, thereby leading to a reduction in profits.

(2)   The Bank of England is likely to **increase interest rates** in an attempt to control inflation. Higher interest rates mean that the cost of investment will increase, and this may lead to the company's investment plans being cut back.

(3)   Long-term inflation will lead to the **devaluation of the currency.** This will benefit exporters, but lead to an increase in the cost of imported raw materials.

(4)   The government may seek to control inflation by **imposing price and wage controls.** This will impact on the operating flexibility of business.

(5)   High inflation results in an **increased level of economic uncertainty** since prices are continually changing. This leads to companies adopting more cautious investment policies than would otherwise be the case, or worst still seeking to cut labour costs by redundancies. **Unemployment** may therefore **rise.**

Examiner's marking scheme

				Marks
(a)	(i)	Financial intermediary explained		2
		Examples	(2 × 1 mark)	2
				4
	(ii)	Each role identified and briefly described	(4 × 2 marks)	8
(b)	(i)	Each role briefly explained	(4 × 1 mark)	4
	(ii)	Each consequence identified and briefly explained	(4 × 1 mark)	4
				20

DO YOU KNOW? - RAISING AND INVESTING MONEY

- *Check that you know the following basic points before you attempt any questions. If in doubt, you should go back to your BPP Interactive Text and revise first.*

- A bank's decision to lend will be based on the following factors.

  C   ....
  A   ....
  M   ....
  P   ....
  A   ....
  R   ....
  I   ....

- A key form of short-term finance is bank overdrafts, for which key factors to consider are:

  ○   ....   ○   ....
  ○   ....   ○   ....
  ○   ....   ○   ....

- Bank loans are more appropriate over the medium or long term, and there are three possible types of repayment: ...., ... and ....

- Obligations attached to the loan, over and above interest payments and repayment of capital, are called ....

- Leases come in two forms: the ...., for which the lessee is responsible for the upkeep of the asset, and the ...., which is a form of rental agreement. An arrangement similar to leasing, but where ownership of the goods passes on payment of the final credit instalment, is called ....

  TRY QUESTIONS 27 AND 28

- A stock exchange can operate as a .... market, enabling businesses to raise new finance, or as a .... market, enabling investors to sell their investments.

- A company may issue one of the following forms of long-term capital.

  ○   ....
  ○   ....

- Other forms of long-term finance for businesses are:

  ○   ....   ○   ....
  ○   ....   ○   ....
  ○   For larger companies only: ....

- A .... is a right given by a company to an investor, allowing him to subscribe for new shares at a future date at a fixed, pre-determined price (called the ....).

- .... shares are shares with a fixed percentage dividend, payable in priority to any dividend paid to ordinary shareholders.

- The alternative ways in which venture capitalists may realise their investment are commonly called ....

- Possible uses of surplus cash held by a business are:

  ○   ....   ○   ....
  ○   ....   ○   ....

- Alternatively, a business may wish to invest its surplus cash.

- The two main types of security are .... and .... securities.

- A commonly used name for government securities is ....

- Strictly speaking, a cheque is a type of ....

- Spreading available funds across a range of separate investments can reduce risk and is called ....

  TRY QUESTIONS 29, 30, 31 AND 32

- *Possible pitfalls*

  Write down the mistakes you know you should avoid

DID YOU KNOW? - RAISING AND INVESTING MONEY

- *Could you fill in the blanks? The answers are in bold. Use this page for revision purposes as you approach the exam.*
- A bank's decision to lend will be based on the following factors.

  C **haracter of the customer**
  A **bility to borrow and repay**
  M **argin of profit**
  P **urpose of the borrowing**
  A **mount of the borrowing**
  R **epayment terms**
  I **nsurance against non-payment**

- A key form of short-term finance is bank overdrafts, for which key factors to consider are:
  - **Amount**
  - **Purpose**
  - **Security**
  - **Margin**
  - **Repayment**
  - **Benefits**

- Bank loans are more appropriate over the medium or long term, and there are three possible types of repayment: **bullet**, **balloon** and **amortising**.
- Obligations attached to the loan, over and above interest payments and repayment of capital, are called **covenants**.
- Leases come in two forms: the **finance lease**, for which the lessee is responsible for the upkeep of the asset, and the **operating lease**, which is a form of rental agreement. An arrangement similar to leasing, but where ownership of the goods passes on payment of the final credit instalment, is called **hire purchase**.

  TRY QUESTIONS 27 AND 28

- A stock exchange can operate as a **primary** market, enabling businesses to raise new finance, or as a **secondary** market, enabling investors to sell their investments.
- A company may issue one of the following forms of long-term capital.
  - **Shares**
  - **Debentures (or loan stock)**
- Other forms of long-term finance for business are:
  - **Cash from retained earnings**
  - **Venture capital**
  - For larger companies only: **international money and capital markets**
  - **Bank borrowings**
  - **Government grants**
- A **warrant** is a right given by a company to an investor, allowing him to subscribe for new shares at a future date at a fixed, pre-determined price (called the **exercise price**).
- **Preference** shares are shares with a fixed percentage dividend, payable in priority to any dividend paid to ordinary shareholders.
- The alternative ways in which venture capitalists may realise their investment are commonly called **exit routes**.
- Possible uses of surplus cash held by a business are:
  - **Purchases of fixed assets**
  - **Payment of dividends**
  - **Acquisitions of other businesses**
  - **Share buy-backs**
- Alternatively, a business may wish to invest its surplus cash.
- The two main types of security are **equity (share)** and **debt** securities.
- A commonly used name for government securities is **gilts**.
- Strictly speaking, a cheque is a type of **bill of exchange**.
- Spreading available funds across a range of separate investments can reduce risk and is called **diversification**.

  TRY QUESTIONS 29, 30, 31 and 32

- *Possible pitfalls*
  - **Remember to match the time period of borrowing with the period over which finance is needed.**
  - **Remember to match types of borrowing to the type and size of the business.**
  - **Remember the different risks of different investments.**

27   QUESTION WITH HELP: A BRICKIE (BUILDERS) LTD

Alan Brickie is 45 years old. He and his wife are the directors and only shareholders of A Brickie (Builders) Ltd. The company has banked with Southern Bank for the seven years since its incorporation. The company is engaged in contract building work, carrying out repairs and extensions to domestic property, including modernising and repairing houses owned by the local authority. In the past the bank has allowed overdraft facilities of up to £15,000.

Mr Brickie has tendered to build six houses for the local authority at a price of £234,000. Payment will be made against architects' certificates. It seems likely that his bid will be successful and he will require a temporary increase in his overdraft facility from the bank to £30,000. By the time he starts the contract he expects the company's balance at the bank to be £7,000, with full payment having been received from his present contracts and his creditors up to date. In addition, he has £20,000 on deposit account with his bank in his own name which he is prepared to inject into the company as a temporary loan.

The details of the local authority contract are as follows.

Contract price	£234,000
Time allowed for work	nine months
Architects' certificates	monthly
Period for honouring architects' certificates	14 days
Retentions to be at the rate of	10%
Limit of retention fund	5% of the contract

Mr Brickie estimates the cost to himself will be £189,000 giving an estimated profit of £45,000 on the contract. He has calculated that 2/3 of the cost of the contract will be labour and 1/3 materials, spread evenly over the period of the contract. He is able to obtain 30 days' credit from his materials supplier, but he knows from experience that the 14 days period for honouring architects' certificates is rarely met and often extends up to 30 days.

'Now' is May 20X8.

Required

As Mr Brickie's adviser on cash flow, advise him as to the bank's likely response to his request for an increased overdraft facility of £30,000. Draw up a cash flow forecast as part of your answer.   **(20 marks)**

> *If you are stuck, look at the next page for detailed help as to how you should tackle this question.*

APPROACHING THE ANSWER

Use this answer plan to construct your answer if you are stuck.

Relevant factors for forecast:

- Period of contract
- Value of work done per month
- Cost of work per month
- Components of cost
- Date first receipts received
- Retentions

Forecasts should show opening and closing monthly balances.

Discussion

- Maximum balance needed
- Other costs
- Allowance for uncertainties
- Should balance be lent
- Feasibility of contract
- Possibility of losses

27   **ANSWER: A BRICKIE (BUILDERS) LTD**

It is important to establish whether an overdraft facility of £30,000 will be sufficient for what Mr Brickie will need. To do this, we can prepare a cash flow forecast, using Mr Brickie's estimates of revenues and payments.

(a)   Period of contract: 9 months (assumed to be completed on time).

(b)   Value of work done per month (£234,000 ÷ 9) = £26,000.

(c)   Cost of work per month (£189,000 ÷ 9) = £21,000.

(d)   Costs per month will consist of £14,000 labour and £7,000 materials.

(e)   First receipts end of month 2 (say, start of month 3).

(f)   Retentions = 10% of £26,000 = £2,600 per month, building up to a maximum of 5% of £234,000 = £11,700.

	Value of work done	Receipts for work done (A)	Cumulative retentions	Payments (1 month credit on materials) (B)	Receipts less payments (A-B)	Starting cash balance	Closing cash balance
	£'000	£'000	£'000	£'000	£'000	£'000	£'000
Start							
Cash in bank						7	
Loan						20	
						27	
Month 1	26	0	0	14	(14)	27	13
Month 2	26	0	0	21	(21)	13	(8)
Month 3	26	23.4	2.6	21	2.4	(8)	(5.6)
Month 4	26	23.4	5.2	21	2.4	(5.6)	(3.2)
Month 5	26	23.4	7.8	21	2.4	(3.2)	(0.8)
Month 6	26	23.4	10.4	21	2.4	(0.8)	1.6
Month 7	26	24.7	11.7(max)	21	3.7	1.6	5.3
Month 8	26	26	11.7	21	5	5.3	10.3
Month 9	26	26	11.7	21	5	10.3	15.3
Month 10	0	26	11.7	7	19	15.3	34.3
Month 11	0	37.7	0	0	37.7	34.3	72.0
Total	234	234.0		189	45.0		

From this cash flow forecast, it is difficult to see why Mr Brickie should need an overdraft facility of £30,000, since a maximum overdraft of £8,000 is indicated, on the basis of the figures and the assumptions used.

Presumably, Mr Brickie wishes to **make other payments** during this period, without income from other sources to cover them. Salaries for himself and his wife must be paid, also possibly plant hire costs. In addition, Mr Brickie might have allowed for **higher costs** and **lower values of work done** in the earlier months, or he might be making a provision for unforeseen delays due to bad weather, or delays caused by local council officials.

Mr Brickie should be asked to explain in more detail the reason for needing an overdraft facility of £30,000.

On the assumption that the request for £30,000 is realistic, the overall profitability of the contract appears to be good. Several other questions need to be asked, however.

(a)   The **contract is large**, in comparison with the amount of business done by the company in the past. Can the business handle a job of such a large size? An answer to this question will call for answers to two subsidiary questions.

(i)   Can Mr Brickie **obtain the skilled labour** he will need to complete a job of this size?

(ii) Will he have to **hire much plant and equipment** for the contract, and if so, has he provided for this in his costings? (Given the data available, this seems doubtful.)

(b) The **draft contract** for the work needs to be **checked**. There might be unfavourable clauses, such as penalties for late completion of work.

Conclusion

Satisfactory answers need to be obtained to the questions discussed above, but provided that these are forthcoming, the bank will probably be prepared to grant the extended facility.

28   BORROWER LTD (12/00)

Borrower Ltd is a medium-sized private company to which you have recently been appointed as the assistant financial controller. The company is currently engaged in a business expansion programme for which additional finance will be required. It is not currently feasible to raise additional equity finance, consequently debt finance is being considered. The decision has not yet been finalised whether this debt finance will be short or long term and if it is to be at fixed or variable rates. The financial controller has asked you, as part of your first assignment, to assist her in the preparation of information for a forthcoming meeting of the Board of Directors.

Required

(a)   Prepare a draft report to the Board of Directors which identifies and briefly discusses:

    (i)   FOUR main factors to be considered when deciding on the appropriate mix of long-term or short-term sources of debt finance for Borrower Ltd.   (10 marks)

    (ii)   Two main advantages of fixing interest rates on debt.   (2 marks)

(b)   (i)   Explain what is meant by a covenant in a loan agreement.   (2 marks)

    (ii)   Briefly outline THREE types of loan covenant, giving specific examples of covenants which may be included in loan agreements and explain the purpose of each type of covenant.   (6 marks)

(20 marks)

Helping hand

In (a) remember that the report is being prepared for a private company. In (b) you need to explain clearly why lenders are interested in obtaining covenants.

---

28   ANSWER: BORROWER LTD

Helping hand

In (a), make sure that you match your answer to the information provided in the question. For example, we know that the company in question is a private company that requires funds for business expansion. Discussions on areas such as the effect on the share price are therefore inappropriate.

In (b) you must not only describe the different types of covenant, but also explain the purpose of the examples that you have included.

What the examiner said

Generally this question was badly answered. Candidates should ensure they study these topics; answers to (b) on loan covenants were poor despite this topic featuring in previous papers.

(a) To: Board of Directors of Borrower Ltd
    From: Assistant Financial Controller
    Date: 29 January 20X1
    Subject: Factors to be considered in deciding the financing mix

Introduction

The purpose of this report is to identify the main factors to be considered when deciding on the appropriate mix of long-term or short-term sources of debt finance, and to consider the advantages of fixing interest rates on debt.

Main factors to be considered

1   **The purpose of the borrowing**

    The type of funds must be matched to the **purpose** for which they are required. The **business expansion programme** is likely to **require finance** both for the purchase of additional fixed assets, and for an increase in the level of working capital. In general cheaper **short-term funds** should only be used to **finance short-term requirements**, such as a larger level of fluctuations in the level of working capital. Short-term debt, usually in the form of an overdraft, is repayable on demand, and it would therefore be risky to finance long-term capital investments in this way.

2   **Flexibility**

    Short-term finance is a **more flexible** source of finance; there may be penalties for repaying long-term debt early. However, we do have to be sure that further short-term debt will be available if we need to renew our facility.

3   **Our ability to borrow and repay**

    We must be able to convince a lender of our ability to service the debt and to repay it at the end of the term. We must therefore put together a **business plan** for the expansion that shows how earnings from the additional sales will be sufficient to cover interest costs, and also shows how we intend to fund repayment at the end of the loan period. We must also confirm that we have the **legal capacity** to borrow in the manner required by checking the articles of association, and that we will not breach any restrictive covenants on our existing borrowings.

4   **The cost of the debt and the repayment terms**

    The **relative costs** of the alternative sources of finance must be considered. For example, short-term debt is usually cheaper than long-term debt, but will carry a higher level of risk, as discussed above. The interest rate charged will also depend on the **perceived risk** of the investment to the lender, and this is another reason for putting together a comprehensive business plan. The **repayment terms** must also be **matched** to the pattern of cash flows coming from the new enterprise. In general there are three types of repayment arrangement for fixed term debt.

Bullet

No principal is repaid until the end of the loan, at which point it is then repaid in full.

Balloon

Some of the loan principal is repaid during the term of the loan, but the majority is not repaid until the end of the loan period.

Amortising

The loan principal is repaid gradually over the term of the loan.

5   **The effect on gearing**

The gearing of the business is a measure of the amount of debt relative to equity. If a company is seen as being too highly geared, finance providers will judge that the **risk of default** is high, and are likely to seek higher compensation for this risk. This could take the form of a higher interest rate, restrictive covenants, or shorter repayment terms. If they perceive the risk to be high, some finance providers may be unwilling to lend at all. If gearing is likely to be a problem, we could consider acquiring some of the new assets using leases, since operating leases are not included in the company's balance sheet.

The advantages of fixing interest rates on debt

The two main advantages of fixed interest rates are as follows:

1   **Cash flow planning**

   With a fixed rate loan, we will know exactly how much we need to pay, and when. This will make it easier to **plan** the **cash flow** and to ensure that we have **funds available** when required.

2   **Cost**

   If we believe that interest rates are likely to rise over the period of the loan, then taking out a **fixed rate loan** will **limit our interest rate liability.**

Conclusions

The key factor in the choice of financing method is the purpose for which the funds are required. A detailed business plan for the new investment should be prepared in order to identify the most appropriate financing mix, and to support our case to potential lenders.

(b) (i)   A covenant in a loan agreement is an obligation placed on the borrower over and above repaying the loan according to terms.

     (ii)   The three types of covenant are:

Positive covenants

These require a borrower to do something, for example to **provide the bank** with its **annual financial statements**. This would allow the bank to **check** on the **financial performance** of the company, and to ensure that it is likely to be able to repay the loan as planned.

Negative or restrictive covenants

These are **promises** by a borrower **not to do something**. For example, the borrower may pledge **not to take out further loans** until the current loan has been repaid. The purpose of this is to protect the position of the lender, and to ensure that the risk of default is not increased, or the level of security diluted.

Quantitative covenants

These set **limitations on the borrower's financial position.** For example, the company might agree that its total borrowings should not exceed 100% of shareholder's funds. The purpose of this is to keep the gearing, and hence the level of risk to the lender, within certain limits.

		Examiner's marking scheme		**Marks**	
(a)	(i)	Report format/presentation			
		Each factor identified		2	
		and briefly explained	(4 × 2 marks)	8	
					10
	(ii)	Each advantage briefly explained	(2 × 1 mark)		2
(b)	(i)	Covenant explained		2	
	(ii)	Covenant type with an example	(3 × 1 mark)	3	
		Purpose of the types of covenant identified	(3 × 1 mark)	3	
					8
					20

29 LOAN LTD (12/01)

Loan Ltd is currently considering a major capital investment project for which additional finance will be required. It is not currently feasible to raise additional equity finance, consequently debt finance is being considered. The decision has not yet been finalised whether this debt finance will be short or long term and if it is to be at fixed or variable rates. One of the directors has suggested that debt finance be raised by a debenture issue. The managing director is not sure exactly what a debenture issue means. The financial controller has asked you for your assistance in the preparation of a report for a forthcoming meeting of the board of directors.

Required

Prepare a draft report to the board of directors which identifies and briefly explains:

(a) FOUR main factors to be considered when deciding on the appropriate mix of short, medium or long-term debt finance for Loan Ltd. (10 marks)

(b) What is meant by a debenture. (4 marks)

(c) THREE practical considerations which could be factors in restricting the amount of debt which Loan Ltd would raise. (6 marks)

(20 marks)

29   ANSWER: LOAN LTD

(a)   To: Board
      From: Technician
      Date: 8 January 20X2

The term of the finance

The term should be appropriate to the **asset** being acquired. As a general rule, long-term **assets** should be **financed** from **long-term finance** sources. Cheaper short-term funds should be used to finance short-term requirements, such as fluctuations in the level of working capital.

Flexibility

Short-term debt is a **more flexible** source of finance; there may be penalties for repaying long-term debt early. If the company takes out long-term debt and interest rates fall, it will find itself locked into unfavourable terms.

Repayment terms

The company must have **sufficient funds** to be able to **meet repayment schedules** laid down in loan agreements, and to cover interest costs. Although there may be no specific terms of repayment laid down for short-term debt, it may possibly be **repayable on demand**, so it may be risky to finance long-term capital investments in this way.

Costs

Interest on short-term debt is usually **less** than on long-term debt. However, if short-term debt has to be renewed frequently, issue expenses may raise its cost significantly.

Availability

It may be **difficult to renew short-term finance** in the future if the company's position or economic conditions change adversely.

Effect on gearing

Certain types of short-term debt (bank overdrafts, increased credit from suppliers) will not be included in gearing calculations. If a company is seen as **too highly geared**, lenders may be **unwilling to lend money,** or judge that the high risk of default must be compensated by higher interest rates or restrictive covenants.

(b)   A **debenture** is a document that sets out the terms of a loan including **interest** and **date** and **terms of repayment** (redemption).

Debentures can be issued to single lenders, or they can be subscribed by a large number of lenders. Debentures are usually **secured** on a company's assets, although **unsecured** debentures are sometimes issued (generally these carry a higher rate of interest then equivalent secured debentures). If the debenture is secured, and interest is not paid or other conditions are breached, the debentureholders can have the asset(s) pledged as security sold to recover their investment.

Convertible debentures are debentures that can be converted on pre-determined dates, and at the option of the holder, into ordinary shares at a pre-determined rate. Conversion terms would be set out when the debenture is issued.

(c) **Previous record of company**

If the company (or possibly its directors or even shareholders) has a **low credit rating** with credit reference agencies, investors may be unwilling to subscribe for debentures. Banks may be influenced by this, and also by their own experiences of the company as customer (has the company exceeded overdraft limits in the past on a regular basis).

Restrictions in memorandum and articles

The company should examine the **legal documents** carefully to see if they place any restrictions on what the company can borrow, and for what purposes.

Restrictions of current borrowing

The **terms of** any **loans** to the company that are **currently outstanding** may contain restrictions about further borrowing that can be taken out.

Uncertainty over project

The project is a significant one, and presumably the **interest and ultimately repayment** that lenders obtain may be very dependent on the success of the project. If the results are uncertain, lenders may not be willing to take the risk.

Security

The company may be **unwilling to provide the security** that lenders require, particularly if it is faced **with restrictions** on what it can do with the **assets secured**.

Alternatively it may have **insufficient assets** to provide the necessary security.

	Examiner's marking scheme		Marks	
(a)	Report format/presentation		2	
	Each factor identified and briefly explained	(4 × 2 marks)	8	
				10
(b)	Debentures explained		1	
	Secured debentures		1	
	Unsecured debentures		1	
	Convertible debentures		1	
				4
(c)	Each practical consideration identified and briefly described	(3 × 2 marks)		6
				20

30   MARKETABLE SECURITIES

RT plc has forecast the following cash movements for the next six months.

Cash available now	£2,000,000
Inflow in two months	£4,000,000
Outflow in four months	£2,000,000
Outflow in six months	£4,000,000

Assume that all movements of cash take place on the *last day* of each two-month period.

The structure of short-term interest rates is as follows.

Current		*Expected in 2 months*		*Expected in 4 months*	
Maturity period	*Annual yield* %	*Maturity period*	*Annual yield* %	*Maturity period*	*Annual yield* %
2 months	7.3	2 months	8.0	2 months	8.3
4 months	7.4	4 months	8.1	4 months	8.4
6 months	7.5	6 months	8.2	6 months	8.3

The company invests surplus cash balances in marketable securities. Company policy is to hold such securities to maturity once they are purchased. Every purchase transaction of marketable securities costs £100.

Required

(a) Calculate which securities should be purchased to maximise income.   (11 marks)

(b) Discuss the criteria that would influence a company's procedure for selecting marketable securities.   (9 marks)

(20 marks)

Helping hand

For (a), you should set out calculations for different options which take advantage of the fact that interest rates are expected to rise. Then calculate the total interest received under each option, remembering to deduct transaction costs. The option that yields the best return should then be identified. In (b) think about the key factors that the company is weighing against each other.

---

30   ANSWER: MARKETABLE SECURITIES

> **Helping hand**
>
> In (a) taking advantage of the expected rise in interest rates leaves us with six options to calculate.
>
> In (b) risk and return are central elements, but don't forget flexibility.

(a)   Since interest rates are forecast to rise, the best solution is likely to be one in which only **short-term deposits** are made, thus allowing advantage to be taken of the rise in rates. Options structured in this way include the following.

	Amount £'000	Month invested	Period (in months)	Rate	Value £
1	2,000	0	2	7.3%	24,333
	6,000	2	2	8.0%	80,000
	4,000	4	2	8.3%	55,333
	Transaction costs				(300)
					159,366
2	2,000	0	4	7.4%	49,333
	4,000	2	4	8.1%	108,000
	Transaction costs				(200)
					157,133
3	2,000	0	4	7.4%	49,333
	4,000	2	2	8.0%	53,333
	4,000	4	2	8.3%	55,333
	Transaction costs				(300)
					157,699
4	2,000	0	2	7.3%	24,333
	2,000	2	2	8.0%	26,667
	4,000	2	4	8.1%	108,000
	Transaction costs				(300)
					158,700
5	2,000	0	6	7.5%	75,000
	2,000	2	4	8.1%	54,000
	2,000	2	2	8.0%	26,667
	Transaction costs				(300)
					155,367
6	2,000	0	6	7.5%	75,000
	4,000	2	2	8.0%	53,333
	2,000	4	2	8.3%	27,667
	Transaction costs				(300)
					155,700

It can be seen that Option 1 yields the best return.

(b)   When selecting marketable securities, the company is normally doing so with the aim of maximising the return on short-term cash surpluses. With this aim in mind, the criteria are likely to include the following.

   (i)   The level of **risk** should be as **low as possible** since the company is not seeking a speculative gain, but to ensure that funds which are intended for specific purposes in the future do not lie idle.

(ii)   The level of **return** should be as **high as possible** within the class of risk which the company is prepared to accept.

(iii)   The level of **transaction costs** and the **degree of complexity** of administration should be as **low as possible**.

(iv)   Ideally the securities will be easily **marketable** so that if the funds are required at an earlier date than anticipated this can be achieved without significant loss of revenue.

(v)   The **amount of funds to be invested** will influence the **types of security** that will be appropriate.

31   **BUGS LTD (6/99)**

Bugs Ltd is a software development company which was established five years ago by three computer programmers. The company has been very successful with the development of custom-written software solutions. Recently, the founder shareholders who are also the directors have identified certain frequent computer problems combined with the introduction of the single european currency as an ideal opportunity to launch a new range of software products.

This new range will require considerable investment in human resources and involve relocation to a more modern office.

At a recent board meeting, it was suggested that the company consider either a launch on a recognised stock exchange, or raising long-term debt finance.

Required

(a) Identify and briefly explain THREE key considerations when deciding between raising debt and equity finance.   (6 marks)

(b) Briefly discuss THREE factors which will limit the amount of loan capital Bugs Ltd is able to raise.   (6 marks)

(c) (i)   Briefly outline the TWO main functions of a stock exchange.   (2 marks)

     (ii) Identify and briefly discuss THREE reasons why Bugs Ltd might wish to obtain a stock exchange listing.   (6 marks)

                                                                        (20 marks)

Helping hand

In (a) you should bring the circumstances of Bugs Ltd into your discussion. Try and think of what else would be important to the owners in addition to the costs of each option.

In (b) think about the documentation that may be relevant, and also how Bugs can guarantee the loan.

In (c) you need to consider some of the wider, non-financial implications of obtaining a stock market liability.

---

31   ANSWER: BUGS LTD

> **Helping hand**
>
> This question deals with the raising of finance and the role of the stock exchange. You should take into account the specific circumstances of Bugs Ltd in your answer, and not just write about these areas in general terms.
>
> Control is a key factor in (a): few shareholders means a significant input into control which will not be given up lightly. Security is important in (b), implications to consider in (c) include obtaining the finance and reputation to make growth easier.
>
> **What the examiner said**
>
> (a) required the identification of three considerations when deciding between debt and equity finance. Most answers to this part were satisfactory, but very few good answers were received.
>
> Answers to (b) were generally good.
>
> (c) dealt with the stock exchange functions and reasons why the company might wish to obtain a stock exchange listing. Most candidates could identify the functions of the stock exchange, but many could not elaborate on the merits of obtaining a stock exchange listing.

(a) Key considerations in the choice between debt and equity finance include the following.

    (i)   **Cost**. Debt finance is normally cheaper than equity finance, partly due to the lower level of risk that it attracts, and partly because debt interest (unlike dividend payments) is allowable for tax.

    (ii)   **Control**. The three founders of the company currently have full control over the company. The issue of further equity is likely to dilute this control, particularly if the company becomes quoted.

    (iii)   **Risk**. If there is a high level of business risk associated with the new projects, then it may be dangerous to use a high level of debt finance. If the company becomes unable to meet its interest costs due to poor performance, it could be forced into liquidation. Additionally, if the company already has a high level of gearing and/or is perceived by investors to be a risky investment, then it may be difficult and costly to raise additional debt.

(b) Factors that may limit the amount of loan capital that Bugs Ltd can raise include the following.

    (i)   **Memorandum and articles of association**. These may restrict the amount of debt that the company is allowed to raise.

    (ii)   **Loan covenants**. Bugs Ltd may have existing loans in place with covenants that restrict the issue of further debt in various ways.

    (iii)   **Security**. Bugs Ltd is essentially a knowledge based service business. It is therefore unlikely to have a high level of tangible assets that can be offered as security against new loans. However, since the company is considering relocation, it may be able to arrange a mortgage on the new property. Similarly, it may be able to finance new equipment purchases using some form of leasing arrangement.

    Other factors that could be included are the earnings and liquidity forecasts of the company, and the quality of its reputation.

(c)   (i)   The main **functions of a stock exchange** are:

         (1)   To allow companies to **raise new finance** through the issue of securities

         (2)   To provide a **well regulated secondary market** in securities

(ii)   Reasons why Bugs Ltd might seek a stock exchange listing include:

(1)   **Access to a wider pool of capital.** This is important for companies like Bugs Ltd that are expanding. Quotation on the stock exchange gives the company access to a wider range of investors who may be willing to put money into the company.

(2)   **Improved image.** Quotation gives a company a better image and reputation for financial stability. This can enhance its sales and marketing efforts and may lead to an improved credit rating with both lenders and suppliers.

(3)   **Growth by acquisition.** This becomes easier since a quoted company can offer shares in consideration for a takeover.

(4)   **The owners can realise a part of their investment.** Once the shares are quoted it is easy for the owners to sell a part of their holdings if they so wish, and thus release value from the business.

(5)   **Lower cost of equity.** This is likely to fall due to the reduction in the perceived risk for shareholders and the improved marketability of the shares.

Note. Only three reasons are required in your answer.

Examiner's marking scheme

			Marks	
(a)		Each consideration identified (3 × 1 mark)	3	
		Brief explanation of each (3 × 1 mark)	3	
				6
(b)		Each factor identified (3 × 1 mark)	3	
		Brief discussion of each (3 x 1 mark)	3	
				6
(c)	(i)	Each main function identified (2 x 1 mark)	2	
	(ii)	Each reason identified (3 × 1 mark)	3	
		Brief discussion of each (3 × 1 mark)	3	
				8
				20

32   FASHIONS LTD (6/98)

Fashion Ltd is a high quality fashion house founded by a former model and a clothes designer. In the period from its foundation eight years ago, the business has been very successful. Sales are currently £2m per annum and profits after tax are £0.25m per annum.

The directors consider that it is now an ideal time to expand the business to a number of new geographical locations. This expansion will require considerable long-term finance to acquire new premises and establish the new centres.

The directors are considering various sources of finance for the expansion, including approaching a venture capital organisation.

Required

(a) Identify the main items to consider when choosing a source of finance.   (7 marks)

(b) Briefly explain FIVE factors a venture capital organisation will take into account when deciding whether or not to invest in Fashions Ltd.   (10 marks)

(c) Identify THREE ways in which a venture capital organisation may finally realise its investment.   (3 marks)

(20 marks)

Helping hand

In (a) think about every aspect of the conditions of loans. In (b) remember that venture capitalists are seeking to make a return and your answer should focus on the matters that will most affect returns. In (c) who will be interested in buying shares?

---

32   ANSWER: FASHIONS LTD

Helping hand

In (a) go though what has to be decided before a loan can be granted. Don't forget the implications for control of the business.

In (b) venture capitalists will be interested in the factors determining demand, and also how much control they can exercise over their investment. They will eventually want to sell, and hopefully the success of the business will make it attractive to other investors.

What the examiner said

Answers to (a) and (b) were often too brief. Most answers to part (c) failed to focus sufficiently on the fact that the requirement sought discussion of the *final* exit routes - evidence of failure by candidates to read the question carefully.

(a)   The main factors to consider in choosing a source of finance are as follows.

The purpose of the loan. The reason for seeking finance should be fully evaluated to ensure that it is financially justified.

The amount of the loan. The company should prepare a cash budget to check that the amount of finance sought is sufficient for the required purpose.

Repayment of the loan. The detailed projections should identify repayment schedules clearly.

The term of the loan. This should be appropriate to the type of asset being acquired. As a general rule, long-term assets should be financed from long-term finance sources. In the case of Fashions Ltd, the main use of funds appears to be the acquisition of premises, in which case long-term finance is most appropriate.

The cost of finance. The relative costs of the different forms of finance available should be compared.

Security. Providers of debt finance will be concerned that the security for the finance they provide is adequate. A fixed charge relates to specific assets, typically land and buildings.

Restrictive covenants. Debt providers may place limitations on the business through restrictive covenants set out in a debenture deed. For example, covenants may restrict the right of the directors to pay out dividends for a specified period or until the loan is below a specified amount.

Taxation. The tax treatment of the cost of financing needs to be considered. Interest on loans will be tax-deductible. If equity finance is raised, dividends paid to the finance provider will need to be paid out of post-tax profits.

Control of the business. If finance is raised through an issue of equity shares, the new equity holders become part-owners of the business. The current owners of the business should consider whether it is desirable to share ownership in this way.

The effect of gearing. The gearing of the business is a measure of the amount of debt relative to equity. If a company is seen as being too highly geared, finance providers will judge that the level of risk of default is high, and are likely to seek higher compensation (for example, in the form of interest payments) for this risk. If they perceive the risk to be high, some finance providers may be unwilling to lend at all.

(b)   A **venture capital organisation** (below, 'VC') is likely to take the following factors into account when deciding whether or not to invest in Fashions Ltd.

The nature of the company's product. The VC will consider whether the good or service can be produced viably and has potential to sell, in the light of any market research which the company has carried out.

Expertise in production. The VC will want to be sure that the company has the necessary technical ability to implement production plans with efficiency.

Expertise in management. Venture capitalists pay much attention to the quality of management, since they believe that this is crucial to the success of the enterprise. Not only should the management team be committed to the enterprise; they should also have appropriate skills and experience.

The market and competition. The nature of the market for the product will be considered, including the threat which rival producers or future new entrants to the market may present.

Future prospects. The VC will want to be sure that the possible prospects of profits in the future compensate for the risks involved in the enterprise. The VC will expect the company to have prepared a detailed business plan detailing its future strategy.

Board membership. The VC is likely to require a place on the Board of Directors. Board representation will ensure that the VC's interests will be taken account of, and that the VC has a say in matters relating to the future strategy of the business.

The risk borne by the existing owners. The VC is likely to wish to ensure that the existing owners of the business bear a significant part of the investment risk relating to the expansion. If they are owner-managers, bearing part of the risk will provide an incentive for them to ensure the success of the venture. Although the VC may be providing most of the investment, the amounts provided by the owners should be significant in relation to their overall personal wealth.

Exit routes. The means by which the VC can eventually realise its investment are called 'exit routes'. Ideally, the VC will try to ensure that there are a number of exit routes.

(c) The VC may be able to realise their investment through the following possible exit routes.

   (i)   The **sale of shares** to the public or to institutional investors **following a flotation** of the company's shares on a recognised stock exchange, or on the Alternative Investment Market or equivalent

   (ii) The **sale of shares** to another **business in a takeover**

   (iii) The **sale of shares to the original owners**, if they later have the resources to make such a purchase

	Examiner's marking scheme	Marks
(a)	Each relevant factor	7
(b)	Each relevant factor (only 5 required - 5 × 2 marks)	10
(c)	Each exit route identified and explained (only 3 required)	3
		20

DO YOU KNOW? - MONITORING AND APPRAISING CAPITAL INVESTMENTS

- *Check that you know the following basic points before you attempt any questions. If in doubt, you should go back to your BPP Interactive Text and revise first.*

- .... expenditure is expenditure on fixed assets, examples of which are:

    - ....   - ....
    - ....   - ....

- Expenditure for the purpose of the trade, or to maintain fixed assets, is called .... expenditure.

- There are various methods of evaluating capital projects.

- The .... method, also called the return on investment method, calculates the estimated average profits as a percentage of the estimated average investment.

- The .... is the time taken for the initial investment to be recovered in the cash inflows from the project. This is particularly relevant if there are liquidity problems, or if distant forecasts are very uncertain.

- .... techniques take account of the time value of money. As with payback, these techniques use cash figures before depreciation in the calculations.

- A future cash flow arising directly from a decision is called a ....

- A cost already incurred is called a .... and should not be taken account of in decision making.

- A future cost that will be incurred whatever decision is taken now is called a ....

- The .... method calculates the present value of all cash flows, and sums them to give the NPV. If this is positive, then the project is acceptable. The .... is the period by which the .... is expected to become positive.

- The .... technique uses a trial and error method to discover the discount rate which produces a .... of zero. This discount rate will be the return forecast for the project.

- DCF methods of appraisal have a number of advantages over other appraisal methods.

    - ....
    - ....
    - ....
    - ....

    TRY QUESTIONS 33, 34 AND 35

- The opportunity cost of finance is ....

- The weighted average ...., reflecting a company's various sources of finance, may be calculated.

- In dealing with inflation in investment appraisal, all cash flows need to be treated consistently, on either a ....or .... basis.

    TRY QUESTIONS 36, 37, 38, 39, 40, 41 AND 42

- *Possible pitfalls*

    Write down the mistakes you know you should avoid.

DID YOU KNOW? - MONITORING AND APPRAISING CAPITAL INVESTMENTS

- *Could you fill in the blanks? The answers are in bold. Use this page for revision purposes as you approach the exam.*

- **Capital** expenditure is expenditure on fixed assets, examples of which are:

  - **Land and buildings**
  - **Motor vehicles**
  - **Plant and machinery**
  - **Fixtures and fittings**

- Expenditure for the purpose of the trade, or to maintain fixed assets, is called **revenue** expenditure.

- There are various methods of evaluating capital projects.

- The **accounting rate of return** method, also called the return on investment method, calculates the estimated average profits as a percentage of the estimated average investment.

- The **payback period** is the time taken for the initial investment to be recovered in the cash inflows from the project. This is particularly relevant if there are liquidity problems, or if distant forecasts are very uncertain.

- **Discounted cash flow** techniques take account of the time value of money. As with payback, these techniques use cash figures before depreciation in the calculations.

- A future cash flow arising directly from a decision is called a **relevant cost**.

- A cost already incurred is called a **sunk cost** and should not be taken account of in decision making.

- A future cost that will be incurred whatever decision is taken now is called a **committed cost**.

- The **net present value** method calculates the present value of all cash flows, and sums them to give the NPV. If this is positive, then the project is acceptable. The **discounted payback period** is the period by which the **net present value** is expected to become positive.

- The **internal rate of return** technique uses a trial and error method to discover the discount rate which produces a **net present value** of zero. This discount rate will be the return forecast for the project.

- DCF methods of appraisal have a number of advantages over other appraisal methods.

  - **The time value of money is taken into account.**
  - **All of a project's cash flows are taken into account.**
  - **The timing of cash flows is allowed for.**
  - **There are universally accepted methods of calculating the NPV and IRR.**

  TRY QUESTIONS 33, 34 AND 35

- The opportunity cost of finance is **the best return that investors can receive from alternative investments.**

- The weighted average **cost of capital**, reflecting a company's various sources of finance, may be calculated.

- In dealing with inflation in investment appraisal, all cash flows need to be treated consistently, on either a '**real**' or **nominal ('money')** basis.

  TRY QUESTIONS 36, 37, 38, 39, 40, 41 AND 42

- *Possible pitfalls*

  - **Take care to exclude non-relevant costs and sunk costs when appraising investments.**

  - **Depreciation, remember, is not a cash flow.**

  - **Remember to state your assumptions.**

33   QUESTON WITH HELP: TWO CAPITAL PROJECTS

The following information relates to two possible capital projects of which you have to select one to invest in. Both projects have an initial capital cost of £200,000 and only one can be undertaken. Profit is calculated after deducting straight line depreciation.

Project	X	Y
Expected profits	£	£
Year 1	80,000	30,000
2	80,000	50,000
3	40,000	90,000
4	20,000	120,000
Estimated resale value at end of Year 4	40,000	40,000

The cost of capital is 16%, relevant discount factors being as follows.

End of year	1	0.862
	2	0.743
	3	0.641
	4	0.552
	5	0.476

Required

(a)   Calculate:

   (i)   The payback period to one decimal place
   (ii)   The accounting rate of return using average investment
   (iii)   The net present value   (11 marks)

(b)   Advise the board which project in your opinion should be undertaken, giving reasons for your decision.   (3 marks)

(c)   The board have looked at your proposal and you have been asked to clarify a number of issues.

   (i)   Explain what is meant by the term 'cost of capital' and why is it important in coming to an investment decision.

   (ii)   State TWO ways in which risk can be taken into account when making a capital investment decision.   (6 marks)

                                                              (20 marks)

If you are stuck, look at the next page for detailed help as to how you should tackle this question.

APPROACHING THE ANSWER

Use this answer plan to construct your answer if you are stuck.

(a) will give you some basic practice of three commonly used appraisal techniques. Remember the following rules.

- Cash flows are used in payback and net present value calculations. If you are given accounting profits (as in this question) you must add back the depreciation charge in order to convert the figures from profits to cash flows.

- Accounting profits are used in calculating the accounting rate of return. Accounting profits are taken after depreciation.

(b) involves explaining which is the best of the three methods, and why, and also what the implications might be if either of the other methods suggest a different recommendation.

In (c)(i) you need to discuss what the cost actually is, and how important the cost is in relation to returns from the project.

Risks can be accounted for in a number of different ways in (c)(ii). Risk criteria can be set, an adjustment made to the calculation or a range of outcomes considered.

33   ANSWER TO QUESTION WITH HELP: TWO CAPITAL PROJECTS

(a)   Annual depreciation $= \dfrac{£200,000 - £40,000}{4}$

   $= £40,000$ per annum

(i)   **Payback period**

	Year	Project X £'000	Project Y £'000
Cash flows	1	120	70
	2	120	90
	3	80	130
	4	60	160
Project resale value		40	40
Payback period		1 + (80/120) years	2 + (40/130) years
		= 1.7 years	= 2.3 years

(ii)   **Accounting rate of return**

The accounting profits are given in the question and we need to calculate the average over the four years. The average investment will be the same for both projects.

Average investment $= \dfrac{£200,000 + £40,000}{2} = £120,000$

	Year	Project X £'000	Project Y £'000
Accounting profits	1	80	30
	2	80	50
	3	40	90
	4	20	120
		220	290
Average (÷ 4)		55	72.5
Average investment		120	120
∴ Average accounting rate of return		$\left(\dfrac{55}{120}\right)$ 45.8%	$\left(\dfrac{72.5}{120}\right)$ 60.4%

(iii)   **Using the cash flows from (i)**

Year	Discount factor 16%	Project X Cash flow £'000	Project X Present value £'000	Project Y Cash flow £'000	Project Y Present value £'000
1	0.862	120	103.44	70	60.34
2	0.743	120	89.16	90	66.87
3	0.641	80	51.28	130	83.33
4	0.552	100	55.20	200	110.40
			299.08		320.94
Initial capital cost			200.00		200.00
Net present value			99.08		120.94

(b)   Project Y should be undertaken because it gives the highest **net present value**. This is a more important measure than the accounting rate of return because it takes account of the timing of cash flows and the time value of money. However the directors should bear in mind that project Y has a longer payback period which can lead to increased risk and reduced liquidity.

(c) (i)   The **cost of capital** is the cost to the company of raising finance for capital expenditure projects, that is the cost of shareholders capital and the cost of any loans raised.

It is important in an investment decision because it is the minimum return that a project should earn. If a project does not earn a return which is at least equal to the cost of funds invested in it then it is not worthwhile.

(ii)   There are a number of ways in which **risk** can be taken into account when making a capital investment decision.

(1)   **Set a short payback period.** If risk is deemed to increase with the length of time a company waits for its returns, then selecting only those projects with a short payback period will tend to reduce the risk.

(2)   **Use a higher discount rate.** This is referred to as adding a 'risk premium' to the discount rate. If a project is considered to be fairly risky then, say, 2% could be added to the basic cost of capital. If it is considered to be very risky then, say, 5% could be added.

(3)   **Use probabilities to assess the range of possible outcomes.** Managers could be asked to forecast a number of different values for sales, costs and so on, together with their associated probabilities.

(4)   **Undertake a sensitivity analysis.** This involves asking a series of 'what if' questions and re-evaluating the project with different sets of assumptions. For example managers might ask, 'what if sales volume is 5% lower than expected?' The project would be re-evaluated to see how sensitive the final result is to this particular change. By carrying out a number of such sensitivity tests it is possible to highlight which particular forecasts are most important to the outcome of the project.

34   PROJECTS T AND R

(a) Explain why net present value is considered technically superior to payback and accounting rate of return as an investment appraisal technique even though the latter are said to be easier to understand by management. Highlight the strengths of the net present value method and the weaknesses of the other two methods.

(8 marks)

(b) Your company has the option to invest in projects T and R but finance is only available to invest in one of them.

You are given the following projected data.

		Project	
		T	R
		£	£
Initial cost		70,000	60,000
Profits:	Year 1	15,000	20,000
	Year 2	18,000	25,000
	Year 3	20,000	(50,000)
	Year 4	32,000	10,000
	Year 5	18,000	3,000
	Year 6		2,000

You are told the following.

1   All cash flows take place at the end of the year apart from the original investment in the project which takes place at the beginning of the project.

2   Project T machinery is to be disposed of at the end of year 5 with a scrap value of £10,000.

3   Project R machinery is to be disposed of at the end of year 3 with a nil scrap value and replaced with new project machinery that will cost £75,000.

4   The cost of this additional machinery has been deducted in arriving at the profit projections for R for year 3. It is projected that it will last for three years and have a nil scrap value.

5   The company's policy is to depreciate its assets on a straight line basis.

6   The discount rate to be used by the company is 14% and appropriate discount factors are as follows.

Year	
1	0.877
2	0.769
3	0.675
4	0.592
5	0.519
6	0.465

Required

(i)   If investment was to be made in project R, determine whether the machinery should be replaced at the end of year 3.

(ii)   Calculate the following for projects T and R, taking into consideration your decision in (i) above.

(1) Payback period
(2) Net present value

Advise which project should be invested in, stating your reasons.   (9 marks)

(c) Explain what the discount rate of 14% represents and state TWO ways of how it might have been arrived at.

(3 marks)

(20 marks)

Helping hand

Time value and cash flow are key elements in (a).

Part (b)(i) requires you to determine whether machinery should be replaced. This means that you have to calculate the net present value of the inflows resulting from the new machinery and the cost of the new machinery but at present day values since the decision is to be made now and not in three years time.

In (b) (ii) consider whether any adjustment will be needed to profits to arrive at cash flows.

In (c) think about what is relevant when you make an investment.

---

34   ANSWER: PROJECTS T AND R

Helping hand

(a) is allocated eight marks, and so the amount of detail you put into your answer should reflect this relatively large allocation.

You answer to (b) (i) impacts upon (b) (ii); depreciation needs to be removed in (b) (ii). In (c) what is important is how the investment is financed, and to what other uses funds could have been put.

(a)   The **net present value method** of investment appraisal is considered technically superior to payback period and accounting rate of return appraisal methods because it takes account of the time value of money.

The **time value of money** means that £1 received now is **worth more** to the individual/ organisation than £1 received in n years time. This is because the £1 received now can be invested today and earn interest so that its quantitative value in n years time is greater than its value now. There is therefore an opportunity cost attached to the delay of cash receipts since there will be an alternative investment opportunity forgone. Net present value appraisal techniques, however, incorporate the concept of the time value of money by **discounting all future cash flows** back to their present day value using a rate called the **cost of capital**. The project's **net present value** is the **sum of all the discounted cash inflows and outflows**. The quantitative worth at today's values allows a ranking of projects to be carried out: the project with the highest net present value is the most advantageous to the individual/organisation.

There is an obvious advantage to the **payback period** and **accounting rate of return** methods of appraisal: they are **relatively straightforward** and easy to understand. There are, however, several disadvantages to their use.

The **payback method ignores any cash flows** that **occur after the project** has paid for itself. A project that takes time to get off the ground but earns substantial profits once it is established might therefore be rejected if the payback method is used.

The **accounting rate of return method** is based on **accounting profits rather than cash** and it may therefore give too much emphasis to notional costs which are merely accounting conventions and not truly relevant to a project's performance. There are also differing views about the way in which ARR should be calculated.

Most importantly, both methods ignore the time value of money. None of these objections apply to the net present value method.

(b)   (i)   To assess whether the machinery should be replaced at the end of year 3, we need to ascertain whether the net present value of the cash inflows following replacement are greater than the initial cost.

The profits include depreciation of £75,000/3 = £25,000. Cash flows are therefore £25,000 pa greater than profits.

Year	Cash flow £	Discount factor	Present value £
3	(75,000)	0.675	(50,625)
4	35,000	0.592	20,720
5	28,000	0.519	14,532
6	27,000	0.465	12,555
		NPV =	(2,818)

The machine should therefore **not be replaced** because the net present value of the case inflows resulting from the purchase are less than the net present value of the purchase. The machinery does not generate enough income to cover its purchase price in present value terms.

(ii)　(1)　The profits of project T include depreciation of

$$\frac{£70,000 - £10,000}{5} = £12,000.$$

∴ Cash flows are £12,000 per annum greater than profits.

Cash flows

Year	T £'000	R £'000
1	27	40
2	30	45
3	32	45
4	44	
5	40*	
Cost	70	60
Payback period	2.41 years	1.44 years

*Includes sale proceeds of £10,000

(2)

Year	T Cash flow £'000	R Cash flow £'000	Discount factor	T Present value £	R Present value £
0	(70)	(60)	1.000	(70,000)	(60,000)
1	27	40	0.877	23,679	35,080
2	30	45	0.769	23,070	34,605
3	32	45	0.675	21,600	30,375
4	44		0.592	26,048	
5	40		0.519	20,760	
			Net present value	45,157	40,060

> **Helping hand**. Because we are not replacing the machine, project R runs for three years only.

Project T should be invested in because, although project R has the shorter payback period, project T has the higher net present value.

(c)　The discount rate of 14% represents the firm's cost of capital which could be the **weighted average cost of the sources** of capital which the company uses to finance the project or it could be the **weighted average of the return** required by shareholders and loan stock investors. It could also be the **opportunity cost of an investment opportunity foregone** (that is, the rate of interest that could have been earned on an investment) that was the next best alternative for the company.

35   CAT LTD (6/00)

CAT Ltd is evaluating a capital expenditure project. The details are as follows:

1   The project has an immediate cost of £110,000 and after its five year life, has a nil residual value. There are no capital allowances available.

2   Sales are expected to be £80,000 per annum for years 1 and 2, £60,000 per annum for years 3, 4 and 5.

3   Cost of sales is 50% of sales.

4   Tax at 10% is payable in the year the profit is earned.

5   The company's cost of capital is 10%.

n(years)	10% factors	15% factors
1	0.909	0.870
2	0.826	0.756
3	0.751	0.658
4	0.683	0.572
5	0.621	0.497

Required

(a) (i)   Calculate the project's IRR (assuming that all cash flows arise annually in arrears).   (8 marks)

     (ii)   Identify and briefly describe TWO advantages and TWO disadvantages of IRR.

(4 marks)

(b) (i)   Calculate the project's simple payback period.   (4 marks)

     (ii)   Identify and briefly describe TWO advantages and TWO disadvantages of payback.   (4 marks)

(20 marks)

Helping hand

When considering how to do the calculations in (a)(i), think also about what you need to do in (b)(i), and how what you do in (a)(i) may help you. In (a)(ii) and (b)(ii) think about what the two methods show, the significance of the time value of money and how important project size is.

---

35   ANSWER: CAT LTD

> **Helping hand**
>
> In part (a) (i) you should tabulate the calculations in order to avoid mistakes, even though the calculations are relatively simple. The tabulation will then provide a basis for the calculations in part (b)(i), enabling them to be completed more quickly. The advantages and disadvantages of IRRs and payback are core topics, and will appear frequently in the exam.

(a)   (i)   The first stage in calculating the IRR is to find the NPV of the project at different discount rates in order to estimate the rate at which the NPV is zero.

Before the NPVs can be calculated, we need to find the after tax cash flows of the project. These can then be discounted to arrive at the NPV.

	Year 0 £	Year 1 £	Year 2 £	Year 3 £	Year 4 £	Year 5 £	Total £
Sales		80,000	80,000	60,000	60,000	60,000	
Cost of sales (50% sales)	———	40,000	40,000	30,000	30,000	30,000	
Taxable revenue		40,000	40,000	30,000	30,000	30,000	
Tax at 10%	———	4,000	4,000	3,000	3,000	3,000	
		36,000	36,000	27,000	27,000	27,000	
Initial cost (non-taxable)	(110,000)						
Net cash flow	(110,000)	36,000	36,000	27,000	27,000	27,000	
10% discount factors	1.000	0.909	0.826	0.751	0.683	0.621	
PV at 10%	(110,000)	32,724	29,736	20,277	18,441	16,767	7,945
15% discount factors	1.000	0.870	0.756	0.658	0.572	0.497	
PV at 15%	(110,000)	31,320	27,216	17,766	15,444	13,419	(4,835)

The IRR can now be found by interpolation, using the following formula:

$$IRR = A + ((a/(a + b)) \times (B - A))$$

where

IRR = Internal rate of return
A   = the discount rate which provides the positive NPV
a   = the amount of the positive NPV
B   = the discount rate which provides the negative NPV
b   = the amount of the negative NPV (ignoring the minus sign)

$$IRR = 10\% + ((7,945/(7,945 + 4,835)) \times (15\% - 10\%))$$
$$IRR = 10\% + (0.6217 \times 5\%)$$
$$IRR = 13.1\%$$

(ii)   Advantages of the IRR method of project appraisal include:

(1)   It takes into account the **time value of money**, unlike other approaches such as payback.

(2)   Results are expressed as a **simple percentage**, and are more easily understood than some other methods.

(3)   It indicates how **sensitive** calculations are to changes in interest rates.

Disadvantages include:

(1)   The method takes **no account** of the **relative sizes** of projects under consideration. It may be that a larger project with a lower IRR will actually add more value to the business than a small project with a high IRR. The IRR may thus **conflict** with the project rankings given by the **NPV** method.

(2) Where the pattern of project cash flows is unusual, there may be **multiple IRRs**. This situation is hard to understand and interpret.

(3) IRR may be **confused** with the **return on capital employed** (ROCE) since both are expressed in percentage terms. In practice, the two are very different since the IRR is based on cash flows while the ROCE is based on profits.

(b) (i) The simple payback period can be found by examining the cumulative cash flow:

	Year 0 £	Year 1 £	Year 2 £	Year 3 £	Year 4 £	Year 5 £
Net cash flow (see above)	(110,000)	36,000	36,000	27,000	27,000	27,000
Cumulative cash flow	(110,000)	(74,000)	(38,000)	(11,000)	16,000	43,000

If all the cash flows take place at the end of the year, the project has a payback period of **four years**. However, it is more realistic to assume that the cash flows occur evenly during the year. In this case the payback period can be approximated as follows:

Payback = 3 years + (11,000/(11,000 + 16,000)) = 3.4 years

(ii) Advantages of the payback method of project appraisal include the following.

(1) It is **easy to calculate** and **understand**.

(2) It provides a rough **guide** to the **risk** of a project, since a project with a shorter payback is likely to be less risky than one with a longer payback.

(3) It is useful to use as a **first screening method** to identify projects for which it is worth undertaking a more detailed evaluation.

Disadvantages include:

(1) As with the IRR, the method **ignores** the **relative size** of projects. It thus tends to discriminate in favour of smaller projects that payback more quickly than larger projects. However, it is the latter that may have a **higher NPV** and do more to add value to the business in the long term.

(2) The simple payback method **ignores** the **time value** of money.

(3) The **cut-off period** for deciding on what is acceptable is **arbitrary**, and takes no account of the level of operating risk that attaches to different projects.

Examiner's marking scheme

				Marks
(a)	(i)	Sales and cost of sales	1	
		Taxation	1	
		Investment cash flows	1	
		NPV at 10% and at 15%	2	
		IRR formula and calculation	2	
		Presentation/conclusion	1	
				8
	(ii)	Each advantage (2 × 1 mark)	2	
		Each disadvantage (2 × 1 mark)	2	
				4
(b)	(i)	Cumulative cash flows	1	
		Formula and calculation	2	
		Presentation/conclusion	1	
				4
	(ii)	Each advantage (2 × 1 mark)	2	
		Each disadvantage (2 × 1 mark)	2	
				4
				20

36   BUNKERS LTD (12/00)

Bunkers Ltd, as one of its many projects, has recently acquired a site for £3 million on the outskirts of an industrialised town with a population of 1 million.

Market research consultants have been recruited, at a cost of £200,000, to advise the management of Bunkers Ltd whether to develop the site as either a golf course or an apartment complex. The consultant's report has just been presented to management and contains the following findings:

'Pay as You Play' Golf Course Development

(1)   The cost of course design by a leading professional golfer, Cat Woods, will cost a total of £1,000,000, 40% payable immediately, with the remaining 60% payable in 12 months time, when the course will be completed.

(2)   Clubhouse, course development and associated facilities will cost an estimated £4,000,000, payable in 12 months time. This cost will be depreciated on a straight line basis over a 10 year period from the date the course is operational. This development is expected to have a zero residual value at the end of the 10 year operating period (ie at the end of year 11).

(3)   Once the course is operational, it is estimated that there will be an average of 200 peak-time players per week, each paying green fees of £100. In addition, it is expected that there will be 100 off-peak time players per week, each paying £30 green fees. The course will be open for 52 weeks a year.

(4)   It is anticipated that two in ten of the peak-time players and one in ten of the off-peak time players will hire trolleys at £10 per trolley hire.

(5)   On average, all players are expected to purchase consumables (tee and golf balls, gloves, light refreshments, etc) which generate £12 contribution per player per round.

(6)   A manager, green keeper and administration staff, costing a total of £275,000 per annum will be needed to run the club.

(7)   Central office overheads of £250,000 per annum are being allocated to this project. The directors have assessed that 40% of these overheads arise as a direct consequence of the golf course project.

(8)   Bar receipts of £1,000,000 per annum are forecast. These bar receipts have a contribution to sales ratio of 50%.

(9)   The site is expected to have a residual value of £6,000,000 at the end of its ten year operational period as a golf course.

Apartment Development

(1)   Planning permission, preparation and submission is expected to cost £200,000 payable immediately.

(2)   Project design team fees will amount to £250,000, and will be payable in 12 months' time.

(3)   Construction costs will amount to £5,000,000 with 20% payable immediately and the remainder due in 12 months time on completion of the apartments.

(4)   The entire development is expected to have a residual value in 11 years time of £10,000,000.

(5)   An existing member of staff, employed on another property development could be retained for a further year as project manager during this apartment construction

phase. Her salary for this one year project would be £50,000, after which time she will be made redundant. If not employed as project manager, she will be made redundant immediately. Whenever she is made redundant, she will receive £40,000.

(6) The development will comprise 200 apartments. It is anticipated that there will be an 80% occupancy rate. Each occupied apartment is expected to generate a net income of £12,500 per annum.

(7) Estate management costs of £475,000 per annum are expected.

General notes

(1) You may ignore inflation and taxation.
(2) The company requires all projects to be evaluated over a 11 year period.
(3) The company's costs of capital is 10%.

(n) period	10% factors	Cumulative 10% factors
1	0.909	0.909
2	0.826	1.735
3	0.751	2.486
4	0.683	3.169
5	0.621	3.790
6	0.564	4.354
7	0.513	4.867
8	0.467	5.334
9	0.424	5.758
10	0.386	6.144
11	0.351	6.495

Required

(a) (i) Calculate the net present value of the 'Pay-as-You-Play' Golf Course Development. (15 marks)

(ii) Calculate the net present value of the Apartment Development. (9 marks)

(iii) On the basis of financial analysis, recommend which project should be undertaken (2 marks)

(b) (i) Identify and briefly discuss FOUR non-financial factors which need to be considered prior to a final decision being made. (6 marks)

(ii) Briefly explain the major stages involved in evaluating, monitoring and controlling capital expenditure projects. (8 marks)

(40 marks)

Helping hand

In (a) you will need to explain why certain costs are excluded, as well as treating relevant costs correctly. In (b)(i) think about the assumptions Bunker is making, what may change over time and the importance of the local infrastructure. In (b)(ii) think about the criteria that will be used to decide whether the project is viable, and how control will be exercised.

---

36   ANSWER: BUNKERS LTD

(a) (i)   The first stage is to identify the annual cash flows that will arise from undertaking the project, assuming the course operates from Year 2.

The following costs will be ignored.

(1)   The site has already been acquired, and therefore the £3m paid for the land is a **sunk cost**.

(2)   The cost of the market research study has **already** been **committed**, and is therefore not relevant

(3)   Depreciation of the facilities is a **non-cash item**, and is therefore not relevant.

(4)   Only 40% of the overheads are incremental, and therefore the **remainder** will be **excluded**.

Net annual income from operations in years 2 - 11 is as follows:

		£'000
Green fees		
Peak	200 × 52 × £100	1,040
Off-peak	100 × 52 × £30	156
		1,196
Trolley hire	200 × 52 × 20% × £10	21
Peak	100 × 52 × 10% × £10	5
Off-peak		26
Consumable purchases	300 × 52 × £12	187
Bar contribution	£1m × 50%	500
Staff costs		(275)
Overheads	£250,000 × 40%	(100)
Total net annual income		1,534

The net present value can now be calculated:

			Discount factor 10%	*Present value* £'000
Year 0	Course design	(400)	1.000	(400)
Year 1	Course design	(600)	0.909	(545)
Year 2	Development cost	(4,000)	0.909	(3,636)
Year 2-11	Annual income	1,534	5.586*	8,569
Year 11	Residual value	6,000	0.351	2,106
				6,094

* The factor to be applied for years 2 - 11 is 6.495 – 0.909 = 5.586.

(ii) The first stage is to identify the annual cash flows that will arise from undertaking the project.

The salary of the existing member of staff retained for an additional year will be included since is a **direct incremental cost**. The redundancy cost saved in year 0 must be included as well, as must the redundancy cost incurred at the end of year 1.

The annual cash flows can now be found:

		£'000
Year 0	Planning costs	(200)
	Construction costs	(1,000)
	Redundancy costs saved	40
		(1,160)
Year 1	Project design fees	(250)
	Construction costs	(4,000)
	Salary costs	(50)
	Redundancy costs	(40)
		(4,340)
Annual income years 2 – 11	Rent 200 × 80% × £12,500	2,000
	Management costs	(475)
		1,525

The net present value can now be calculated:

		Discount factor 10%	Present value £'000
Year 0 Net cost	(1,160)	1.000	(1,160)
Year 1 Course design	(4,340)	0.909	(3,945)
Year 2-11 Annual income	1,525	5.586★	8,519
Year 11 Residual value	10,000	0.351	3,510
Net present value			6,924

★ The annuity value to be applied for years 2 – 11 is 6.495 - 0.909 = 5.586

(iii) On the basis of the figures provided, both projects show a positive net present value at the cost of capital of 10%. However, the apartment development has a higher net present value than does the golf course development, and therefore is to be preferred on financial grounds.

(b) (i) Non-financial factors that should be considered include the following.

(1) Bunkers Ltd has not yet obtained **planning permission** for the developments. It should not therefore proceed with the apartment development unless it is confident that planning permission will be granted within the timescales considered. It is possible that this could cause problems, given that the site seems to be a greenfield site on the edge of the town, and may therefore not be scheduled for residential development.

(2) A related point is that if there was **significant local opposition** to the developments, the cost of gaining planning permission could escalate significantly.

(3) The projections assume that income will be **even** throughout the life of the projects. However, in reality, the economic cycle over a ten-year period is likely to mean that annual figures will **vary significantly**, and this could affect the actual out-turn.

(4)   Bunkers seems to be very optimistic in its projection that both developments will be fully operational in just one year's time. The effect of **over-runs,** and a slow build up of income should be evaluated.

(5)   Bunkers Ltd should consider the **level of competition** that it is likely to face from other property developers over the ten-year operating period. In addition, if another golf course were to open locally, this could affect the financial projections.

(6)   **Population figures** should be examined to see if there will be a significant demand for the types of apartment planned.

(7)   **Apartments** will be more attractive if there are **good transport links** to the city centre.

(8)   The evaluations are likely to be **very sensitive** to changes in the residual values. If economic or market conditions changed during the life of the project, this could have a significant impact on financial performance.

(ii)   The major stages in evaluating, monitoring and controlling capital expenditure projects are as follows.

Initial investigation of the project

(1)   Is it **feasible**, technically and commercially?
(2)   What are its **main risks**?
(3)   Does it match the company's **long-term strategic objectives**?

Detailed evaluation

(1)   Once the feasibility of the project has been established, a detailed investigation should be made of expected cash flows arising from the projects, ideally using **discounted cash flow** techniques.

(2)   **Sensitivity analysis** can be used to analyse the effects of risk.

(3)   **Sources of finance** should be considered.

(4)   In the event of finance being restricted, **projects** should be **ranked** in order of priority.

Authorisation

(1)   Rules should be established on the **level of management** that can authorise projects of different size, and their relation to the **capital expenditure budget**.

(2)   Those making the decision must be satisfied that an appropriately detailed evaluation has been carried out, that the proposal meets the profitability criteria, and that it is **consistent** with the overall **strategy** of the company.

Implementation

(1)   **Responsibility** for the project should be **assigned** to a project manager, who is given specific targets to achieve.

(2)   **Resources** should be **allocated** to the project.

Project monitoring

(1)   **Progress** should be **monitored**, and regular reports made to senior management.

(2)   **Projects** can be **monitored more effectively** if the costs and benefits originally expected are reassessed in the light of unforeseen events happening in the course of the project.

Post-completion audit

This should be **carried out** at the **end of the project** in order to make use of what can be learned from the experience in the planning of future projects.

Examiner's marking scheme

				Marks
(a)	(i)	**Golf development**		
		Design	1	
		Development	1	
		Residual value	1	
		Green fees	2	
		Trolley hire	2	
		Golf consumables	2	
		Staff costs	1	
		Overheads	1	
		Bar contribution	1	
		NPV calculation	2	
				14
	(ii)	**Apartment development**		
		Planning permission	1	
		Design team	1	
		Construction	1	
		Residual value	1	
		Project manager's – redundancy	1	
		– salary	1	
		Net rental – income	1	
		Estate manager	1	
		NPV calculation	2	
				10
	(iii)	Recommendation		
				2
(b)	(i)	Each non-financial factor and briefly discussed ($4 \times 1\frac{1}{2}$ marks)	6	
	(ii)	Each stage briefly discussed (8×1 mark)	8	
				14
				40

37   QUICK FREEZE FOODS PLC (12/98)

Quick Freeze Foods plc produces a range of convenience processed foods for a number of supermarket chain stores. Its success has been based on the expertise and customer-driven emphasis of its research and development team.

The R&D team has identified three mutually exclusive projects which could be undertaken. The finance director has recruited you as assistant accountant to carry out a financial evaluation of each project.

Details of the three projects' cash flows are shown below.

Cash flow timing

	Indian range £	Chinese range £	Italian range £
Initial outlay	(80,000)	(20,000)	(20,000)
1	26,500	5,000	12,000
2	26,500	6,000	8,000
3	26,500	8,000	6,000
4	26,500	10,000	Nil

Ignore taxation and inflation. Assume that cash flows occur at the ends of each of the years shown.

Note. The present value of £1 in n years is as follows.

n (year)	at 10%	at 15%
1	0.909	0.870
2	0.826	0.756
3	0.751	0.658
4	0.683	0.572

Required

(a) Using each of the following appraisal methods rank the projects in order of their investment potential.

  (i)   Net present value (NPV) at 10%   (7 marks)
  (ii)   Approximate internal rate of return (IRR)   (7 marks)

(b) (i)   Critically compare each of the above investment appraisal methods.   (4 marks)

  (ii)   Explain which method you regard as the most useful for project appraisal and which project you would recommend.   (2 marks)

(20 marks)

Helping hand

The question does not require you to calculate the IRR for each of the three projects, but simply to use the technique to rank them. Since only the 10% and 15% discount factors are provided, it is not possible to use interpolation to estimate an IRR for the Italian projects; however, there is still sufficient information to be able to rank the three projects in IRR order.

In (b) important considerations are size, results and how each method can accommodate uncertainty and risk.

---

37   ANSWER: QUICK FREEZE FOODS PLC

> **Helping hand**
>
> In (a) all you need to do for the Italian project is to identify that its IRR exceeds the other two's. The reasons discussed in (b) for preferring NPV are fundamental to this area of the syllabus.
>
> **What the examiner said**
>
> Some answers to part (a) showed difficulty with the calculation of IRR and some confused IRR with ARR.

(a)   The projects will be discounted at both 10% and 15% for the purpose of calculating the IRR.

Indian range

	Year 0 £	Year 1 £	Year 2 £	Year 3 £	Year 4 £	Total £
Cash flow	(80,000)	26,500	26,500	26,500	26,500	
10% discount factors	1.000	0.909	0.826	0.751	0.683	
Discounted cash flow at 10%	(80,000)	24,089	21,889	19,902	18,100	3,980
15% discount factors	1.000	0.870	0.756	0.658	0.572	
Discounted cash flow at 15%	(80,000)	23,055	20,034	17,437	15,158	(4,316)

Net present value at 10% = £3,980

The IRR can be found by interpolation using the following formula:

$$IRR = A + \left[\frac{a}{a+b} \times (B-A)\right]$$

where   A is the rate of return with a positive NPV

B is the rate of return with a negative NPV

a is the amount of the positive NPV

b is the amount of the negative NPV

In this case:

IRR = 10% + [(3,980/(3,980 + 4,316) × (15% − 10%)]% = 12.4%

Chinese range

	Year 0 £	Year 1 £	Year 2 £	Year 3 £	Year 4 £	Total £
Cash flow	(20,000)	5,000	6,000	8,000	10,000	
10% discount factors	1.000	0.909	0.826	0.751	0.683	
Discounted cash flow at 10%	(20,000)	4,545	4,956	6,008	6,830	2,339
15% discount factors	1.000	0.870	0.756	0.658	0.572	
Discounted cash flow at 15%	(20,000)	4,350	4,536	5,264	5,720	(130)

Net present value at 10% = £2,339

The IRR can be found by interpolation as above:

IRR = 10% + [(2,339/(2,339 + 130) × (15% − 10%)]% = 14.7%

Italian range

	Year 0 £	Year 1 £	Year 2 £	Year 3 £	Year 4 £	Total £
Cash flow	(20,000)	12,000	8,000	6,000	0	
10% discount factors	1.000	0.909	0.826	0.751	0.683	
Discounted cash flow at 10%	(20,000)	10,908	6,608	4,506	0	2,022
15% discount factors	1.000	0.870	0.756	0.658	0.572	
Discounted cash flow at 15%	(20,000)	10,440	6,048	3,948	0	436

Net present value at 10% = £2,022

Since the NPV is positive at 15%, this means that the IRR of the project is in excess of 15%.

The results can be summarised and the projects ranked as follows:

	NPV	*Ranking*	*IRR*	*Ranking*
Indian range	£3,979	1st	12.4%	3rd
Chinese range	£2,339	2nd	14.7%	2nd
Italian range	£2,022	3rd	>15%	1st

(b) (i) The IRR and NPV approaches are similar in that they are both based on the principle of **discounted cash flow** (DCF). The main advantage of the IRR method is that the information it provides is **more easily understood** by managers, especially non-financial managers. However, since the results are expressed in percentage terms, the method can be **confused** with the **accounting return on capital employed**. A fundamental drawback to the IRR method is that it **ignores the relative size of investments**. This is not the case with the NPV technique, which measures the amount by which the net worth of the firm will be increased by undertaking the project. This method is therefore superior for **ranking mutually exclusive projects**. A further advantage of the NPV approach is that when discount rates are expected to differ over the life of the project, such variations can be incorporated easily into NPV calculations, but not into IRR calculations.

(ii) The NPV method is the preferred approach for project appraisal since it gives **unambiguous results** and can be **adjusted to account for varying discount rates, uncertainty and risk**. It can be used to **compare mutually exclusive projects** of different lifespan and risk levels. In this case, it is recommended that Quick Freeze Foods plc should develop the Indian range since this will generate the highest NPV cash flow of the three projects. This assumes that 10% is an appropriate discount rate for the evaluation of the investment. However, before a final decision is reached Quick Freeze Foods plc should also consider the non-financial factors, such as competition, marketing and production issues.

Examiner's marking scheme

				Marks
(a)	(i)	NPV of each project	(3 × 2 marks)	6
		Ranking		1
	(ii)	IRR of each project	(3 × 2 marks)	6
		Ranking		1
				14
(b)	(i)	Critical evaluation of NPV		2
		Critical evaluation of IRR		2
	(ii)	Selection of NPV for mutual projects		1
		Selection of highest NPV		1
				6
				20

38   WEAVERS LTD (6/98)

Weavers Ltd is engaged in the manufacture of carpets and is considering an expansion of production facilities to meet an anticipated increase in demand over the next five years. The board of directors is currently considering two mutually exclusive options.

The first option is to acquire an additional loom.

(i)   The loom will have an initial cost of £800,000 and will have a life of five years. At the end of year five it will have a zero scrap value.

(ii)   The loom will produce an additional 1,000 carpets per annum for the next five years.

(iii)   The sales price of each carpet is £1,000 which has been fixed for the next five years by Government price control.

(iv)   Each carpet produced by this loom requires:

    (1)   Material costing £400.
    This will remain constant for the next five years.

    (2)   Direct labour of 10 hours at £10 per hour in year one.
    For each of the subsequent four years, pay will increase by 2% of the preceding year's level.

    (3)   Machine time of 20 hours at £10 per hour.
    This will remain constant for the next five years.

(v)   Depreciation is on a straight line basis.

The second option is to subcontract production of an additional 1,000 carpets per annum under a fixed contract for the next five years.

(i)   There is an annual subcontract fee payable at the end of each of the next five years commencing at the end of year one at £150,000. For each of the subsequent four years this fee will increase by 5% of the preceding year's level.

(ii)   Over the next five years the subcontractor has agreed to produce and deliver up to a maximum 1,000 carpets each year to the company for an agreed cost per carpet of £700 (in addition to the annual fee in (i)).

(iii)   The sales price of each carpet is £1,000 which has been fixed for the next five years by Government price control.

(iv)   Under the contract Weavers Ltd must agree to accept a minimum of 750 carpets per annum.

(v)   Weavers Ltd has already spent £100,000 conducting research into the viability of this subcontract arrangement.

The cost of capital is 10%. See discount factors below.

Ignore taxation.

Required

(a)   Calculate the net present value of each of the options to the nearest £'000.

    State clearly any assumptions made.   (18 marks)

(b)   (i)   On the basis of the calculation made in (a) above, which of the two options would you choose and why?   (2 marks)

    (ii)   Briefly outline FOUR key factors which should be considered before a final decision is reached.   (4 marks)

(c) (i) Explain why it is important to evaluate carefully capital investment decisions.
(4 marks)

(ii) Identify and discuss the key stages in the capital investment appraisal decision making and control cycle.
(10 marks)

(iii) Outline TWO key advantages of auditing the performance of a capital investment project.
(2 marks)

Note. The present value of £1 in n years at 10%:

n (year)	*10%*
1	0.909
2	0.826
3	0.751
4	0.683
5	0.621

(40 marks)

Helping hand

In (a) make clear what you're including and excluding. In (b) think about the conditions, risks and contract operation. For (c) consider the extent of the business's commitment and go through the various stages highlighting what each stage is designed to achieve, and also considering the criteria used to assess the project.

---

38   **ANSWER: WEAVERS LTD**

> **Helping hand**
>
> In (a) don't forget to exclude sunk and non-cash costs. For (b) the conditions imposed may be onerous, and the company is dependent upon the sub-contractor. Capital expenditure is at the heart of a business's development and strategy, hence each stage listed in (c) (ii) is important. Some projects will fall at the initial feasibility stage before detailed evaluation is undertaken. Management involvement must be significant.
>
> **What the examiner said**
>
> Part (c) was the worst answered, with many candidates failing to answer the question as set.

(a)

Year	0	1	2	3	4	5
	£'000	£'000	£'000	£'000	£'000	£'000
Option 1						
Cost of loom	(800)					
Sales		1,000	1,000	1,000	1,000	1,000
Materials		(400)	(400)	(400)	(400)	(400)
Labour (2% inflation)		(100)	(102)	(104)	(106)	(108)
Machine time		(200)	(200)	(200)	(200)	(200)
Cash flows	(800)	300	298	296	294	292
10% discount factors	1.000	0.909	0.826	0.751	0.683	0.621
Discounted cash flow	(800)	273	246	222	201	181

Net present value = £323,000.

Year	0	1	2	3	4	5
	£'000	£'000	£'000	£'000	£'000	£'000
Option 2						
Sales		1,000	1,000	1,000	1,000	1,000
Subcontractor costs (£700 per carpet)		(700)	(700)	(700)	(700)	(700)
Annual fee (5% infl'n)		(150)	(158)	(165)	(174)	(182)
	-	150	142	135	126	118
10% discount factors	1.000	0.909	0.826	0.751	0.683	0.621
Discounted cash flow	-	136	117	101	86	73

Net present value = £513,000.

Notes

1   **Depreciation** is not a cash flow and therefore has not been included in the NPV calculations.

2   The £100,000 costs of research into the subcontracting arrangement is a **sunk cost,** and is therefore not relevant.

3   Revenues and costs are assumed to arise at the end of each year.

(b) (i)   The two options concerned are mutually exclusive. Therefore, the option with the higher NPV, in this case Option 2, should be chosen.

(ii)   Other factors which should be considered include the following.

(1)   **The effect of the fixed contract fee.** With Option 2, Weavers Ltd is committed to a fixed annual fee regardless of the volume of carpets required.

(2)   **The requirement to accept a minimum quantity.** The requirement under Option 2 to accept at least 750 carpets per annum would be disadvantageous in the event that demand for the carpets is insufficient to sell this number.

(3) **Risk of failure of the subcontractor's business.** There is the risk that after the subcontracting agreement has been entered into, the subcontractor's business could fail during the life of the agreement.

(4) **Quality control.** Under Option 1, Weavers Ltd will keep control of production quality assurance. With a subcontractor, the quality of the product may be more difficult to control.

(5) **Cash flow profiles.** Under Option 1, substantial funds will be needed early on for the initial investment, while Option 2 requires no expenditure initially.

(c) (i) Careful evaluation of capital investment decisions is important for the following reasons.

(1) Capital investment will involve a **large amount** of the **resources** of the enterprise, and making a wrong decision could prove to be costly.

(2) Capital investment decisions are often closely **tied in with the overall strategy** of the enterprise and need to be considered in the light of the long-term objectives of the business.

(3) **Abandonment** of a capital investment programme at a later stage can be **expensive**.

(4) The **risks and uncertainties** of making capital investments can be **high** because their benefits generally accrue over the medium to long term. Over this timescale, projected benefits can be difficult to predict.

(ii) **Initial feasibility study.** Before a detailed evaluation of a capital investment proposal can be carried out, a brief initial investigation should generally be carried out to establish in broad terms whether the project is feasible. This initial investigation should take into account such factors as the availability of the required resources, the risks of the project, its technical and commercial feasibility, its risks, and the place of the project in the context of the strategic objectives of the enterprise.

Detailed evaluation. If the project is feasible, a detailed evaluation should be undertaken. This investigation will take into account all the relevant expected cash flows deriving from the project. Net present value (NPV), internal rate of return, or other appraisal techniques, may be employed. The project should be appraised alongside any alternative projects which are also being considered. The NPV method is to be preferred because it is consistent with the objective of maximising shareholder wealth. An assessment of the sources of finance available for the project, and their relative costs, should be incorporated in the detailed appraisal. Any non-financial factors arising from the project should also be considered. The degree of risk in the project may be assessed with the help of sensitivity analysis.

Approval of the project. Except for minor projects which are within the specified authorisation limits of other staff, senior management and possibly the Board of Directors, will make the final decision about whether to go ahead with the project. Those making the decision must be satisfied that an appropriately detailed evaluation has been carried out, that the proposal meets the necessary criteria to contribute to profitability, and that it is consistent with the overall strategy of the enterprise.

Implementation. Once the decision has been made that the project will be undertaken, responsibility for the project should be assigned to a project manager or other responsible person. The required resources will need to be made available to this manager, who should be given specific targets to achieve.

Project monitoring. After commencement of the project, progress should be monitored and senior management should be informed on the progress of the project regularly. The project can be monitored more effectively if the costs and benefits originally expected are reassessed in the light of unforeseen events happening in the course of the project.

Post-completion audit. At the end of the project, a post-completion audit should be carried out in order to make use of what can be learned from the experience in the planning of future projects.

(iii)   Audit of project performance can bring the following advantages.

(1) **Better future investment decisions.** The audit can be helpful in identifying where mistakes have been made, so that similar mistakes can be avoided in the future. It may also identify areas of success which might be replicated in future projects.

(2) **Better current investment decisions.** Knowledge that an audit will be carried out at a later date may encourage managers involved to be more realistic and not unduly optimistic in their judgements. The data used in current appraisals may be improved as a result.

(3) **Contribution to performance evaluation**. A project audit can be useful to project managers and to senior management in providing feedback which is of use to the process of management control and performance assessment.

Examiner's marking scheme

				Marks
(a)	*Option 1*			
		Sales/Materials/Labour/Machine costs	4	
		Loom cost & scrap	1	
		Discount factors	1	
		NPV	2	
		Assumptions/notes	2	
	Option 2			
		Sales	1	
		Subcontractor costs (Contract fee)	2	
		Subcontractor cost (Per unit)	2	
		NPV	2	
		Summary	1	
				18
(b)	(i)	Accept higher NPV in mutually exclusive projects		2
	(ii)	Each factor briefly explained (Only 4 needed)		4
(c)	(i)	Maximisation of shareholder wealth	2	
		Risk and quantum of resources required	2	
				4
	(ii)	Each main phase properly explained (Only 5 needed – 5 × 2 marks)		10
	(iii)	Each advantage explained (Only 2 needed)		2
				40

39   NOKE PLC (12/99)

Noke plc is a manufacturer of sports footwear and is proposing to start a new range called Zoomer. It is expected that the Zoomer range will have a life of four years from the start of year 20X1 to the end of 20X4. Production and sales of the new Zoomer range will cease at the end of 20X4.

You have recently joined the company's accounting and finance team and have been provided with the following information relating to the project.

Capital expenditure

A feasibility study which cost £50,000 has just been completed. This study recommended that the company buy new plant and machinery costing £1,500,000 to be paid for at the start of the project. The machinery and plant would be depreciated at 20% of cost per annum and sold for £300,000 receivable at the end of 20X4.

As a result of undertaking the proposed project it is also recommended that an existing machine be sold for cash at the start of the project for its current book value of £25,000. This machine had been scheduled to be sold for cash at the end of 20X2 £10,000.

Sales and purchases relating to the new Zoomer range

	20X1	20X2	20X3	20X4
	£'000	£'000	£'000	£'000
Sales revenue	1,000	1,250	1,500	1,750
Debtors (at year end)	100	125	150	175
Purchases	400	500	600	700
Creditors (at year end)	40	50	60	70
Payments to sub contractors	50	100	100	100
Fixed overheads and advertising				
With the Zoomer range	1,300	1,100	1,000	900
Without the Zoomer range	1,200	1,000	900	800

Labour costs

From the start of the project, two employees currently working in another department and earning £12,500 per annum each will be transferred to work on the new product line. Another employee currently earning £20,000 per annum will be promoted to work on the new line at a revised salary of £25,000 per annum.

If the project is not undertaken, these employees will immediately have to be made redundant at a cost of a full year's salary each. In any event, when the new project ceases at the end of 20X4, they will be made redundant on similar terms.

These labour and redundancy costs have not been included in the above figures.

Material costs

Recycled nylon for which the company has no other use is already in stock and cost the company £10,000 last year. It can be used in the manufacture of the new product range. If it is not used, it would have to be disposed of at a cost to the company of £5,000 at the end of 20X1.

Recycled rubber is also in stock and can be used on the new product range. It cost the company £15,000 some years ago. The company has no other use for it, but could sell it on the open market for £10,000 at the end of 20X1.

These cash flows associated with the nylon and rubber have *not* been included in the above purchases figures.

Notes

1   The year-end debtors and creditors are received and paid during the following year.

2   The net tax liabilities payable on 31 December each year, as a direct consequence of this project, are as follows.

20X1	20X2	20X3	20X4
£'000	£'000	£'000	£'000
20	46	84	109

The net tax payable has taken into account the effect of all relevant costs, any capital allowances and the one year time-lag in the payment of tax.

(Capital allowances are tax allowable depreciation.)

3   The company's cost of capital is a constant 10% per annum.

The present value of £1 in n years at 10% is as follows.

N (year)	Present value at 10%
	£'000
1	0.909
2	0.286
3	0.751
4	0.683
5	0.621

Assume that cash flows occur at the end of each respective year apart from those stated to occur immediately.

Required

(a) (i)   Calculate the net present value (NPV) of the new Zoomer range project to the nearest £'000 assuming it is now the beginning of 20X1.   (22 marks)

     (ii) Give TWO reasons, with a brief explanation, why NPV is considered superior to other methods of evaluating capital expenditure projects.   (2 marks)

(b) Write a short report to the board of directors which:

     (i)   Advises whether or not to accept the project on financial grounds   (2 marks)

     (ii) Explains why certain figures which were provided in the question were excluded from the net present value calculations   (6 marks)

     (iii) Identifies and briefly explains FOUR other factors which would need to be considered before a final decision is reached   (8 marks)

(40 marks)

Helping hand

In (a) the best way to show the adjustments you will need to make to sales and purchases will be to set up workings for each time period. Remember for (b) (ii) that sunk, non-relevant and non-cash costs should be excluded.

Your answer to (b) (iii) does not need to be confined to financial matters.

---

39   ANSWER: NOKE PLC

> **Helping hand**
>
> In (a) there are a large number of adjustments that must be made to the figures provided. You may find it helpful to list these out separately in your workings before trying to incorporate them into the cash flow itself. In (b) (ii) try to understand why some costs are relevant and others are not. In (b) (iii) you can include both financial and non-financial factors in your discussion.

(a) (i)   It is assumed that all costs and revenues arise at the end of the year. Those that arise immediately will therefore be treated as occurring at the end of 20X0.

Cash flow projections

		20X0 £'000	20X1 £'000	20X2 £'000	20X3 £'000	20X4 £'000	20X5 £'000
Capital expenditure							
New plant & machinery	1b	(1,500)				300	
Existing machinery	2	25		(10)			
Operating revenues							
Sales	3		900	1,225	1,475	1,725	175
Purchases	3		(360)	(490)	(590)	(690)	(70)
Sub-contractors			(50)	(100)	(100)	(100)	
Labour	4b		(50)	(50)	(50)	(50)	
Redundancy costs	4a, c	45				(50)	
Existing material stocks	1c		(5)				
Fixed overheads and Advertising	5		(100)	(100)	(100)	(100)	
Taxation				(20)	(46)	(84)	(109)
Net cash flow		(1,430)	335	455	589	951	(4)
10% discount factors		1.000	0.909	0.826	0.751	0.683	0.621
Discounted cash flow		(1,430)	305	376	442	650	(2)

The net present value of the project is £341,000.

Notes

1   The following items will be excluded from the calculations.

(a) The feasibility study has already been completed. It should therefore be treated as a **sunk cost** and excluded from the cash flow.

(b) Depreciation of plant and machinery is a **non-cash item**, and should therefore be excluded.

(c) The original purchase cost of the recycled nylon and the recycled rubber has already been incurred, and is therefore also a **sunk cost**. However, the cost of disposing of the nylon will be avoided as a result of undertaking the project, and this will therefore be included as a **relevant revenue**. Similarly the income forgone from the sale of the rubber on the open market must be included as a **relevant cost**.

2   The rescheduled sale of the existing machine will take place as a direct result of undertaking the project, and is therefore a **relevant cost**. The proceeds of £25,000 must be included at the end of 20X0, and the proceeds of £10,000 forgone at the end of 20X2 must be included as a cost to the project.

3   The NPV cash flow must include only **actual cash movements** that arise as a result of undertaking the project. The figures for sales and purchases must therefore be adjusted to take account of the movement in debtors and creditors.

	20X1 £'000	20X2 £'000	20X3 £'000	20X4 £'000	20X5 £'000
Sales revenue	1,000	1,250	1,500	1,750	
Less debtors at end of year	(100)	(125)	(150)	(175)	
Add debtors at start of year		100	125	150	175
Cash flow arising from sales	900	1,225	1,475	1,725	175
Purchases	400	500	600	700	
Less creditors at end of year	(40)	(50)	(60)	(70)	
Add creditors at start of year		40	50	60	70
Cash flow arising from purchases	360	490	590	690	70

4   The three employees transferred to work on the new product would otherwise have been made redundant, and all costs and savings arising are therefore a direct consequence of the project being undertaken. The following cash flows will therefore be included.

(a) An immediate saving of £45,000 in redundancy costs.

(b) Annual salary costs of £50,000 from 20X1 to 20X4.

(c) Redundancy costs of £50,000 at the end of 20X4.

5   Only the **incremental costs** of fixed overheads and advertising should be charged to the project.

(ii)   Reasons why NPV is superior to other methods of evaluating capital expenditure projects

(1) It takes into account the **time value of money**. Given the choice of receiving £100 today and £100 in one year's time, most people would choose to receive £100 today because they could spend it or invest it to earn interest. A future receipt is also inherently more uncertain than a present receipt. The NPV approach allows this effect to be quantified and included in the appraisal by means of the discount rate.

(2) Unlike other methods, the project is assessed in terms of its effect upon the **net worth of the company**. Thus the tendency of some other methods to discriminate in favour of smaller short-term projects with a high rate of return is avoided.

(b) To: Board of Directors
     From: Accountant
     Date: 15 December 20X0
     Subject: Net present value appraisal of the new Zoomer range project

Discounted cash flow projections

When discounted at the cost of capital of 10%, the project shows a positive NPV of £341,000. It is therefore recommended that on financial grounds the project should be accepted, although the broader strategic and non-financial factors must be taken into account in arriving at the final decision.

Figures excluded from net present value calculations

1   The feasibility study has already been completed, and is therefore a **sunk cost**.

2   Depreciation is excluded because this is a **non-cash item**.

3   The original purchase cost of both the recycled nylon and the recycled rubber has already been incurred and is therefore a **sunk cost**.

4   Fixed overheads and advertising expenditure that would have been incurred without the Zoomer range are excluded since these are **not relevant costs**.

Other factors to be considered

1   There is no information included that relates to the relative risk associated with this particular project. If it is anticipated that the Zoomer range has a higher **level of risk** than the existing operations of Noke plc, then the **discount rate** should be adjusted to reflect this.

2   The project requires an **immediate cash investment** of £1.5m, and will not become cash positive until 20X4. The company must therefore consider how it intends to finance this considerable investment.

3   It is likely that the **actual operating cash flows** will **vary from the estimates** used in the appraisal. It would be useful to assess the sensitivity of the project to variations in the key variables such as sales revenue.

4   The **position** of the new product range in the **overall strategic plan** for the company will influence the final decision. If the project is crucial to the strategic development and long-term security of the company, it may be subject to less stringent financial criteria than might otherwise be the case.

BPP
PROFESSIONAL EDUCATION

40 **CRUSHER LTD (12/01)**

Crusher Ltd is a medium sized engineering business, engaged in the design and manufacture of crushing equipment for processing rock into sand and gravel.

Two years ago, the company undertook an investment in a new range of crushing equipment, which was launched into the North American market. This investment was estimated to have a four year life. At the end of four years, it was anticipated that new technology would render the investment obsolete with no residual value.

The first two years of the investment have shown considerable losses and the directors have requested an immediate review of the project. The financial controller has asked you, as assistant accountant, to review the financial performance of the investment.

The original project proposal, as approved by the board of directors two years ago, showed an internal rate of return (IRR) of 17.9% and a net present value (NPV) of £174,000 at a cost of capital of 15%. These calculations were based on the following cash flows.

Original project cash flows	Time 0 Cash flows £'000	Year 1 Cash flows £'000	Year 2 Cash flows £'000	Year 3 Cash flows £'000	Year 4 Cash flows £'000
Market research	(100)				
Research and development	(450)				
Equipment design	(150)				
Tooling and equipment	(1,500)				
Sales revenue		1,200	2,000	3,600	3,200
Variable manufacturing costs		(600)	(950)	(1,620)	(1,360)
Variable selling costs		(120)	(160)	(216)	(128)
Directly attributable cash fixed costs		(300)	(300)	(300)	(300)
Originally projected net cashflows	(2,200)	180	590	1,464	1,412

The profit statements in respect of this particular project for the last two years and the revised budget for the new two years show the following.

Actual results and revised forecasts	Actual profit Year 1 £'000	Actual profit Year 2 £'000	Budget profit Year 3 £'000	Budget profit Year 4 £'000
Sales revenue	1,000	2,200	3,500	3,000
Variable manufacturing costs	(600)	(1,210)	(1,750)	(1,350)
Directly attributable cash fixed costs	(200)	(300)	(300)	(100)
Depreciation	(375)	(375)	(375)	(375)
Variable selling costs	(125)	(175)	(200)	(100)
Allocated fixed selling costs	(250)	(300)	(350)	(350)
Allocated head office costs	(125)	(250)	(375)	(375)
Profit/Loss	(675)	(410)	150	350

The following notes have also been drawn to your attention.

1 The investment incurred at the start of the project was the same as the original proposal.

2 Crusher Ltd ignores taxation for capital investment appraisal analysis and for financial statement preparation relating to any particular investment project.

3 Crusher Ltd's cost of capital is 15%.

4 Crusher Ltd has been offered £1,600,000 by another company who wishes to take ownership of the entire project for the remaining two years of its life.

Required

(a) Prepare a draft report for the financial controller to present to the board of directors, which:

    (i) Recalculates the project's original net present value (NPV) and internal rate of return (IRR) based on the most up to date information. (14 marks)

    (ii) Sets out the current minimum acceptable abandonment value and recommends whether to abandon the investment given the current offer of £1,600,000 for the transfer of the entire investment to the other company. (8 marks)

(b) (i) Identify and briefly explain FOUR main advantages of conducting post completion audits on all main projects. (8 marks)

    (ii) Identify and briefly explain FIVE key principles for incorporation into post completion audits, making reference to this particular project. (10 marks)

(40 marks)

Helping hand

In (a) remember that not every cost will be included in the investment appraisal. Make sure you're clear on the timescale in (a) (ii). In (b) think back to earlier questions in this kit.

---

40   ANSWER: CRUSHER LTD

Helping hand

Other layouts are possible for the NPV and IRR calculations in (a) but our layout avoids repetition. (a) (i) and (ii) are about costs relevant to the project; allocated costs and depreciation should be ignored. (a) (ii) is effectively an appraisal of the last two years of the project with the end of year 2 being time 0. Similar questions to (b) have been set on other papers, and the question indicates the understanding you need of the objectives of post-completion audits, also how they are organised, where they are focused, and how their results are communicated.

What the examiner said

Most candidates made very good attempts at the NPV calculations, but answers to the IRR calculation were poor. Many candidates mixed up IRR with accounting rate of return (ARR). Candidates must ensure that they can distinguish between the two.

A number of candidates failed to attempt the abandonment calculation in (a) (ii).

Most candidates answered (b) (i) well, and many evidently had read past exam questions and relevant articles. However, a significant number failed to answer (b) (ii) when what was needed was a general discussion of auditing principles.

(a) (i)   To: Financial Controller
            From: Technician
            Date: 7 January
            Subject: Project Continuation

Introduction

Current estimates indicate that the project's net present value (NPV) and internal rate of return (IRR) will differ significantly from original estimates. A decision is now needed on whether or not to abandon the project.

NPV and IRR

	Original	Revised
NPV (£'000)	174	(94)
IRR (%)	17.9	13.4

The NPV and IRR have been calculated as follows:

	0	1	2	3	4
	£'000	£'000	£'000	£'000	£'000
Market research	(100)				
R&D	(450)				
Equipment design	(150)				
Tooling	(1,500)				
Sales revenue		1,000	2,200	3,500	3,000
Variable manufacturing		(600)	(1,210)	(1,750)	(1,350)
Cash fixed costs		(200)	(300)	(300)	(100)
Variable selling costs		(125)	(175)	(200)	(100)
	(2,200)	75	515	1,250	1,450
15% discount factor	1.000	0.870	0.756	0.658	0.572
Discounted cash flow	(2,200)	65	389	823	829
NPV	(94)				
13% discount factor	1.000	0.885	0.783	0.693	0.613
Discounted cash flow	(2,200)	66	403	866	889
NPV	24				

NPV at 15% = (£94,000)

$$\text{IRR} = A + \left[\frac{a}{a+b} \times (B - A)\right]$$

$$= 13 + \left[\frac{24}{24+94} \times (15-13)\right]$$

$$= 13.4\%$$

(ii) To calculate the minimum acceptable abandonment value, the revenues and costs for years 3 and 4 are discounted with end of year 2 being time 0.

	3	4
	£'000	£'000
Sales revenue	3,500	3,000
Variable manufacturing costs	(1,750)	(1,350)
Cash fixed costs	(300)	(100)
Variable selling cots	(200)	(100)
	1,250	1,450
15% discount factor	0.870	0.756
Discounted cash flow	1,088	1,096
Net present value	2,184	

The minimum acceptable abandonment value is £2,184,000 and thus the offer should not be accepted.

(b) (i) Advantages of post-completion audits include the following.

1 **Better forecasting techniques**

The post-completion audit can identify weaknesses in the forecasting and estimating techniques used to evaluate projects, and should help to improve the discipline and quality of forecasting.

2 **Better future investment decisions**

The post-completion audit can identify where mistakes have been made such as lack of research or unrealistic assumptions. This should ensure that similar mistakes are avoided in the future. It may also identify areas of success that might be replicated in future projects.

3 **Better current investment decisions**

Awareness that a post-completion audit will be carried out at a later date may encourage managers involved to be more realistic and not unduly optimistic in their judgements.

4 **Contribution to performance evaluation**

A post-completion audit can provide feedback to project managers and to senior management which is of use in the process of management control, performance assessment and market evaluation.

(ii) Principles for inclusion in post-completion audits include the following.

1 **Staffing**

The staff responsible for carrying out the audit should **not** have been **involved** in the implementation of the project. However, they should have **sufficient expertise** and **business awareness** to be able to make reasonable judgements about it.

2   **Participation of project staff**

Project staff should be **consulted** by the audit team, and should be kept informed of the audit's progress.

3   **Timing**

On some occasions it will be appropriate to carry out post-completion audits before the end of the investment's life. With the crushing equipment project, an audit undertaken before the end of the project may identify **inefficiencies** which have caused the variable manufacturing costs to be much greater than other projects. These can be corrected on this or indeed other projects. In addition an audit at that stage can help identify the appropriateness of **abandonment** of the project.

4   **Focus**

A post-completion audit does not need to focus on all aspects of an investment, but just those aspects that have been identified as **particularly sensitive or critical,** or which have deviated significantly from what was originally planned. Some attention should be given to sales as a key variable, but sales for the first two years combined have been in line with original expectations.

5   **Future figures**

If the completion audit takes place before the end of the project, it should analyse whether the forecasts (here the revised forecasts) are based on **realistic assumptions.** Is the assumption that variable manufacturing costs can be brought under control realistic? Are the assumptions about sales revenue unduly pessimistic? (Sales are forecast to be less than originally expected in years 3 and 4, despite being greater than expected in year 2).

6   **Results and recommendations**

The conclusions of the audit should highlight the reasons why the project has been **successful**, or, as here, why the project has not gone as well as anticipated. This should include an analysis of how much the project's losses have been due to controllable factors, and how much due to factors outside the company's control (unexpected price increases by suppliers). It should also include recommendations for specific improvements.

7   **Feedback to managers**

Feedback must be given to the managers responsible for the projects and anyone else responsible for implementing changes to procedures. Any feedback should **not be unduly critical**, as managers might become risk-averse and less willing to undertake future projects. In this project the sales results have been as anticipated, and the cost over-runs may not mean that similar future projects should not be undertaken, either because lessons have been learnt, or because the over-runs were due to one-off factors.

Examiner's marking scheme

				Marks
(a)	(i)	Report format		2
		Investment costs		2
		Sales revenue		1
		Variable manufacturing costs		1
		Variable selling costs		1
		Directly attributable fixed costs		1
		NPV calculation at 15%		2
		NPV calculation at 13%		2
		IRR formula/calculation		2
				14
	(ii)	Remaining two years' cash flows:		
		Sales		1
		Variable manufacturing costs		1
		Variable selling costs		1
		Directly attributable cash fixed costs		1
		NPV calculation at 15%		2
		Recommendation with justification		2
				8
(b)	(i)	Identification of each criterion	(4 × 1 mark)	4
		Brief explanation of each	(4 × 1 mark)	4
				8
	(ii)	Identification of each criterion	(5 × 1 mark)	5
		Brief explanation of each	(5 × 1 mark)	5
				10
				40

41   PENSIONS SYSTEM (Pilot Paper)

You are an assistant accountant in the pension department of a large life assurance and pensions company. You have been co-opted onto a systems feasibility study team which is investigating an upgrade in your department's current computer systems. In particular, the project team is investigating the adoption of a new method of capturing on-line, customer employee data for certain group pension policy products.

The economic aspects of the study show that the use of on-line as opposed to manual data entry could provide an average time saving of 45 minutes for each new group pension policy file set up on the system. The estimated total cost per hour of the administrative staff who currently enter policy data is £30 per hour and about 3,000 policies of the type under review are sold each year. The sales volume of group pension business is expected to be 3,000 policies next year rising to 3,500 the following year, 4,000 the next and settling at 4,500 policies thereafter.

The new system can be developed and implemented at a cost of £350,000. The new system will replace an existing system which was only implemented two years ago at a cost of £200,000. Both systems could operate for a further five years at which time the method of administering pension products is expected to change. Neither system would be required after this time.

The written down value of the current system stands at £100,000 and the resale value of the hardware component is currently £75,000. This system would be expected to have a resale value of no more than £10,000 five years from now. The resale value of the new system would be about £65,000 five years from now.

Finally the new system would incur maintenance charges of £35,000 per annum as opposed to £20,000 per annum for the current system.

You have been asked to contribute to the study by providing a financial analysis of the proposed investment.

Required

(a) Using the net present value method prepare a discounted cash flow analysis of the proposed new systems. The cost of finance of the pensions company is estimated at 11%. Ignore the effects of taxation and inflation.   (25 marks)

(b) Briefly explain how you could have introduced the effects of taxation and of inflation into your analysis.   (15 marks)

Year	Discount factor at 11%
1	0.901
2	0.812
3	0.731
4	0.659
5	0.593

(40 marks)

41   ANSWER: PENSIONS SYSTEM

(a)   The **net present value** of the project is calculated below.

Year	Asset purchase £	Asset disposal £	Labour saving £	Main-tenance £	Net cash flow £	Discount factor	DCF £
0	(350,000)	75,000			(275,000)	1.000	(275,000)
1			67,500	(15,000)	52,500	0.901	47,303
2			78,750	(15,000)	63,750	0.812	51,765
3			90,000	(15,000)	75,000	0.731	54,825
4			101,250	(15,000)	86,250	0.659	56,839
5		65,000	101,250	(15,000)	151,250	0.593	89,691
Net present value							25,423

Notes

1   It is assumed that the hardware component of the current system is sold on acquisition of the new system.

2   It is assumed that the resale value of the current system will be no more than £10,000 five years from now whether or not the project is undertaken. Therefore, this resale value is ignored.

3   Labour cost savings are assumed to arise at the end of each period, at a value of:

Number of policies × 0.75 hours × £30

Conclusion

The positive net present value is favourable for the project. In practice, non-financial factors such as the effect on quality, personnel and intangibles should also be taken into consideration.

(b)   **Taxation**

If the company has a tax liability, then this is likely to have an effect on the **appraisal** of the project. The net cash flows arising from the project would be adjusted by an amount reflecting the tax effect in each year.

Tax is likely to affect **capital acquisitions** and non-capital cash flows in different ways.

In the UK, for example, **capital allowances** are normally available at a rate of 25% per annum on the tax written-down value of the investment. When assets are eventually sold, as in the case of the computer system in the example, there will be a balancing charge or allowance to reflect the difference between the tax written-down value and the sale proceeds. The net cash flow effect is represented by the tax allowance (or charge) multiplied by the effective tax rate which the company faces.

There will be a **loss in tax saving** on the **expenses** of the business arising from the reduction in the cost of administration, less the additional maintenance costs. This would also be adjusted for at the relevant point in the NPV calculation.

It may be that tax becomes payable at some time after the relevant expenses are incurred or assets acquired, and this **time delay** should be taken into account. For example, if tax becomes payable with a **one year delay**, the tax adjustments should be shown in the next year, so that the adjustments are discounted at the rate appropriate to tax payments.

Inflation

There are two approaches to dealing with increases in costs and prices in a project appraisal.

(i)   All cash flows may be **adjusted** by the **anticipated rate or rates of inflation** in order to reflect the amount in pounds which will be received or paid at the future dates. The, the discount rate used should be a '**money' or nominal discount rate.**

(ii)   Inflation may be ignored in the cash flows, so that cash flows are expressed in constant price level terms, and a '**real' discount rate** should then be used.

The **money discount rate** is the real rate adjusted by the **rate of inflation**. In the equation below, each rate is expressed as a decimal, eg 10% is shown as 0.1.

$(1 + \text{money rate}) = (1 + \text{real rate}) \times (1 + \text{inflation rate})$

If the inflation rate is positive, the money rate will be higher than the real rate.

Provided that all costs and revenues are expected to inflate at the same rate, the two different approaches will lead to the same result. However, it may be that **different rates of inflation** are anticipated for different components in the cash flow. For example, it might be that staff costs are expected to rise by 4% per annum but maintenance costs are expected to rise by only 2% per annum. If so, approach (i) can be used, and each cash flow component adjusted accordingly.

42   PILLS LTD (6/99)

Pills Ltd is a medium sized medical research company, engaged in the development of new medical treatments. To date, the company has invested £250,000 in the development of a new product called 'Gravia'. It is estimated that it will take a further two years of development and testing before 'Gravia' is fully approved by medical industry regulators.

The company believes it can sell the patent for Gravia to a multinational pharmaceutical company for £1,000,000, when it has been fully developed.

The directors of Pills Ltd are currently reviewing the Gravia project, as there is some concern about the size of the required finance to complete the development work.

The project manager has provided the following information.

1   To complete the development, Pills Ltd will need to acquire additional type A material expected to cost £150,000 per annum over the next two years.

2   Type B material will also be required. Currently, there is a sufficient stock of type B material to last for the two years of the project. This material originally cost £50,000. Its replacement cost is £75,000. Instead of using it on this project, it could immediately be sold as scrap for £20,000. It has no other alternative use.

3   If it is decided to continue with the Gravia project, specialist equipment will need to be purchased immediately for £100,000. This equipment could eventually be sold at the end of the project for £25,000.

4   Two chemists currently employed for an annual salary of £20,000 each will be made redundant whenever the Gravia project ends. Redundancy payments are expected to be one full year's salary each.

5   Laboratory technicians currently employed by Pills Ltd are working on the Gravia project at a total annual cost of £85,000. The company has a variety of other projects to which the technicians could be transferred whenever the Gravia project ends.

6   Annual fixed overheads allocated to this project of £100,000 include £60,000 general Head Office overheads and £40,000 overheads which are specifically incurred as a direct consequence of the project.

7   If the development project does not proceed, a foreign dictator has offered immediately to buy the existing Gravia formula from Pills Ltd for military use at a cost of £250,000.

8   Interest on money borrowed to finance the project will cost £20,000 per annum.

9   All cash flows occur at the end of the year unless otherwise stated.

The cost of capital for Pills Ltd has been estimated at 10%.

Ignore inflation and taxation.

Note. The present value of £1 in *n* years at 10%.

n (year)	PV at 10%
1	0.909
2	0.816

Required

(a)   Briefly explain the main principles used to identify relevant costs for decision-making examples from the question.   (8 marks)

(b)   (i)   Calculate the project's NPV to the nearest £'000.   (12 marks)

       (ii)   Calculate the break-even minimum amount to the nearest £'000 required from the sale of the patent to ensure an NPV of at least zero.   (4 marks)

(iii)   Based on financial analysis, determine whether the company should proceed with the project.   (2 marks)

(c) (i)   Briefly outline THREE additional non-financial factors which need to be considered in reaching a final decision.   (6 marks)

(ii)   Briefly explain how the effects of taxation and inflation could have been included in the financial analysis.   (8 marks)

(40 marks)

Helping hand

In (a) think about the differences that a decision to undertake a project will make.

For (b) (i) work systematically through the cost information deciding which costs are relevant.

In (c) (i) you must restrict your answer to non-financial factors.

Calculations are not required in (c) (ii).

---

42   ANSWER: PILLS LTD

> **Helping hand**
>
> (a) and (b) require you to understand how to identify relevant costs in capital investment appraisal, and then to use this knowledge to disentangle the relevant costs in relation to a specific development project. The NPV calculations themselves are relatively simple since they only cover a two-year timescale. Don't, however, forget to take account of time factors when calculating the breakeven value in (b) (ii).
>
> (c) is looking for *non-financial* factors only, and not for other factors in general. Therefore it is a waste of time to write about other financial factors that could have been included.
>
> (c) (ii) requires a basic understanding of how inflation and taxation should be included in NPV investment appraisal, but you do not need to perform any actual calculations.
>
> **What the examiner said**
>
> In general, candidates gave reasonable answers to part (a).
>
> Most of the marks were given for the calculation of a simple net present value in part (a), with only two year's cash flows to analyse. A significant majority of candidates gave very poor answers to this part. Candidates need considerable practice in identifying relevant costs, appropriately timing them and calculating a net present value.
>
> Most answers to part (c)(i) were satisfactory, although a number of answers mentioned financial issues, indicating that sufficient attention had not been given to studying the pilot paper.
>
> (c)(ii) required an explanation of how taxation and inflation could be factored into the financial analysis. Many seemed unable to deal with this issue, indicating that insufficient attention was given to studying the pilot paper.

(a)   **A relevant cost** is a future cash flow that arises as a direct consequence of the decision being considered. Non-cash items such as depreciation should be ignored. The main principles used to identify relevant costs are as follows.

(i)   **Relevant costs are future costs**. A decision is about the future; it cannot alter what has been done already. A cost that has been incurred in the past is totally irrelevant to any decision that is being made now. Such costs are known as **sunk costs** and include payments that have been contractually committed (**committed costs**), even if payment has not yet been made. An example of a sunk cost in this case is the £250,000 that has already been invested in the development of Gravia.

(ii)   **Relevant costs are incremental costs**. A relevant cost is one that arises as a direct consequence of a decision. In this case, the cost of the lab technicians should be excluded, since they can be transferred to other work and they will continue to be employed whether or not the project goes ahead.

(iii)   **Opportunity costs**. These are the benefits which could have been earned, but which have been given up, by choosing one option instead of another, ie they are cash flows that are foregone as a result of the project being undertaken. In this case, the income that is foregone as a result of not scrapping material B is an opportunity cost.

It should be noted that the **costs of financing the investment project** is not included as relevant costs within the cash flow projections, even though they meet the above conditions. This is because they are accounted for in the process of discounting, and therefore to include them in the cash flows would be to double count them.

(b) (i)

	Note	Year 0 £	Year 1 £	Year 2 £
Sale of patent				1,000,000
Type A material			(150,000)	(150,000)
Type B material	1	(20,000)		
Specialist equipment	2	(100,000)		25,000
Chemist salaries	3		(40,000)	(40,000)
Chemist redundancies	3	40,000		(40,000)
Fixed overheads	4		(40,000)	(40,000)
Sale of formula foregone		(250,000)		
Net cash flow		(330,000)	(230,000)	755,000
10% discount factors		1.000	0.909	0.826
Discounted cash flow		(330,000)	(209,070)	623,630
Total net present value		£84,560	(£85,000 to the nearest £'000)	

Notes

1   Neither the **original cost** of the material nor its **replacement cost** are relevant to the decision. However, Pills will forego the proceeds from the sale of the material as scrap, and this should therefore be included in the cash flow.

2   The specialist equipment would only be purchased if the **project is undertaken,** and therefore its cost is relevant to the decision.

3   The chemists will only continue to be employed if the **project is undertaken,** and therefore their salaries should be included. If the project does not go ahead, Pills would have to make them redundant now, and therefore this payment that is saved as a result of the project being undertaken should be included as a positive cash flow. However, since they will be made redundant at the end of the project, the cost of redundancy must be included in year 2.

4   Only that element of the overheads that are **specifically incurred** as a direct consequence of the project should be included.

(ii)   If the patent income is excluded from the above figures, the NPV becomes:

	Year 0 £	Year 1 £	Year 2 £
Net relevant cash flows	(330,000)	(230,000)	(245,000)
10% discount factors	1.000	0.909	0.826
Discounted cash flow	(330,000)	(209,070)	(202,370)
Total net present value	(£741,440)		

The minimum required from the sale of the patent is an amount in year 2 (the earliest possible date of sale) that is equivalent to an NPV of £741,440. If S = undiscounted sale proceeds, then this can be expressed as follows:

$$0.826 \times S = £741,440$$

$$S = £897,627$$

The **breakeven value** is therefore £898,000 to the nearest £'000.

(iii)   Since the project has a positive NPV it should add to the net worth of the company. It is therefore recommended that, on the basis of the information provided, Pills should proceed with the Gravia development project.

(c) (i)   Additional **non-financial factors** could include the following.

     (1) **Legal issues**. There may be political reasons why the company would not be permitted to sell the formula to the foreign dictator.

     (2) **Ethical policy**. Although it may be possible to sell the drug to the foreign dictator, this may not be in line with its ethical policy, and could result in bad publicity.

     (3) **Patent competition**. Pills must be satisfied that they will be able to patent the drug successfully. If other companies are also patenting similar drugs, Pills may not succeed with its application since the drug may not be deemed to meet the novelty criterion.

     (4) **Technical competition**. Pills must be confident that there are not competing products in development elsewhere that could render Gravia obsolete.

     (5) **Access to customers**. Pills is planning to sell the patent for £1m once it is fully developed. However, it must be confident that this sale can be achieved in reality before proceeding with the development.

Note. Only three factors are required in your answer.

(ii)   **Taxation**. All companies are liable to tax, and the effect of undertaking a project will be to increase or decrease tax payments each year. These incremental cash flows should be included in the cash flows of the project for discounting to arrive at the project's NPV. As with all project cash flows, these payments or benefits must be included at the point in time at which they are made, and not at the point in time at which the liability becomes apparent.

In the case of Pills, there would be two types of tax to account for, as follows.

     (1) **Tax on capital expenditure**. The company is planning to purchase specialist equipment that will be used for two years before being sold. **Capital allowances** are generally allowed on the cost of plant and machinery at the rate of 25% on a reducing balance basis. Capital allowances are used to reduce taxable profits, and the consequent reduction in a tax payment should be treated as a cash saving arising from the acceptance of the project. When the plant is eventually sold, the difference between the sale price and the reducing balance amount at the time of the sale will be treated as a taxable profit if the sale price exceeds the reducing balance. If the reducing balance exceeds the sale price, then the difference will be treated as a tax allowable loss.

     (2) **Tax on revenue expenditure**. The company must determine which of the revenue receipts and payments are subject to tax, and then compute the tax liability in the normal way for inclusion in the DCF calculations.

Inflation. Inflation can be included in capital investment appraisal in two ways.

     (1) Each **element of the cash flow** is **adjusted** by the appropriate forecast **inflation rate** for that element over the life of the project. The inflation-adjusted cash flows are then discounted at the money (nominal) cost of capital, which reflects the effect of forecast future inflation rates. This method is appropriate where there are a variety of inflation rates that affect the different elements of the cash flow, and is the method most widely used in practice.

(2) Each **element of the cash flow** is **stated in real terms,** ie without being adjusted for inflation. They are then **discounted using a real cost of capital** that excludes the effect of forecast inflation rates. This approach is only valid if all the revenues and costs are increasing at a broadly similar rate. In practice, this is often not realistic, for example, at the moment in the UK wage rates are increasing at a significantly faster rate than are factory gate prices.

Examiner's marking scheme

			Marks	
(a)		Future/cash flow/direct consequence (3 × 1 mark)	3	
		Exception (finance costs)	1	
		1 example from question for each of 4 above (4 × 1 mark)	4	
				8
(b)	(i)	Sale of patent	1	
		Materials type A and type B (2 × 1 mark)	2	
		Equipment	2	
		Redundancy deferred (2 × 1 mark)	2	
		Chemist salaries	1	
		Directly attributable fixed cost	1	
		Formula sale	1	
		NPV calculation	1	
		Notes or assumptions explained	1	
				12
	(ii)	Break-even principle identified	1	
		NPV calculation with zero residual value	1	
		Formulation to solve	1	
		Correct breakeven figure (to nearest £'000)	1	
				4
	(iii)	Positive NPV therefore accept		2
(c)	(i)	Each non-financial factor (3 × 1 mark)	3	
		Brief explanation of each (3 × 1 mark)	3	
				6
	(ii)	Tax on relevant costs is relevant	1	
		Include in cash flows correctly timed	1	
		Capital allowances comment	1	
		Balance allowance/charge comment	1	
		Existence of inflation must be considered	1	
		Inflation flows with money cost of capital	1	
		Real flows with real cost of capital	1	
		Understanding of inflation demonstrated	1	
				8
				40

Mock exam 1

Managing Finances

June 2002

Question Paper:	
Time allowed	**3 hours**
All FOUR questions are compulsory and MUST be attempted	

Level C

Paper 5

DO NOT OPEN THIS PAPER UNTIL YOU ARE READY TO START

UNDER EXAMINATION CONDITIONS

ALL FOUR questions are compulsory and MUST be attempted

1   Mirrors Ltd has been engaged in the manufacture of mirrors and glass for the past 20 years. The company is family owned and it has 10 equal shareholders. The company has been facing increasing competition, particularly from cheap imports, with a consequential reduction in market share and profit margin. In order to combat the erosion of profit, the company has invested approximately £500,000 over the past year in an effort to embrace new technology. The research and development team has developed two new product types. As funds are limited, it is believed that only one product type can be successfully launched.

Product A

Product A is a mirror with an in-built microprocessor which can digitally enhance the image of the person it is reflecting, to make them appear more attractive. The product is to be called 'The Vanity mirror'.

Details of the Vanity mirror are as follows:

(i)   Capital investment will be required, totalling £1,750,000, £250,000 of which is payable immediately and the remainder in one year's time. The investment is needed to acquire the rights to use the digital technology for the project and the necessary plant and equipment.

(ii)   Production and sales will commence in one year's time, with sales volumes projected as follows:

-    Sales for the first two years of Product A are anticipated to be 5,000 mirrors per annum.

-    For the subsequent three years, sales are expected to increase to 7,500 per annum.

(iii)   At the end of the estimated five-year life of the project, it is expected that the product range will become completely obsolete and will need to be terminated.

(iv)   The terminal value of the plant and equipment is expected to be nil at the end of the project's life (ie in six years' time).

(v)   Selling prices per mirror, in two years' time, are projected to be £220.50. Thereafter selling prices are expected to increase by 5% per annum.

(vi)   Material costs at today's value are projected at £70 per mirror. Labour and overhead costs per mirror at today's values are £30 and £25 respectively. Material costs per mirror are expected to remain at this level for the foreseeable future. Labour and overhead costs per mirror are expected to increase by 10% per annum.

Product B

Product B is a plug-in mirror, which absorbs light during the day and can store and subsequently reflect it during the night. This product range is to be referred to as 'The illuminator mirror'.

Details of the Illuminator mirror are as follows:

(i)   Total capital expenditure of £2,500,000 is required. £500,000 of this is required immediately to purchase a new factory site. The remaining £2,000,000 is required to build a new factory and is payable in one year's time.

(ii)   The terminal value of the project at the end of its five-year life is expected to be £2,500,000 after tax.

(iii)   Production and sales will commence in one year's time. Total sales volume is expected to be 5,000 units per annum in the first year of operation, and is expected to grow at a compound rate of 50% per annum thereafter.

(iv)   Sales prices in two years' time are projected at £250 per mirror, thereafter sales prices will be reduced by 5% per annum, in order to stimulate the growth in volume.

(v)   Material costs are projected at £50 per mirror, with labour costs projected at £20 and variable overheads estimated at £80 per mirror. These costs are all expressed to today's value.

(vi)   Material and labour costs per mirror are expected to inflate at 10% per annum. Variable overhead cost per mirror are expected to remain constant for the duration of the project.

Note: All cash flows can be assumed to occur at year-end unless otherwise stated. Mirrors Ltd pays corporate tax at the rate of 20% per annum, one year in arrears. Mirrors Ltd's cost of capital in money 'nominal' terms is 10%.

N (periods)	10%
1	0.909
2	0.826
3	0.751
4	0.683
5	0.621
6	0.564
7	0.513

Required

(a) (i) Calculate the net present value of launching either the Vanity mirror or the Illuminator mirror (to the nearest £000) and evaluate on financial grounds which of the two projects should be accepted.
(30 marks)

(ii) Identify and briefly discuss three non-financial factors which need to be taken into account before a final decision is reached.
(6 marks)

(b) Briefly describe two sources of finance, other than bank loans, for projects of this nature, which Mirrors Ltd could have considered.
(4 marks)

(40 marks)

2   Books Ltd publishes, prints and distributes educational textbooks to a large number of customers. It supplies directly to schools, retail bookshops and libraries.

Up until now the company published, printed and distributed a limited range of educational texts. It has recently won an exclusive contract to supply a wider range of texts to all schools throughout the country. This has resulted in a huge expansion in business, and while the new business is potentially very profitable, the company is currently experiencing cash flow difficulties.

The bank manager has expressed concern at the increase in the level of the company's bank overdraft. The managing director has decided that immediate action is required to rectify the problem. The controller has contacted a factoring institution, Factor Ltd, with a view to factoring debtors.

Credit sales for the year just ended were £2,555,000, with average debtors of £1,050,000. Debtors days are expected to remain at current levels if the factoring arrangement is not entered into. Standard industry average credit terms are 120 days.

Factor Ltd has put forward the following proposal:

(i) Factoring facilities will be provided to Books Ltd with advances of 75% of the value of sales invoices. If the factoring proposal is accepted, Books Ltd will be required to utilise the full advances facility.

(ii) Factor Ltd will charge 1.25% of Book Ltd's turnover for the factoring service.

(iii) Interest on advances will be charged at 14% per annum.

The financial controller of Books Ltd has also provided the following information:

(i) Sales revenue is expected to double in the coming year and remain at this increased level for the foreseeable future.

(ii) All sales are on credit and as a result of the stricter credit control procedures adopted by Factor Ltd, average debtors are expected to be reduced to the industry average of 120 days.

(iii) The existing credit control function can be reduced by one member of staff, saving £25,000 per annum.

(iv) A member of the general administration staff, who spends approximately 25% of her time on sales administration, will no longer be required to carry out this function. She will, however, still be retained by the company on the same salary as at present, whether or not the factoring proposal is accepted.

(v) Current overdraft rates are 12% per annum.

Required

(a) Calculate for the coming year if it is financially beneficial for Books Ltd to factor its debtors. (Note: a net present value analysis is not required).
(12 marks)

(b)   Identify and briefly describe four specific other actions which could be instigated by Books Ltd in the management of stocks and debtors, to help reduce the cash operating cycle.   (8 marks)

(20 marks)

3   Bags Ltd is a chain of retail outlets, specialising in high quality leather bags and briefcases. One of the products purchased by Bags Ltd for resale is an executive briefcase.

Bags Ltd sells a fixed quantity of 100 briefcases per week. The estimated holding cost for a briefcase is £10.00 per annum per briefcase.

Delivery from Bags Ltd's existing supplier takes two weeks and the purchase price per briefcase delivered to Bags Ltd is £100. The current supplier charges a fixed £75 order processing charge for each order regardless of the order size.

Bags Ltd has recently been approached by an alternative supplier of leather briefcases, which are very similar to the existing briefcase range. It is expected that this alternative briefcase can be sold in the same quantities and price as the existing range.

The alternative supplier's offer is as follows:

1   The cost to Bags Ltd per briefcase will be £96.

2   There will be a fixed order processing charge of £250, regardless of order size.

3   Delivery will take one week.

4   Bags Ltd estimates that due to packaging differences, the storage cost per briefcase will fall to £9.20 per annum per briefcase.

Note

The economic order quantity Q, which will minimise costs, is:

$$Q = \sqrt{\frac{2CoD}{Ch}}$$

Where   Co = The cost of making one order = *Processing cost.*
        D   = Annual demand
        Ch = The holding cost per unit per annum

Required

(a)   Assuming Bags Ltd continues to purchase from the existing supplier, calculate the:

    (i)   Economic order quantity   (2 marks)
    (ii)   Total cost of stocking the briefcase for one year to the nearest £   (3 marks)

(b)   Assuming Bags Ltd switches to the new supplier of briefcases, calculate the:

    (i)   Economic order quantity   (2 marks)

    (ii)   Total cost of stocking the alternative briefcase for one year to the nearest £, and determine if it is financially viable to change to this new supplier.   (3 marks)

(c)   Discuss two limitations of the above calculations and briefly describe three non-financial factors to be taken into account before a final decision is made.   (5 marks)

(d)   Assuming there is an upfront investment cost for Bags Ltd of £40,000, payable immediately, and that the annual saving from switching to the new supplier arises at the end of each of the next three years, calculate the net present value of switching, if the cost of capital for Bags Ltd is 10% per annum.   (5 marks)

(20 marks)

N (periods)	10%
1	0.909
2	0.826
3	0.751

4   Trader Ltd is a company operating in a European Union country, which is currently not a member of the European Monetary Union.

Trader Ltd imports raw materials from a variety of European countries. It sells its products domestically and exports to other European Union countries and the USA.

The government of the country has stated that there will be a referendum within the next 12 months to determine if the electorate wishes the country to join the European Monetary Union.

Currently Trader Ltd experiences corporate tax rates, interest rates and inflation rates higher than the average rates prevailing in the European Monetary Union countries. Over the past number of years, the country's exchange rate has fluctuated significantly in relation to the Euro.

Required

(a)   (i)   In the context of the European Union, briefly explain what is meant by:

European economic union;
And
European monetary union   (4 marks)

      (ii)   Identify and briefly describe two of the main objectives of the European Monetary System.
                                                                                  (4 marks)

(b)   (i)   Identify and briefly explain three favourable implications for Trader Ltd of entry into the Single European Currency zone, and   (6 marks)

      (ii)   Identify and briefly explain three adverse implications for Trader Ltd of entry into the Single European Currency zone.   (6 marks)

                                                                                 (20 marks)

ANSWERS TO MOCK EXAM 1

DO NOT TURN THIS PAGE UNTIL YOU
HAVE COMPLETED MOCK EXAM 1

WARNING! APPLYING THE MARKING SCHEME

If you decide to mark your mock exam using the ACCA marking scheme (reproduced at the end of each BPP answer), you should bear in mind the following points.

1 The BPP answers are not definitive: you will see that we have applied our own interpretation of the marking scheme to our answers to show how good answers should gain marks, but there may be more than one way to answer the question. You must try to judge fairly whether different points made in your answers are correct and relevant and therefore worth marks according to the ACCA marking scheme.

2 In numerical answers, do not penalise yourself too much for minor arithmetical errors: if you have followed the correct principles you should gain most of the marks. This emphasises the importance of including workings, which show the marker which principles you were following.

3 If you have a friend or colleague who is studying or has studied this paper, you might ask him or her to mark your paper for you, thus gaining a more objective assessment. Remember you and your friend are not trained or objective markers, so try to avoid complacency or pessimism if you appear to have done very well or very badly.

1

Helping hand

You may find the time frame of this question confusing, in which case a diagram may help. Remember if sales and production start in one year's time, then revenues and costs will occur for the first time at the end of the following year, at year 2. Given the products' five year lives, the revenues and costs will be received and paid from years 2-6, and the tax will be paid with a one year time delay, from years 3-7. In fact you are given the discount factor for year 7, and that indicates that it is probably relevant.

You may have presented the net present value calculations in an alternative way. This will be fine provided the presentation is clear, and you have not confused yourself.

In (b) you were only required to give two methods of raising funds. Going public and raising money on the stock market is probably inappropriate for this company, given that it is currently a family owned company with no other shareholders.

(a) (i)   **Product A Vanity mirror**

	0	1	2	3	4	5	6	7
	£'000	£'000	£'000	£'000	£'000	£'000	£'000	£'000
Capital investment	(250)	(1,500)						
Sales (W)			1,103	1,158	1,823	1,914	2,010	
Material costs (W)			(350)	(350)	(525)	(525)	(525)	
Labour (W)			(182)	(200)	(329)	(362)	(399)	
Overheads (W)			(151)	(166)	(275)	(302)	(332)	
Tax (W)				(84)	(88)	(139)	(145)	(151)
	(250)	(1,500)	420	358	606	586	609	(151)
Discount factor	1.000	0.909	0.826	0.751	0.683	0.621	0.564	0.513
DCF	(250)	(1,364)	347	269	414	364	343	(77)
NPV	46							

Working

	2	3	4	5	6	7
Quantity	5,000	5,000	7,500	7,500	7,500	
Sales price (+ 5% after year 2) £	220.50	231.53	243.10	255.26	268.02	
Sales revenues £'000	1,103	1,158	1,823	1,914	2,010	
Material cost per unit £	70	70	70	70	70	
Material costs £'000	350	350	525	525	525	
Labour costs per unit (+10% after year 0) £	36.30	39.93	43.92	48.32	53.15	
Labour costs £'000	182	200	329	362	399	
Overheads per unit (+10% after year 0) £	30.25	33.28	36.60	40.26	44.29	
Overheads £'000	151	166	275	302	332	
Revenues – costs £'000	420	442	694	725	754	
Tax at 20% year in arrears £'000		84	88	139	145	151

Product B Illuminator mirror

	0	1	2	3	4	5	6	7
	£'000	£'000	£'000	£'000	£'000	£'000	£'000	£'000
Capital investment	(500)	(2,000)						
Terminal value							2,500	
Sales (W)			1,250	1,781	2,538	3,617	5,154	
Material costs (W)			(303)	(499)	(824)	(1,359)	(2,242)	
Labour (W)			(121)	(200)	(329)	(544)	(897)	
Overheads (W)			(400)	(600)	(900)	(1,350)	(2,025)	
Tax (W)				(85)	(96)	(97)	(73)	2
	(500)	(2,000)	426	397	389	267	2,417	2
Discount factor	1.000	0.909	0.826	0.751	0.683	0.621	0.564	0.513
DCF	(500)	(1,818)	352	298	266	166	1,363	1
NPV	128							

Working

	2	3	4	5	6	7
Quantity (+ 50% after year 2)	5,000	7,500	11,250	16,875	25,313	
Sales price (- 5% after year 2) £	250	237.50	225.63	214.34	203.63	
Sales revenues £'000	1,250	1,781	2,538	3,617	5,154	
Material cost per unit (+10% after year 0) £	60.50	66.55	73.21	80.53	88.58	
Material costs £'000	303	499	824	1,359	2,242	
Labour costs per unit (+10% after year 0) £	24.20	26.62	29.28	32.21	35.43	
Labour costs £'000	121	200	329	544	897	
Overheads per unit £	80	80	80	80	80	
Overheads £'000	400	600	900	1,350	2,025	
Revenues – costs £'000	426	482	485	364	(10)	
Tax at 20% year in arrears £'000		85	96	97	73	2 CR

The **NPV** of the **Illuminator mirror** (£128,000) is larger than that of the **Vanity mirror** (£46,000), and so on the grounds of NPV alone the Illuminator project should be chosen.

(ii)   Relevant non-financial factors would include the following:

(1)   **Reasonableness of assumptions**

The forecasts are dependent on a large number of assumptions, which may not hold in practice. In particular the assumptions about **increased demand** may not hold if competition is stronger than expected. The positive NPV of the Illuminator mirror is also rather dependent upon the **terminal value** being as forecast.

(2)   **Attitudes to risk**

Managers and shareholders may feel that there is too high a risk of either or both projects having a **negative present value**. The **payback** period of both projects is very close to their lives, and the positive net present value of both to shareholders may be insufficiently large to compensate for the risks.

(3)   **Technological changes**

Technological changes may cause problems of **compatibility** with the microprocessor in the Vanity mirror, or may even render it **obsolete**.

(4)   **Product problems**

The success of both projects will be jeopardised if the products **fail to work** properly. In particular the quality of the digital image on the Vanity mirror may not be satisfactory for customers.

(b) (i) **Rights issue**

A rights issue is an offer of shares to **existing shareholders** enabling them to buy more shares in proportion to their current holdings. Problems could arise with this method if some shareholders are **unable or unwilling to subscribe** for rights; other shareholders might then take the rights up and change the **balance of control** within the company. However given the current limited circle of shareholders, the directors should be able to assess in advance how likely this is to happen.

(ii) **Venture capital**

Venture capital is money provided by outsiders either as a loan to the company or for shares in the company. Venture capital organisations often provide **development finance** for companies wishing to invest in new products or new markets. However venture capitalists will be looking for evidence that the development will be successful. They may wish to appoint a **representative** to the company's board, to look after their interests. They will also wish to **realise their investment**; the **timescale** of the two projects under review would probably be acceptable but whether the **level of returns** would be sufficient is more questionable.

(iii) **Debenture**

A debenture is a loan (not a bank loan), the terms of which are set out in a written document. Debentures can be issued to single lenders or they can be subscribed by a number of lenders. Many debentures are **secured** on **asset(s)** owned by the company. The debentureholder can **realise the security** by selling the assets if the company fails to pay interest or breaches the terms of the debenture in other ways. Interest will be **tax deductible.**

(iv) **Commercial mortgage**

As an alternative to debentures, the company can take out a mortgage **secured on an asset.** It must possess an asset that is valuable enough to offer sufficient security to the mortgage lender. Again the interest would be tax deductible.

Examiner's marking scheme		Marks
(a) (i) Vanity range		
Sales revenue		2
Materials/labour/variable overheads		6
Taxation		2
Capital investment		1
Discounting process/NPV		2
Presentation		1
Illuminator range		
Sales revenue		2
Materials/labour/variable overheads		6
Taxation		2
Capital investment		2
Discounting process/NPV		1
Conclusion		2
Presentation		1
		30
(ii) Each factor identified and discussed	(3 × 2 marks)	6
(b) Each source identified and explained	(2 × 2 marks)	4
		40

2

(a) **Maintaining current arrangement**

	£
Costs of holding debtors $(1,050,000 \times 2 \times 0.12)$	252,000

Factoring

	£
Costs of service $(2,555,000 \times 2 \times 0.0125)$	63,875
Costs of advance $(2,555,000 \times 2 \times {}^{120}/_{365} \times 0.75 \times 0.14)$	176,400
Costs of overdraft interest on non-advance debtors $(2,555,000 \times 2 \times {}^{120}/_{365} \times 0.25 \times 0.12)$	50,400
Savings of staff costs	(25,000)
	265,675

On the basis of these calculations, it does not appear beneficial for Books Ltd to factor its debts. However it might be cheaper just to use the Factory company to tighten up debt collection procedures; this should be investigated.

(b) The company could use the following methods.

(i) **Invoicing**

Books Ltd should ensure that all dispatches are **invoiced promptly**.

(ii) **Payment means**

Books Ltd could encourage schools to pay by quicker methods, in particular **direct debit**.

(iii) **Discounts or special offers**

Books could give schools **discounts** for **quicker payments,** or give special offers, for example **free titles**.

(iv) **Just-in-time system**

The company could introduce a just-in-time stock system so that materials are ordered from suppliers only when needed. However the seasonal peaks of demand may cause suppliers problems.

(v) **Improvements in production process**

All stages of the production process should be investigated to see if increased efficiency can reduce work-in-progress, and whether changes in the sequence of production would speed it up. In particular new computer packages may **decrease typing** time, and improvements in the **printing** and **binding** processes may save time at the end of the process.

(vi) **Total quality management**

Better staff training to **improve** the **efficiency** of the 'manual' elements of the production process (typing, proofing) and also **reduce the number of errors** that have to be corrected will improve the efficiency of the production process.

(vii) **Reduced stocks**

It is likely that many stocks will be held for only a short time as they will be produced in time for the new academic year. However Books Ltd should **investigate stocks** that are held for **any length of time**. In a number of subjects textbooks will become out of date as syllabuses change, new theories emerge or real-world developments occur. However if Books Ltd was to reduce its print runs to minimise the level of stock holdings, there is an increased chance of stock running out and the need for costly reprints.

Examiner's marking scheme

			Marks	
(a)	Finance cost of debtors pre-factoring		2	
	Reduction of debtors days		2	
	New level of debtors (75% & 25%)	(2 × 2 marks)	4	
	Factoring service fee		2	
	Administration/credit control saving		1	
	Conclusion		1	
				12
(b)	Reducing cash operating cycle			
	Each action described	(4 × 2 marks)	8	
				20

3

Helping hand

You might have presented your economic order quantity calculations in (a) (ii) and (b) (ii) slightly differently. Note our answer to (a) (ii) sets out the formula for calculating each element of total costs (these also apply to (b) (ii)).

(a) (i) $Q = \sqrt{\dfrac{2\,Co\,D}{Ch}}$

$= \dfrac{\sqrt{2\times75\times100\times52}}{10}$

$= 279$ briefcases

(a) (ii) Number of orders per annum $= \dfrac{D}{Q}$

Total costs

			£
Ordering costs	$(\dfrac{CoD}{Q})$	$(\dfrac{75\times100\times52}{279})$	1,398
Holding costs	$(\dfrac{ChQ}{2})$	$(\dfrac{10\times279}{2})$	1,395
Purchase costs	(unit cost × D)	(100 × 100 × 52)	520,000
			522,793

(b) (i) $Q = \sqrt{\dfrac{2\,Co\,D}{Ch}}$

$= \dfrac{\sqrt{2\times250\times100\times52}}{9.20}$

$= 532$

(ii) **Total costs**

			£
Ordering costs	$\left(\dfrac{250\times100\times52}{532}\right)$		2,444
Holding costs	$\left(\dfrac{9.20\times532}{2}\right)$		2,447
Purchase costs	$(96 \times 100 \times 52)$		499,200
			504,091

Total costs are less if the alternative supplier is used, so the company should change suppliers.

(c) **Limitations of calculations**

(i) The calculations assume **annual demand** is constant. In reality there may be peaks and troughs, increasing the risk of running out of stock at certain times of the year.

(ii) The calculations do not take into account the **credit terms** offered by both suppliers. If the new supplier offers stricter credit terms, there will be a cost of lost interest on cash balances.

Non-financial factors

(i) Bags will need to consider the **reliability** of the two suppliers. Will the alternative supplier be able to achieve the one-week lead time?

(ii) Bags will need to ensure that the new supplier offers the same (or better) **quality** of goods, and **standard of service.**

(iii) Bags also needs to consider the **brand image** of the new supplier, and also the **product presentation** and packaging of the goods.

(d) Annual savings $= 522,793 - 504,091$
$= 18,702$

		£	Discount factor	£
0	Investment costs	(40,000)	1.000	(40,000)
1	Annual savings	18,702	0.909	17,000
2	Annual savings	18,702	0.826	15,448
3	Annual savings	18,702	0.751	14,045
				6,493

Net present value is £6,493 and on these conditions it would be better to change suppliers.

Examiner's marking scheme

			Marks	
(a)	(i) EOQ formula and solution		2	
	(ii) Cost of holding, ordering and purchasing		3	
				5
(b)	(i) EOQ formula and solution		2	
	(ii) Cost of holding, ordering and purchasing		3	
				5
(c)	Limitations	(2 × 1 mark)	2	
	Non-financial factors	(3 × 1 mark)	3	
				5
(d)	Savings/investment, cash flows		2	
	Discounted cash flows/NPV		2	
	Conclusion		1	
				5
				20

4

Helping hand

This question may have been a surprise to many candidates. Impact of monetary policies is in the syllabus, but you may have found the level of detailed knowledge required disconcerting. If you did struggle with this question, you need to make as much use as possible of the information given – you are told plenty of information about Trader that you can utilise.

(a) (i)   European economic union consists of the common market for trade, with **consequent elimination of barriers** preventing trade between different countries within the union. It involves some **standardisation of regulations** and some **co-ordination of economic policy**.

European monetary union

There are three aspects to monetary union:

(1) **Common currency**

The common currency is the **euro**, which replaced twelve national currencies on 1 January 2002.

(2) **European central bank**

The role of the European central bank includes **issuing euros, conducting monetary policy, acting as lender of last resort** and **managing the exchange rate** of the common currency.

(3) **Centralised monetary policy**

A common monetary policy including **common interest rate levels** will be operated for all countries in the union.

(ii)   **Objectives of the European Monetary System**

(1) **Stabilisation of exchange rates**

Currency union aims to promote a greater degree of exchange rate stability than was possible when each country had its own individual exchange rates.

(2) **Facilitation of trade**

Monetary union will eliminate the constraint of currency risk on trade and investment within the union.

(3) **Economic policy stability**

Businesses and countries will be able to trade in a stable environment. Politicians will no longer be able to pursue short-term economic policies at a national level to gain a political advantage. Economic stability should result in lower interest and inflation rates, and common tax rates across the Union.

(b) (i) **Policy stability**

The **economic conditions** Trader faces domestically may become **more stable** if its home country enters the Currency zone. Lower inflation levels may result in **increased demand**.

Lower tax rates

Tax rates may have to **decrease** as a result of the country entering economic union. Trader will pay less tax itself, and thus **more earnings** will be available for investment or for distribution to shareholders. In addition the lower tax levels will result in consumers having more to spend, and may lead to increased demand for Trader's goods.

Lower interest rates

It seems likely at present that entering the Currency zone in the near future will mean that Trader enjoys **lower interest rates.** This will **reduce** the company's **cost of capital**, and mean a **higher present value** for investment projects and more wealth for shareholders.

Reduction of exchange risk

Trader will not need to worry about **hedging** against adverse movements in its own currency as compared with the Euro. It will also **not** have to **pay foreign currency transaction costs** for exchanging its own currency for the Euro. These are likely to be significant as all Trader's suppliers are European, and much of the demand comes from Europe.

Expansion of overseas demand

Adoption of the Euro will ease trade between Trader and customers in countries that are already in the Euro zone. Customers will no longer face the exchange risk and transactions costs associated with Trader's home country's currency not being the Euro.

(ii) **Costs of introducing Euro**

The company will need to re-price all its goods. There will be **administrative costs** in **changing price lists, showing two prices** on invoices and **modifying computer systems.**

Costs of supplies

Trader Ltd's **suppliers** may take the introduction of the Euro and the consequent re-pricing as an opportunity to **increase prices.** Trader may not be able to pass on these increases to its customers.

Price transparency

Adoption of the Euro will mean customers will find it easier to **compare Trader's prices** with competitors in other countries within the Currency zone. Trader may then come under pressure to reduce its margins.

Inflexible monetary policies

It would appear that the country in which Trader Ltd is based has an economy that is at a different stage of the business cycle to most of the countries within the union. If the country enters monetary union, it may enter at a time when its own economic conditions have eased, but adverse conditions elsewhere in the union have led to the imposition of a **more restrictive monetary policy** than Trader's country's circumstances warrant. This may mean Trader faces **reduced domestic demand,** or **increased cost** and **decreased ease** of borrowing.

Increased competition

Trader may face increased competition, particularly in domestic markets, from **companies elsewhere in the Currency zone** who decide to **invest** in or **export** to Trader's home country because of the removal of currency risk with that country.

Increased threat of takeover

Again this is a consequence of **removal of foreign currency risk** within the **Currency zone. Cross-border mergers** are **likely to increase.** Although the **regulatory regime** in the Currency zone may be as strict or stricter than it used to be in Trader's own country, the government within Trader's country may be less able to intervene to save local companies from acquisition.

Examiner's marking scheme

				Marks	
(a)	(i)	European Economic Union explained		2	
		European Monetary Union explained		2	
					4
	(ii)	Objectives identified	(2 × 1 marks)	2	
		Explanation of each objective	(2 × 1 marks)	2	
					4
(b)	(i)	Each implication identified	(3 × 1 marks)	3	
		Each implication explained	(3 × 1 marks)	3	
					6
	(ii)	Each implication identified	(3 × 1 marks)	3	
		Each implication explained	(3 × 1 marks)	3	
					6
					20

Mock exam 2

Managing Finances
December 2002

Question Paper:	
Time allowed	**3 hours**
All FOUR questions are compulsory and MUST be attempted	

Level C
Paper 5

DO NOT OPEN THIS PAPER UNTIL YOU ARE READY TO START

UNDER EXAMINATION CONDITIONS

BPP
PROFESSIONAL EDUCATION

ALL FOUR questions are compulsory and MUST be attempted

1   Retailer Ltd operates a chain of retail and wholesale stores throughout the country. The Board of Directors undertook a strategic review of operations two years ago, which also involved a detailed profitability analysis of each of the company's outlets. Resulting from this appraisal, a strategic withdrawal from certain markets was agreed and this strategy is now almost complete. The Board of Directors wishes to have the recent financial performance of the company reassessed, relative to the industry average, following the implementation of the withdrawal strategy.

Extracts from the financial statements of Retailer Ltd

	Profit & Loss A/c Y/e 30 Nov 20X2 £'000	Profit & Loss A/c Y/e 30 Nov 20X1 £'000
Sales revenue	2,500.00	3,000.00
Profit before interest and tax	275.00	300.00
Interest	(35.00)	(50.00)
Profit before tax	240.00	250.00
Tax at 25%	(60.00)	(62.50)
Profit after tax	180.00	187.50
Dividends	(100.00)	(100.00)
Retained earnings	80.00	87.50

Balance sheet as at 30 Nov 20X2 / 30 Nov 20X1

	£'000	£'000	£'000	£'000	£'000	£'000
Fixed assets			760.00			862.50
Current assets						
Stock	250.00			300.00		
Debtors	100.00			150.00		
Bank	40.00			-		
		390.00			450.00	
Current liabilities						
Bank overdraft	-			100.00		
Trade creditors	160.00			200.00		
Corporation tax	60.00			62.50		
Dividends	100.00			100.00		
		320.00			462.50	
			70.00			(12.50)
			830.00			850.00
Medium & long-term liabilities						
10% convertible debenture (20X5)			300.00			300.00
12% secured debenture (20X1) Note 3			-			100.00
			530.00			450.00
Financed by:						
Issued share capital						
(5m 5p par value shares)			250.00			250.00
Share premium			100.00			100.00
Retained earnings			180.00			100.00
			530.00			450.00

233

Other information:

		20X2	20X1
1.	Industry average statistics		
	Return on capital employed	29%	30%
	Return on shareholder's capital	28%	28%
	Operating profit margin	10%	10%
	Asset turnover ratio	2.8 times	2.8 times
	Current ratio	1:1	1:1
	Quick ratio (Acid test)	0.7:1	0.7:1
	Debtor days	12 days	12 days
	Gearing ratio	60%	50%
	(Medium and long term debt as a % of equity based on book value)		
	Interest cover (Times interest earned)	4 times	5 times

Note: All averages are based on year end values.

2. Retailer Ltd's operating profit is expected to grow by 10% per annum for the next two years. Dividend per share is expected to increase to three pence per share for the next two years.

3. The secured debenture was redeemed in December 20X1.

4. Each convertible debenture is convertible into 1,000 shares (per £100 nominal value) at any time during 20X5. The convertible debenture is held by a venture capital organisation, which provided finance for Retailer Ltd to modernise its retail outlets in 20W9. The venture capitalist currently also holds 20% of the company's ordinary shares.

Required

(a) (i) Assess the financial performance and financial position of Retailer Ltd in comparison to the industry average.

(13 marks are available for calculations and 9 marks are available for appropriate commentary) (22 marks)

(ii) Calculate the forecast gearing ratio (debt/equity % based on year end book values) for the next two years. (8 marks)

(b) Identify and briefly discuss FOUR reasons why a company such as Retailer Ltd should wish to make a strategic withdrawal from a market sector. (6 marks)

(c) Explain the following terms:

(i) debenture;
(ii) convertible debenture. (4 marks)

(40 marks)

2 Slowpayer Ltd produces a range of kitchenware for the export market. Due to shipping time and customs clearance delays, payment from customers is received on average 90 days from the date of shipment.

Slowpayer Ltd's input costs for materials, employees and other costs are locally sourced. The 90 day period taken by its foreign customers to pay has resulted in some cashflow difficulties for the company.

Credit purchases are currently £2 million per annum and Slowpayer Ltd typically takes on average 90 days to pay its suppliers, which is well in excess of agreed credit terms. Slowpayer Ltd is in effect using its trade credit to help finance working capital.

Suppliers are currently offering 2% discount for payment within 15 days. Slowpayer Ltd's Financial Controller is considering taking the early settlement discount. He has asked you as assistant accountant to evaluate the financial impact of such a decision.

Slowpayer Ltd finances the remaining working capital requirements with a bank overdraft, which has an interest rate of 9%.

Required

(a) (i) Determine if it is financially viable to take advantage of the early settlement discount. (6 marks)

(ii) Identify and briefly discuss THREE additional factors which should be considered in order to determine if the change in payment policy should be made. (6 marks)

(b) (i)   Identify and briefly explain FOUR methods of paying creditors.   (4 marks)

    (ii)   Briefly outline TWO advantages and TWO disadvantages of paying by cheque.   (4 marks)

(20 marks)

3   Puzzler Ltd is investing in new machinery to upgrade its production facilities. Two mutually exclusive machines have been identified and the Managing Director must now make a final decision on which of the two to accept. He has asked for a report setting out key financial data in respect of both machines to assist in the final decision.

The Financial Controller, to whom you report, has provided you with the following information in respect of both machines and has asked for your input to the report.

	Machine A £	Machine B £
Immediate cost	52,000	52,000
Estimated net annual cash inflows		
Year 1	25,000	6,000
Year 2	20,000	16,000
Year 3	15,000	20,000
Year 4	3,000	32,000
Estimated life of the investment	4 years	4 years
Anticipated scrap value at the end of the 4 years	12,000	16,000

The assets will be depreciated using straight line depreciation.

Required

(a) (i)   Explain the term accounting rate of return, (ARR) sometimes referred to as return on capital employed (ROCE).   (2 marks)

    (ii)   Calculate the ARR of both machines (using average annual profit as a percentage of average investment).   (6 marks)

(b) (i)   Calculate the internal rate of return (IRR) of both machines.   (8 marks)

    (ii)   Identify TWO main differences between ARR and IRR.   (4 marks)

(20 marks)

Discount factors

Year	15%	20%
1	0.870	0.833
2	0.756	0.694
3	0.658	0.579
4	0.572	0.482

4   Restaurants plc operates a chain of restaurants. The manager of one of its restaurants has recently been convicted of defrauding the company. He had been paying cash from restaurant receipts to fictitious part-time employees for the past five years, totalling an estimated £100,000. The fraud was discovered only after the company was informed by an acquaintance of the manager.

The Board of Directors has expressed concern that the fraud was not detected by the internal audit function. The Board of Directors has been criticised by many of the company's institutional investors and needs to be seen to take decisive action. The Board has asked that internal audit policies and procedures be extensively revised to attempt to improve fraud prevention and detection.

Required:

(a) (i)   Explain briefly what is meant by segregation of duties and why it is an important aspect of internal control.   (4 marks)

    (ii)   Identify and explain TWO methods by which internal audit can attempt to confirm the effective operation of segregation of duties.   (4 marks)

(b) (i)   Prepare a draft report, identifying FOUR specific steps which could be instigated by internal audit to increase the likelihood of fraud being detected, in the light of the above incident.   (8 marks)

    (ii)   Identify and briefly explain TWO recommended future policy changes regarding fraud detection or prevention, which Restaurants plc could consider.   (4 marks)

(20 marks)

ANSWERS TO MOCK EXAM 2

1

(a)(i)

		Retailer		Industry	
		20X2	20X1	20X2	20X1
(1)	Return on capital employed			29%	30%
	$\dfrac{\text{Profit before interest and tax}}{\text{Shareholders' funds} + \text{medium and long-term liabilities}}$	$\dfrac{275}{530+300} = 33\%$	$\dfrac{300}{450+400} = 35\%$		
(2)	Return on shareholders' capital			28%	28%
	$\dfrac{\text{Profit after tax}}{\text{Shareholders' funds}}$	$\dfrac{180}{530} = 34\%$	$\dfrac{187.50}{450} = 42\%$		
(3)	Operating profit margin			10%	10%
	$\dfrac{\text{Profit before interest and tax}}{\text{Sales revenue}}$	$\dfrac{275}{2,500} = 11\%$	$\dfrac{300}{3,000} = 10\%$		
(4)	Asset turnover ratio			2.8	2.8
	$\dfrac{\text{Sales}}{\text{Shareholders' funds} + \text{Medium and long-term liabilities}}$	$\dfrac{2,500}{830} = 3.0$	$\dfrac{3,000}{850} = 3.5$		
(5)	Current ratio			1:1	1:1
	$\dfrac{\text{Current assets}}{\text{Current liabilities}}$	$\dfrac{390}{320} = 1.22\!:\!1$	$\dfrac{450}{462.50} = 0.97\!:\!1$		
(6)	Quick ratio			0.7:1	0.7:1
	$\dfrac{\text{Current assets excluding stock}}{\text{Current liabilities}}$	$\dfrac{140}{320} = 0.44\!:\!1$	$\dfrac{150}{462.50} = 0.32\!:\!1$		
(7)	Debtor days			12 days	12 days
	$\dfrac{\text{Debtors} \times 365}{\text{Trade sales}}$	$\dfrac{100}{2,500} \times 365 = 15 \text{ days}$	$\dfrac{150}{3,000} \times 365 = 18 \text{ days}$		
(8)	Gearing ratio			60%	50%
	$\dfrac{\text{Medium and long-term debt}}{\text{Equity}}$	$\dfrac{300}{530} = 57\%$	$\dfrac{400}{450} = 89\%$		
(9)	Interest cover			4 times	5 times
	$\dfrac{\text{Profit before interest and tax}}{\text{Interest}}$	$\dfrac{275}{35} = 7.9 \text{ times}$	$\dfrac{300}{50} = 6 \text{ times}$		

(1) **Return on capital employed**

The withdrawal policy appears to have lowered the return, although it still remains in excess of industry average.

(2) **Return on shareholders' funds**

Again the withdrawal policy has lowered the return on funds, although shareholders may be pacified by the maintenance of dividends at the same level, and the return still exceeding industry average. A return based on market values may provide better information than a return based on book values.

(3) **Operating profit margin**

The withdrawal appears to have improved the margin so that it now exceeds industry levels.

(4) **Asset turnover ratio**

The fall in the ratio indicates that Retailer is generating less sales from assets owned, although it is still making better use of its assets than the rest of the industry.

(5) **Current ratio**

The policy of withdrawal from certain sectors has improved Retailer's current ratio so that it now is in excess of the industry average and also 1:1, which is sometimes considered a safe level.

(6) **Quick ratio**

Again withdrawal has increased this ratio, although it is still low compared with industry levels, and may indicate possible liquidity problems.

(7) **Debtor days**

Although this ratio exceeds industry levels, it has fallen since the strategic withdrawal began, and does not appear high. However it is likely that a significant proportion of the company's retail sales are for cash, and it would be more useful to calculate debtor days using credit sales rather than total sales.

(8) **Gearing ratio**

The redemption of the secured debenture has significantly reduced gearing to a point below industry average, indicating Retailer is not suffering excessive financial risk.

(9) **Interest cover**

Again the redemption of the debenture has increased interest cover significantly, and Retailer has no problems in meeting its interest burden. Perhaps therefore Retailer could make more use of debt finance which is low cost and tax deductible.

(ii)

	20X4	20X3
	£'000	£'000
Profit before interest and tax (+ 10% on previous year)	332.75	302.50
Interest $(300 \times 10\%)$	(30.00)	(30.00)
Profit before tax	302.75	272.50
Tax at 25%	(75.69)	(68.13)
Profit after tax	227.06	204.37
Dividends $(0.03 \times 5m)$	(150.00)	(150.00)
Retained earnings	77.06	54.37
Retained earnings b/f	584.37	530.00
Retained earnings c/f	661.43	584.37

$$\text{Gearing} = \frac{\text{Medium and long - term debt}}{\text{Equity}}$$

$$\text{20X3 Gearing} = \frac{300}{584.37}$$

$$= 51\%$$

$$\text{20X4 Gearing} = \frac{300}{661.43}$$

$$= 45\%$$

(b) **Fall in demand**

Demand in the sector may be in long-term decline due to factors such as changes in taste.

Poor margins

Because of **falls in sales price** (due to increased competition in the sector) or **increases in costs,** profit margins may fall to levels below what is acceptable or losses be made.

Other opportunities

Retailer's directors may believe that the **resources** the company has will **earn more** profits if they are taken out of one sector and invested in another. In particular selling retail sites may provide the cash required for investment in other sectors.

Increased risk

The chances of making **insufficient profits or losses** in a sector may **increase to unacceptable levels** because of economic instability (for example recession or adverse exchange rate movements).

(c) (i) **A debenture** is a document setting out the terms of a loan. These may include the payment of fixed or floating rate interest, security, the eventual redemption of capital and the rights of the debentureholder if the conditions in the debenture are not met.

(ii) A **convertible debenture** is a debenture that may be converted, on pre-determined dates and at the option of the holder, into ordinary shares of the company at a predetermined rate. Conversion rights and terms are set out in the debenture deed. If the debenture is not converted, it is held until maturity and then redeemed.

Examiner's marking scheme

				Marks	
(a)	(i)	Calculation of:			
		ROCE		2	
		ROSC		2	
		Margin		1	
		Asset turnover		1	
		Current ratio		1	
		Acid test		1	
		Debtor days		1	
		Gearing		2	
		Interest cover		2	
		Commentary on each ratio		9	
					22
	(ii)	Forecast P&L account			
		PBIT	(2 × ½ mark)	1	
		Interest	(2 × ½ mark)	1	
		Tax	(2 × ½ mark)	1	
		Dividend	(2 × ½ mark)	1	
		Gearing both years	(2 × 2 marks)	4	
					8
(b)		Reasons identified and explained	(4 × 1½ marks)		6
(c)		Debenture		2	
		Convertible		2	
					4
					40

2

Helping hand

Cash discounts are very much core knowledge, (a) illustrating that you need to know formulae and also important non-financial implications of decisions such as accepting discounts. (b) covers another important area; you need to be aware not just of payment methods, but the factors that determine when these methods are used.

(a) (i) Using the formula:

$$\frac{d}{(100-d)} \times \frac{365}{t}$$

where d = 2, t = 90 − 15 = 75

$$\text{Cost of lost discount} = \frac{2}{(100-2)} \times \frac{365}{75}$$

$$= 9.93\%$$

This compares with a bank overdraft rate of 9%, so it is beneficial for Slowpayer to take discounts.

Alternative working

$$\text{Cost of lost discount} = \left[\frac{100}{(100-d)}\right]^{\frac{365}{75}}$$

$$= \left[\frac{100}{(100-2)}\right]^{\frac{365}{75}} - 1$$

$$= 10.33\%$$

(ii)   **Restriction of credit**

Even if Slowpayer does not take the discount, it may **not** be able to continue to **exceed credit terms indefinitely**. Suppliers may restrict credit or stop offering it altogether.

Interest

Suppliers may charge **interest** on overdue accounts.

Administration

Increased time may be taken **dealing with correspondence** from suppliers who are pursuing their money owed, and ultimately defending legal action.

Supplier goodwill

Slowpayer may **gain supplier goodwill** if it takes the discounts. This may mean that suppliers are more willing to provide help when Slowpayer needs it, if for example Slowpayer urgently needs a delivery of supplies. Taking discounts may also facilitate **partnership arrangements** with suppliers such as sharing information.

Improved credit rating

Paying creditors sooner should result in Slowpayer being given a **better rating** with credit agencies, and mean that its suppliers are more likely to give it **favourable references**. This will help Slowpayer if it tries to obtain credit from new suppliers in the future.

Bank overdraft

One problem with taking the discount is the potential **increase in bank overdraft levels**. The bank may be reluctant to allow this or may seek further security from the company.

(b) (i)   **Methods of making payments to suppliers**

Cash

Cash may be used to pay small sums of money to suppliers. It is not generally used for large payments.

Cheques

Cheques are used for many sorts of payment. They are paid out of a **current account** at a bank.

Banker's draft

A banker's draft is an alternative method of bank payment to a cheque, but unlike a cheque, **it cannot be stopped or cancelled after it has been issued**.

Standing order

Standing orders with banks are used to make **regular payments of fixed amounts** to suppliers. Businesses give instructions to banks to make these payments, specifying amounts, dates, frequency of payments and banking details of suppliers.

Direct debits

Direct debits with banks are used for **payments of varying amounts** at **irregular intervals**. They are initiated by suppliers.

Electronic funds transfers

Electronic funds transfers are used to make **immediate payments** between accounts of **large amounts** to suppliers who request them.

(ii)   **Advantages of paying by cheque**

(1)   Cheques are **convenient to use** for payments of any amount.

(2)   The **cheque counterfoil** and **cheque number** can be used to **trace past payments** whenever queries arise.

(3)   **Cheque security** can be enhanced by their being **endorsed or crossed**.

(4)   Cheques are **commonly used** and **widely accepted**.

Disadvantages of paying by cheque

(1)   Cheques can be a **slow method of payment**; a supplier may insist on a method that is **more prompt and reliable** such as standing orders.

(2)   There are **security problems** such as the **need to keep cheques in a safe place**, and the ease with which **signatures on cheques** can be forged.

(3)   **Alterations to cheques** may not always be detected quickly.

Examiner's marking scheme

				Marks	
(a)	(i)	Discount available		1	
		Formula and correct application		2	
		Annualised		2	
		Conclusion		1	
					6
	(ii)	Each factor identified and briefly discussed	(3 × 2 marks)		6
(b)	(i)	Each method identified	(4 × 1 mark)		4
	(ii)	Each advantage	(2 × 1 marks)	2	
			(2 × 1 marks)	2	
					4
					20

3

Helping hand

A key distinction between ARR and IRR is that ARR is based on profits whereas IRR is based on cash flows. Hence the ARR calculation needs to take account of depreciation; don't forget that the realisable value needs to be brought in when calculating the annual depreciation charge. With IRR by contrast depreciation is ignored (as a non-cash payment).

The question provides you with the 15% and 20% discount factors to use in the IRR calculations in (b) (ii).

(a)   (i)   The accounting rate of return is a method for **calculating the return** on an **investment**, and comparing it with a pre-determined target level. The accounting rate of return is calculated as:

$$\frac{\text{Estimated average profits}}{\text{Estimated average investment}} \times 100\%$$

(ii)   **Machine A**

Depreciation charge $= \dfrac{52,000 - 12,000}{4} = £10,000$

Year		Inflows £	Depreciation £	Profits £
1		25,000	(10,000)	15,000
2		20,000	(10,000)	10,000
3		15,000	(10,000)	5,000
4		3,000	(10,000)	(7,000)
				23,000

Average profits $= \dfrac{23,000}{4} = £5,750$

Average investment $= \dfrac{52,000 + 12,000}{2} = £32,000$

ARR $= \dfrac{5,750}{32,000} = 18.0\%$

Machine B

Depreciation charge $= \dfrac{52,000 - 16,000}{4} = £9,000$

Year		Inflows £	Depreciation £	Profits £
1		6,000	(9,000)	(3,000)
2		16,000	(9,000)	7,000
3		20,000	(9,000)	11,000
4		32,000	(9,000)	23,000
				38,000

Average profits $= \dfrac{38,000}{4} = £9,500$

Average investment $= \dfrac{52,000 + 16,000}{2} = £34,000$

ARR $= \dfrac{9,500}{34,000} = 27.9\%$

(b) (i)   **Machine A**

Year		Cash flow £	Discount factor 15%	Present value £	Discount factor 20%	Present value £
0	Cost	(52,000)	1.000	(52,000)	1.000	(52,000)
1	Receipts	25,000	0.870	21,750	0.833	20,825
2	Receipts	20,000	0.756	15,120	0.694	13,880
3	Receipts	15,000	0.658	9,870	0.579	8,685
4	Receipts	3,000	0.572	1,716	0.482	1,446
4	Scrap	12,000	0.572	6,864	0.482	5,784
				3,320		(1,380)

$$IRR = A + \left[\frac{a}{a+b} \times (B-A)\right]$$

$$= 15 + \left[\frac{3,320}{3,320+1,380} \times (20-15)\right]$$

$$= 18.53\%$$

Machine B

Year		Cash flow £	Discount factor 15%	Present value £	Discount factor 20%	Present value £
0	Cost	(52,000)	1.000	(52,000)	1.000	(52,000)
1	Receipts	6,000	0.870	5,220	0.833	4,998
2	Receipts	16,000	0.756	12,096	0.694	11,104
3	Receipts	20,000	0.658	13,160	0.579	11,580
4	Receipts	32,000	0.572	18,304	0.482	15,424
4	Scrap	16,000	0.572	9,152	0.482	7,712
				5,932		(1,182)

$$IRR = A + \left[\frac{a}{a+b} \times (B-A)\right]$$

$$= 15 + \left[\frac{5,932}{5,932+1,182} \times (20-15)\right]$$

$$= 19.17\%$$

(ii) **Differences between ARR and IRR**

(1) **ARR** is based on **profits**, whereas **IRR** is based on **relevant cash flows**.

(2) **IRR** takes into account **the time value of money**, by giving less weight to the more distant cash flows, whereas ARR takes **no account** of **the time value of money**.

(3) **ARR** is a **ratio**, whereas **IRR** is an extrapolation based on **profits**.

Examiner's marking scheme				**Marks**	
(a)	(i)	ARR explained		1	
		Formula		1	
					2
	(ii)	Machine A and Machine B			
		Depreciation	(2 × ½ mark)	1	
		Total profit after depreciation	(2 × 1 mark)	2	
		Average annual profit	(2 × ½ mark)	1	
		Average investment	(2 × ½ mark)	1	
		ARR	(2 × ½ mark)	1	
					6
(b)	(i)	Machine A and Machine B			
		Cash flows	(2 × ½ mark)	1	
		NPV at 10%	(2 × 1 mark)	2	
		NPV at 15%	(2 × 1 mark)	2	
		IRR formula		1	
		IRR calculation	(2 × 1 mark)	2	
					8
	(ii)	Cash versus profit		2	
		Time value of money		2	
					4
					20

Helping hand

In (a) segregation of duties can occur with varying degrees of strictness; the first sentence in the answer defines the minimum. In (a) (ii) auditors need to obtain evidence of how segregation should work and how segregation does work in practice (the two may not be identical!) (b) (i) is about the steps that could be taken to combat the problem of fraudulent restaurant managers, (b) (ii) covers wider issues.

(a) (i) **Segregation of duties** means that **no single person** should be responsible for **recording and carrying out all stages of a transaction**. Segregation of duties can also involve **different people** being responsible for **different accounting operations**.

Segregation of duties makes it **more difficult** for **fraudulent transactions** to be processed, as a **number of people** would have to **collude** in the fraud. It also makes it **more difficult** for **accidental errors** to be processed, since the more people are involved, the **more checking** there will be.

(ii) **Confirmation of segregation of duties**

(1) Auditors can **inspect organisation charts** or records that set out the responsibilities of staff.

(2) Auditors can **check the accounting records of individual transactions** for signatures or other evidence that different staff have carried out different parts of the accounting process.

(3) Auditors can **observe operations** to confirm different staff are carrying out different stages of accounting transactions.

(b) (i) **To:** Board

From: Internal Audit head

Date: 31 January 20X3

Subject: Detection of fraud

The following steps should be taken as a result of the identification of the fraud.

(1) The circumstances of the fraud should be **investigated**, with the **investigation** aiming to **highlight weaknesses in internal controls** that allowed the fraud to go undetected.

(2) The **results of the investigation** should be used to decide whether to **strengthen existing internal controls**, or to **implement new internal controls**.

(3) Internal audit may also **investigate employees and cash accounting** at other restaurants.

(4) As well as these investigations, the company could undertake a **wider risk assessment** of possible problem areas (for example stock pilfering) with a view to changing or adding internal controls.

(5) Internal audit could introduce **surprise visits** to restaurants to see whether **controls** are **being followed** and **verify cash and other asset balances**.

(6) Full audits of restaurants may need to take place **more frequently** and cover a **wider scope**.

(7) **Analytical review** should be carried out regularly, and **additional audits** performed at restaurants showing unusual results.

(ii) The following steps could be taken to prevent and detect fraud in the company as a whole.

    (1) The company could introduce a **code of ethics** covering issues such as fraudulent behaviour, whistleblowing, conflicts of interest.

    (2) **Recruitment procedures** should be rigorous including thorough interview procedures, references and investigation of gaps in employment history.

    (3) **Training procedures** should emphasise the importance of the business's internal controls.

    (4) The chances of staff discontent motivating fraud on the company can be reduced by **reasonable pay and working conditions**, and **appraisal and grievance systems**.

    (5) **Personnel policies** can be used to limit the risk of fraud, for example seeking explanations if an employee's lifestyle changes significantly and requiring employees to take all their holiday entitlement.

    (6) Restaurant managers should be held responsible for **fraud prevention** and **detection** in their area.

Examiner's marking scheme

				Marks
(a)	(i)	Segregation of duties explained		2
		Importance of segregation		2
				4
	(ii)	Methods identified and explained	(2 × 2 marks)	4
(b)	(i)	Each step explained	(4 × 2 marks)	8
	(ii)	Future policy changes	(2 × 2 marks)	4
				20

Topic index

The topic index is provided as a ready reference to aid your revision

251

See overleaf for information on other
BPP products and how to order

CAT Order

To BPP Publishing Ltd, Aldine Place, London W12 8AA
Tel: 020 8740 2211. Fax: 020 8740 1184
email: publishing@bpp.com
online: www.bpp.com

Mr/Mrs/Ms (Full name) _____

Daytime delivery address _____

Postcode _____

Email _____

Daytime Tel _____

Date of exam (month/year) _____

	6/01 Texts	1/02 Kits	i-Learn CD	i-Pass CD	i-Learn Workbook	Virtual Campus enrolment
LEVEL A						
Paper A1 Transaction Accounting	£16.95 ☐		£29.95 ☐	£19.95 ☐	£9.95 ☐	£80 ☐
Paper A2 Office Practice and Procedure	£16.95 ☐	£8.95 ☐	£29.95 ☐		£9.95 ☐	£80 ☐
LEVEL B*						
Paper B1 Maintaining Financial Records and Accounts (UK)	£16.95 ☐	£8.95 ☐	£30.95 ☐	£19.95 ☐	£9.95 ☐	£80 ☐
(International)	£16.95 ☐	£8.95 ☐				
Paper B2 Cost Accounting Systems	£16.95 ☐	£8.95 ☐	£30.95 ☐	£19.95 ☐	£9.95 ☐	£80 ☐
Paper B3 Information Technology Processes	£16.95 ☐	£8.95 ☐	£30.95 ☐	£19.95 ☐	£9.95 ☐	£80 ☐
LEVEL C						
Paper C1 Drafting Financial Statements (Industry and Commerce) (UK)	£16.95 ☐	£8.95 ☐	£30.95 ☐	£21.95 ☐	£9.95 ☐	£80 ☐
(International)	£16.95 ☐	£8.95 ☐				
Paper C2 Information for Management	£16.95 ☐	£8.95 ☐	£30.95 ☐	£21.95 ☐	£9.95 ☐	£80 ☐
Paper C3 Auditing Practice and Procedure (UK)	£16.95 ☐	£8.95 ☐	£30.95 ☐	£21.95 ☐	£9.95 ☐	£80 ☐
(International)	£16.95 ☐	£8.95 ☐				
Paper C4 Preparing Taxation Computations and Returns FA2001 (10/01 Text)	£16.95 ☐	£8.95 ☐				
Paper C5 Managing Finances	£16.95 ☐	£8.95 ☐	£30.95 ☐	£21.95 ☐	£9.95 ☐	£80 ☐
Paper C6 Managing People	£16.95 ☐	£8.95 ☐	£30.95 ☐	£21.95 ☐	£9.95 ☐	£80 ☐

SUBTOTAL £ _____

Register via our website, and pay on-line
www.bpp.com/virtualcampus/cat

POSTAGE & PACKING

Study Texts and Workbooks

	First	Each extra	
UK	£3.00	£2.00	£ ☐
Europe*	£5.00	£4.00	£ ☐
Rest of world	£20.00	£10.00	£ ☐

Kits

	First	Each extra	
UK	£2.00	£1.00	£ ☐
Europe*	£2.50	£1.00	£ ☐
Rest of world	£15.00	£8.00	£ ☐

CDs

	First	Each extra	
UK	£2.00	£2.00	£ ☐
Europe*	£2.00	£2.00	£ ☐
Rest of world	£20.00	£10.00	£ ☐

Grand Total (Cheques to *BPP Publishing*) I enclose a cheque for (incl. Postage) £ ☐☐☐☐

Or charge to Access/Visa/Switch

Card Number ☐☐☐☐☐☐☐☐☐☐☐☐

Expiry date _____ Start Date _____

Issue Number (Switch Only) ☐☐☐☐

Signature _____

We aim to deliver to all UK addresses inside 5 working days; a signature will be required. Orders to all EU addresses should be delivered within 6 working days. All other orders to overseas addresses should be delivered within 8 working days. * Europe includes the Republic of Ireland and the Channel Islands.

REVIEW FORM & FREE PRIZE DRAW

All original review forms from the entire BPP range, completed with genuine comments, will be entered into one of two draws on 31 July 2003 and 31 January 2004. The names on the first four forms picked out on each occasion will be sent a cheque for £50.

Name: _____   **Address:** _____

_____

Date:_____   _____

How have you used this Practice & Revision Kit?
(Tick one box only)

☐ Home study (book only)

☐ On a course: college _____

☐ With 'correspondence' package

☐ Other _____

Why did you decide to purchase this Practice & Revision Kit? *(Tick one box only)*

☐ Have used complementary Interactive Text

☐ Have used BPP Texts in the past

☐ Recommendation by friend/colleague

☐ Recommendation by a lecturer at college

☐ Saw advertising in journals

☐ Saw website

☐ Other _____

During the past six months do you recall seeing/receiving any of the following?
(Tick as many boxes as are relevant)

☐ Our advertisement in *ACCA Student Accountant*

☐ Other advertisement _____

☐ Our brochure with a letter through the post

Which (if any) aspects of our advertising do you find useful?
(Tick as many boxes as are relevant)

☐ Prices and publication dates of new editions

☐ Information on Practice & Revision Kit content

☐ Facility to order books off-the-page

☐ None of the above

Have you used the companion Interactive Text for this subject?   ☐ Yes   ☐ No

Your ratings, comments and suggestions would be appreciated on the following areas

	Very useful	Useful	Not useful
Introductory section (How to use this Practice & Revision Kit)	☐	☐	☐
'Do You Know' checklists	☐	☐	☐
'Did You Know' checklists	☐	☐	☐
Possible pitfalls	☐	☐	☐
Objective test questions	☐	☐	☐
Short-form questions	☐	☐	☐
Content of answers	☐	☐	☐
Mock exams	☐	☐	☐
Structure & presentation	☐	☐	☐
Icons	☐	☐	☐

	Excellent	Good	Adequate	Poor
Overall opinion of this Kit	☐	☐	☐	☐

Do you intend to continue using BPP Interactive Texts/Kits?   ☐ Yes   ☐ No

Please note any further comments and suggestions/errors on the reverse of this page. The BPP author of this edition can be emailed at nickweller@bpp.com

Please return to: Lynn Watkins, BPP Professional Education, FREEPOST, London, W12 8BR

REVIEW FORM & FREE PRIZE DRAW (continued)

Please note any further comments and suggestions/errors below

FREE PRIZE DRAW RULES

1   Closing date for 31 July 2003 draw is 30 June 2003. Closing date for 31 January 2004 draw is 31 December 2003.

2   Restricted to entries with UK and Eire addresses only. BPP employees, their families and business associates are excluded.

3   No purchase necessary. Entry forms are available upon request from BPP Professional Education. No more than one entry per title, per person. Draw restricted to persons aged 16 and over.

4   Winners will be notified by post and receive their cheques not later than 6 weeks after the relevant draw date.

5   The decision of the promoter in all matters is final and binding. No correspondence will be entered into.